A STRIKING LIKENESS

TO MY PARENTS, MALCOLM AND SYBIL CROSS

A Striking Likeness

The Life of George Romney

David A. Cross

ASHGATE

Published by
Ashgate Publishing Limited
Gower House
Croft Road
Aldershot
Hants GU11 3HR
England

Ashgate Publishing Company
Old Post Road
Brookfield
Vermont 05036–9704
USA

British Library Cataloguing-in-Publication data

Cross, David A.
A striking likeness: the life of George Romney
1. Romney, George, 1734–1802 2. Painters – England – Biography
3. Painting, English 4. Painting, Modern – eighteenth century – England
I. Title
759.2

Library of Congress Cataloging-in-Publication data

Cross, David, A., 1951–
A striking likeness: the life of George Romney / David Cross.
p. cm.
Includes bibliographical references and index.
ISBN 1–84014–671–0 (hardback: alk. paper)
1. Romney, George, 1734–1802. 2. Portrait painters – England – Biography.
I. Romney, George, 1734–1802. II. Title.
ND1329.R64C76 1999
759.2-dc21 98–53571
CIP

ISBN 1 84014 671 0

Printed on acid-free paper

Phototypeset in Palatino by Intype London Ltd
Printed in Singapore

Contents

List of illustrations

Colour plates

House of Lords, 208.1 × 146.7 cm (82.2 × 58 in)

XVI *John Milton Dictating to his Daughters*, 1793, oil on canvas, private collection, 193.5 × 206 cm (76.2 × 81.2 in)

Black and white plates

1 *Dr Slop Entering Mr Shandy's Parlour* (engraving by W. Haines), from William Hayley, *The Life of George Romney*, 1809, Chichester Record Office, Sussex, 19 × 15.5 cm (7.5 × 6.1 in)

2 *Memories of Windermere*, c.1761, oil on canvas, sold Christie's, 18 June 1971, 81 × 126.5 cm (32 × 50 in). Photo courtesy of Christie's Images

3 *Mrs Wilbraham Bootle*, c.1764, oil on canvas, sold Christie's, 18 June 1976, 126.5 × 101.2 cm (50 × 40 in). Photo courtesy of Christie's Images

4 *Samson Overpowered*, 1777–80, pen and brown ink over pencil with brown and grey watercolour wash, Yale Center for British Art, New Haven, Connecticut, 49.7 × 39.7 cm (19.7 × 15.6 in). Gift of Mr and Mrs J. Richardson Dilworth

5 *Dr James Ainslie*, c.1765, oil on canvas, Bradford Art Galleries and Museums, 145 × 121 cm (57 × 47.5 in)

6 *Mr and Mrs Lindow*, 1772, oil on canvas, Tate Gallery, London, 139.2 × 113.9 cm (55 × 45 in)

7 *Peter Woodhouse*, c.1765–8, oil on canvas, sold Christie's, 20 April 1990, 192.3 × 126.5 cm (76 × 50 in). Photo courtesy of Christie's Images

8 *The Leigh Family*, 1767–8, oil on canvas, National Gallery of Victoria, Melbourne, Australia, 185.8 × 202 cm (73.4 × 79.8 in)

9 *Richard Cumberland*, c.1772, oil on canvas, National Portrait Gallery, London, 124 × 98.7 cm (49 × 39 in)

10 *Peter and James Romney*, 1766, oil on canvas, Yale Center for British Art, New Haven, Connecticut, Paul Mellon Collection, 92.3 × 91 cm (36.5 × 36 in)

11 *Mirth*, 1770, oil on canvas, sold Christie's, 22 October 1979, 234.7 × 142.9 cm (92.7 × 56.5 in). Photo courtesy of Christie's Images

12 *Melancholy*, 1770, oil on canvas, sold Christie's, 15 April 1988, 234.7 × 142.9 cm (92.7 × 56.5 in). Photo courtesy of Christie's Images

13 *A Wood Nymph* (engraving by Valentine Green), 1778, private collection, 59.5 × 41.7 cm (23.5 × 16.5 in)

14 *Venus Commanding Psyche to Fetch the Waters of the Styx*, c.1777–83, black chalk on paper, Board of Trustees of the National Museums and Galleries on Merseyside (Walker Art Gallery, Liverpool), 101.6 × 124 cm (40.2 × 49 in)

15 *Joseph Brant (Thayendanegea)*, 1776, oil on canvas, National Gallery of Canada, Ottawa, 127 × 101.6 cm (49 × 39 in)

16 *John Flaxman Modelling the Bust of William Hayley*, 1791–2, oil on canvas, Yale Center for British Art, Paul Mellon Collection, New Haven, Connecticut, 226 × 114.7 cm (89 × 57 in)

17 *Mrs Penelope Lee Acton*, 1791–3, oil on canvas, Huntington Art Collection, San Marino, California, 236.6 × 143.8 cm (93.5 × 57.5 in)

18 *Miss Elizabeth Harriet Warren (later Viscountess Bulkeley) as Hebe*, 1776, oil on canvas, private collection, on loan to the National Museums and Galleries of Wales, Cardiff, 238.5 × 148 cm (94.3 × 58.5 in)

19 *The 4th Duke of Marlborough*, 1779–86, oil on canvas, Blenheim Palace, Oxfordshire, 235.3 × 144.2 cm (93 × 57 in). By kind permission of his Grace the Duke of Marlborough

20 *Mrs Maxwell*, 1780, oil on canvas, sold Christie's, 16 July 1982, 237.8 × 146.7 cm (94 × 58 in). Photo courtesy of Christie's Images

21 *Edward Wilbraham Bootle and his Brother Randle*, 1786, oil on canvas, sold Sotheby's

Macbeth), *c*.1791–2, pen with black ink and grey watercolour wash, Fitzwilliam Museum, Cambridge. Photograph Courtauld Institute of Art

45 *Sketch for Circe or Cassandra*, 1782–6, pen with brown ink and wash over pencil, The Folger Shakespeare Library, Washington D.C., 50.3 × 31.1 cm (19.7 × 12.2 in)

46 *The Laocoön*, *c*.1774, black chalk, Yale Center for British Art, New Haven, Connecticut, 43.8 × 30.5 cm (17.2 × 12 in). Gift of Mr and Mrs J. Richardson Dilworth

47 *John, Lord Somers*, *c*.1785–6, oil on canvas, Eastnor Castle, Herefordshire, Hervey-Bathurst Collection, 253 × 143 cm (100 × 57 in)

48 *Head of a Fiend*, *c*.1792–4, Indian ink wash, 35.4 × 36.7 cm (14 × 14.5 in). Reproduced by permission of the Provost and Fellows of Eton College

49 *The Wronged Maid*, late 1770s, pen with dark brown ink and grey water-colour wash over pencil, Fitzwilliam Museum, Cambridge, 31.9 × 50.8 cm (12.5 × 20 in). Photograph Courtauld Institute of Art

50 *The Lapland Witch*, 1780s, pen and brown ink, brown wash over pencil on paper, Fitzwilliam Museum, Cambridge, 31.4 × 47.9 cm (12.6 × 19.2 in). Photograph Courtauld Institute of Art

51 *The Beggar Girl*, 1780s, pen with brown ink and grey watercolour wash over black chalk, Fitzwilliam Museum, Cambridge, 38.1 × 38.7 cm (15.2 × 12.5 in). Photograph Courtauld Institute of Art

52 *John Howard Visiting Prisoners*, 1790s, pen and grey ink, grey watercolour wash over pencil, Fitzwilliam Museum, Cambridge, 35.9 × 49.5 cm (14.1 × 19.5 in). Photograph Courtauld Institute of Art

53 *Thomas Paine* (engraving by William Sharp), 1793, National Portrait Gallery, London, 23 × 19.3 cm (9.1 × 7.6 in)

54 *William Cowper*, 1792, pastels on paper, National Portrait Gallery, London, 57.5 × 47.5 cm (23 × 19 in)

55 *The Fall of the Rebel Angels*, early 1790s, pen with black ink and grey watercolour wash over pencil, Fitzwilliam Museum, Cambridge, 54 × 39 cm (21.2 × 15.2 in). Photograph Courtauld Institute of Art

56 Thomas Hayley, *Portrait of George Romney*, *c*.1796, plaster of Paris medallion, Chichester Record Office, 13.9 cm diameter (5.5 in)

57 *A Head of King Saul*, 1776–7, black chalk partly worked with stump, Fitzwilliam Museum, Cambridge, 43.8 × 31.1 cm (17.2 × 12.2 in). Photograph Courtauld Institute of Art

58 *A Head of Edgar (King Lear)*, 1773–5, black chalk on paper, Fitzwilliam Museum, Cambridge, 35 × 53.3 cm (14 × 21.3 in). Photograph Courtauld Institute of Art

59 Martin Archer Shee, *George Romney* (engraving by W. Bond), 1810, Jackson Collection, Carlisle Library, 19 × 15.5 cm (7.5 × 6.1 in)

60 *Self-portrait*, *c*.1780–82, oil on canvas, National Portrait Gallery, London, 125 × 101.2 cm (50 × 40 in)

Acknowledgements

Although I trained as a scientist to the age of eighteen and as a social scientist to first degree level, numerous people have encouraged me in my exploration of words and images in a great variety of ways. At the age of ten I was introduced to the concept of biography by my first music teacher, the late Margaret Taylor FRCO. While I was at Denstone the late Jack Richards fostered a love of Shakespeare in me, while Barry Trapnell and Hilary Comeau contributed to the genesis of a powerful interest in art, enhanced by a tour of Italy with my late grandfather Colonel Frank Cross of the Royal Welch Fusiliers. Jeffrey Simmons, my agent, suggested biography as a suitable vehicle for my multifarious interests of almost thirty years later, and drew my discussions with Ashgate Publishing to a successful conclusion. On the road to press I have enormously appreciated the experience of Pamela Edwardes, the commissioning editor, who has cheerfully kept me on course; the painstaking labour with chronology and theme of my indefatigable editor Sue Moore, who has considerably improved the fluency of the text; the meticulous work of the copy editor Lindsey Shaw-Miller; the assiduous proof-reading by Elspeth and Martin Orram; and the efforts of all others involved in the production of this biography.

In particular my gratitude is due to four people without whose inspiration and assistance the book would have been neither researched nor completed: Dr William Rollinson, formerly of the Department of Continuing Education, Liverpool University, gave me my first opportunity to lecture in art history and shared his publishing experience; Mary Burkett OBE, former Director of Abbot Hall Art Gallery, Kendal, whose energy led to the purchase of Romney's greatest work, *The Gower Children*, for the benefit of Cumbria, gave me several crucial contacts in the early stages of my project and generously provided an apartment with staggering views of the Derwent valley, where I spent four fruitful years; Dr Brian Allen of the Paul Mellon Centre for

British Art welcomed me to a splendid library, gave much support and advice, read an early version of the text and recommended my eventual publisher; and at an advanced stage Alex Kidson of the Walker Art Gallery, Liverpool, carefully read the text twice, locating several weaknesses, and assisted greatly with the proofs, while his enthusiasm for Romney sustained me through several dark periods.

The endeavours of my distant predecessors in Romney studies proved an inestimable benefit whilst more contemporary Romney scholars who have earned my sincere thanks include Professor Anne Crookshank of Trinity College, Dublin, who generously gave me a huge collection of photographs, and Patricia Jaffé for her superb Fitzwilliam catalogue. Since the inception of the project my warm appreciation must be accorded to Dr Yvonne Romney Dixon of Trinity College, Washington, for her lively correspondence and memorable hospitality; Jennifer Watson for her excellent Canadian catalogue which provided numerous scholarly leads; Professor Victor Chan of the University of Alberta for kindly sending a copy of his PhD; Elizabeth Allen of Muswell Hill for several enlightening conversations; Jean Wallis, an MA student at Reading, whose insights will become important to Romney scholarship; and the late Sarah Cookson, an able 'A' level student who tragically died before she could complete her project on Romney.

Facilities for research were provided by Dr Charles Saumarez Smith, Director of the National Portrait Gallery, and his staff; Lindsay Stainton and her former colleagues at the Department of Prints and Drawings, The British Museum; the staff of the National Art Library, The Victoria and Albert Museum; the staff of the Witt Library and the Photographic Survey, The Courtauld Institute, especially Jane Cunningham and Sarah Wimbush; Jane Munro of the Fitzwilliam Museum; Vicky Slowe, former Director of Abbot Hall Art Gallery and now Director of the Ruskin Museum, Coniston; and Edward King, Philip Dalziel and Christian Barnes of Abbot Hall Art Gallery. It has been a privilege to visit Romney's surviving houses and I am grateful to the owners who kindly gave me access to these significant places.

Although they are already named in my bibliography, I am enormously grateful to numerous scholars whose books and articles I have cited; also to curators, librarians, archivists and fellow researchers all over the world who have responded to legions of queries and frequently sent relevant unsolicited information. In particular I must thank the following: Patrick Noon and his colleagues at the Yale Center for British Art, New Haven; Pierre Rosenberg and his staff at the Musée du Louvre, Paris; Karen Hearn and Elizabeth Einberg of the Tate Gallery; Alastair Laing of the National Trust; the staff of the Paul Mellon Centre for British Art; Helen Valentine of the Royal Academy library; Peter van der Merwe of the National Maritime Museum; the staff of the Museum of London; Elizabeth Knight of the Cowper and Newton

Museum, Olney; Nigel Viney for locating several elusive portraits; Stephen Freeth of the Guildhall Library; Thelma Goodman of Lancaster University Library; Richard Hall of Kendal Record Office; Aidan Jones of Barrow-in-Furness Record Office; Stephen White of Carlisle Reference Library; Ron Smith of Barrow-in-Furness Reference Library; Christine Strickland and Jackie Fay of Kendal Reference Library; and Joan Sharpe and Sue Harris of Cockermouth Library who arranged for numerous inter-library loans.

In accumulating a collection of photographs of Romney paintings and drawings I am in debt to many institutions, to private owners and to Barrow Arts Panel who gave me a photographic grant. James Miller, David Moore-Gwyn and the staff at Sotheby's, Margie Christian and the staff at Christie's and Lowell Libson and David Posnett of the Leger Gallery (now Spink-Leger) have been unfailingly helpful and generous in providing prints. Warm thanks go to the owners who have given permission for their paintings to be reproduced; the names of those not seeking anonymity are printed in the list of illustrations or in brackets after references in the text. Furthermore, I acknowledge the expertise of numerous photographers, known and unknown, including Steve Thomas, George M. Garbutt, John Spragg, Jeremy Whittaker and Beaver Photography, Chichester; and the technical and computing skills of Leslie Leak in Kendal and Matthew and David of Astra Printing in Barrow, when my own computer system failed.

I must also express my gratitude to those who have contributed to the subsidy required to fund the colour plates in this volume: the members of the Arts Panel Barrow-in-Furness, John R.E. Borron, Michael Bottomley, Mary Burkett OBE, Emma Carpenter, Jocelyn Carr-Holland, Humphry and Hilary Chapman, G.P. Clifton and the members of Millom Local History Society, Alan Cross, Lilian Cross, Malcolm and Sybil Cross, Michael and Christina Cross, Moyra Cross, Margaret Cutress, Joan David, Pamela Dickinson, Yvonne Romney Dixon, Ian and Audrey Dunn, Professor and Mrs Philip Edwards, Esther Finch, Peter and Suzanne Greenhill, Richard Hall, John and Peggy Hartley, Captain John Furnival Hayes, Dr Geoffrey and Dr Valerie Howden, Linda Kelly, David Kremen, Alice Leach and the members of Barrow-in-Furness Civic Society, the Paul Mellon Centre for British Art, Charles and Judy Morris, Margaret Oddy, Martin and Elspeth Orrom and the members of the Romney Society, Olive and Harry Pilkington and the Friends of Dalton Castle, Mavis Rimmer and the members of Kirkby Literary Society, Mr and Mrs Frank Schiff, Jean Smith, Chris and Linda Stockbridge, Christine Strickland, Jean Wallis and Joan Wilkinson.

For their generosity, long-suffering encouragement and support I am eternally grateful to my parents and my immediate family: Richard, Angie, Rose, Chris, Paul, Sarah, Tom, Jamie and Owen. Many friends and colleagues have assisted greatly during the long gestation of this book including Stella Barnes for a lifetime of literary stimuli; Christine Tranchant of Haubourdin and Professor Sally Ghaly of the University of Sharjah for triggering important phases in this and other projects; Terence Tookey, the Reverend Nicholas Varnon and Andrew Hunter, three dedicated schoolmasters; Professor Richard Wilson of Lancaster University, my MA tutor, who ably speeded my metamorphosis from scientist to artist; David and Angie Stovell for bolstering my decision to begin independent scholarship; Peter Needham and Pat Blackburn for broad conversation, great understanding, the use of both cottage and car and countless faultlessly administered walks in the Lakes; Joan David, whose sense of beauty is a joy and who provided immense emotional support; Professor Michael Wheeler and the members of the Ruskin Programme, especially Christine Parker, for invitations and collateral stimuli; Jane Murphy for introducing me to my agent; Clare Brockbank and the Friends of the Armitt Library for crucial opportunities; Professor Keith Hanley, editor of the Armitt Journal, for understanding and encouragement; the late Barry Maclean-Eltham, founder Chairman of the Romney Society for his dedication and enthusiasm; Sarah Braddyll for heroically typing countless letters and creating sybaritic week-ends; Finbar O'Suilleabhain for his example of fidelity to a distant goal; Edward and Shizuko Hughes for their powerful determination in creativity; Emma Carpenter, Helen Kirk and Anne Stone (now North) for their spontaneous warmth, helpful encouragement and culinary skills; Dr John Satchell, former editor of Abbot Hall's magazine *Quarto* for several degrees of insight; David Lindley for being a good listener; Tim Cockerill for his keen interest and extensive correspondence; Janice Savage for believing in my project; Phillis Blades for her kind gift of a rare book; Jan Parkin for her dry wit; the members of writing groups in Barrow, Ulverston and Coniston for shared ideas and stimuli; Elspeth Hulme, who encouraged my lecturing activities, and to NADFAS audiences throughout the UK; John and Carolyn Sykes and Jerry and Libby Barton for their neighbourliness; Elizabeth Allen of Great Salkeld and the present committee of the Cumbria Decorative and Fine Arts Society, and numerous students and all others not mentioned who have over many years persisted in the belief that my labours would amount to something in the end.

David A. Cross
Cumbria, Autumn 1998

1

From woodcarver to portraitist 1734–62

In the south of Cumbria, the fertile Furness peninsula is bounded by the broad Duddon estuary to the north-west, by the Irish Sea spanning the horizon to the west, and, to the south-east, by miles of tidal sands across Morecambe Bay.[1] North and east of its undulating, stone-walled fields and its woods rise the high fells of the Lake District. In the twelfth century the remoteness of Low Furness had appealed to the brotherhood of Cistercian monks, who built the red sandstone abbey dedicated by them to St Mary. Over time a wealthy community evolved here around the trading of wool. At the nearby village of Dalton-in-Furness one abbot built a castle, and a market town grew up. After the Dissolution, prosperity declined in Dalton; the neighbouring town of Ulverston expanded to become the principal market on the peninsula, in part through being nearer to Lancaster via the treacherous sands of Morecambe Bay.

In the eighteenth century, in the 'soft and picturesque' landscape of Low Furness, two thirds of the population around Dalton still toiled on small acreages of deep red soil, where they practised successful arable farming and the raising of cattle. Rich deposits of haematite iron ore, mined from the Furness limestone, had supported small-scale charcoal smelting at least since medieval times. This industry throve through a collaboration between the providers of land, ore, charcoal and manpower, when plentiful charcoal from the coppiced woods of High Furness outlasted the fuel famines of other regions.

At Beckside, on the eastern side of the town, stood the family farm where George Romney was born on 15 December 1734, in the eighth year of the reign of George II.[2] The Romneys had come from Colby, near Appleby in the north of Cumbria, where the artist's grandfather, also George Romney, had been born to a family of 'statesmen' or independent yeoman farmers.[3] In 1702, aged sixty, the elder George Romney married a local girl, Jane

Barrow; their first son John, the artist's father, was born at Millwood, close to Furness Abbey, in 1703.[4] Old George lived to see the births of five grandchildren and died aged ninety-six. The Romney property at Beckside, which was probably adjacent to the junction of the present-day Market Street and Station Road, was demolished in the nineteenth century to accommodate the new Town Hall.[5]

Romney's origins have been depicted as humble; but three of his four grandparents evidently had some financial independence. 'Honest' John Romney, the artist's father, was regarded as both industrious and creative. No one occupational title describes this talented man who cultivated his few acres, built furniture and was 'as expert at making a fiddle as in constructing a gentleman's home'.[6] He also worked in metal and is credited with having designed the north of England's first plough with an iron mould-board.[7] His other agricultural innovations included manuring the land with mussels and experimenting with a plough drawn downwind by using a sail.[8] He was also notable for pumping water from flooded mines, initially using horse gins and later by erecting steam engines.[9] Although Captain Savery had patented this invention in 1698, and there were steam pumps in use in Staffordshire by 1716, this was, nevertheless, an early use of such technology.

As the Jethro Tull of Furness, John Romney was not distracted by these adventures from his principal trade. He had links with furniture makers in Lancaster and upholsterers in Kendal and is reputed to have been the first in Furness to have used mahogany for furniture, instead of the indigenous oak or walnut. However, he tended to dissipate his talents on too many schemes; he was not interested in collecting debts and he rarely received adequate recompense for either his industry or his powers of innovation.[10]

The artist's mother, Ann, was born in 1704 at Whitbeck, near Millom, across the Duddon sands to the north of Furness.[11] She was the daughter of John Simpson, also a 'statesman', of Sladebank below Black Combe. Her mother was Bridget Parke, sister of the prosperous ironmaster William Parke of Whicham and daughter of the Reverend Lawrence Parke of Woodhouse, vicar of Whitbeck from 1661 to 1673.[12]

John and Ann Romney married on 30 June 1730 and were to have ten sons and one daughter.[13] William, the firstborn, was delivered at Millwood, like his father, in 1731; George was the third child and consequently old enough to witness the early deaths of several younger siblings. Ann Romney was a clever, frugal woman who kept a neat house and brought her children up in piety and knowledge. But of the eleven children, only the artist, his sister Jane and his younger brother James lived beyond middle age.

George and his brothers grew up frail, in their psychological nature and physical constitution alike. The artist became an absent husband, while James and Peter also suffered much misery through their unsuccessful relationships with women. John was to be incapable of steady work and Lawrence's letters suggest that he endured corresponding symptoms.[14] On the evidence of their father's somewhat eccentric behaviour, it may be that the family's tendency both to creativity and to melancholia had a genetic source. Indeed, the artist himself believed that his tendency to fall 'into some melancholy malady' was 'partly constitutional'.[15] Of the six brothers that survived childhood, five were to show erratic symptoms and at least three were active creatively.[16] Numerous studies of siblings demonstrate the familial nature of manic depressive illness and it could be that the 'emotional convulsions that disabled [Romney's] brothers empowered him to create an art that [was] all the more intense'.[17]

Throughout his life Romney was a person of quirky complexity, and his technical gifts were periodically hampered by 'singular infirmities of mind', which have led to him being inaccurately labelled as 'insane'.[18] The link between mental instability and genius has been a persistent cultural notion since Aristotle, and recent clinical studies locate more mood disorders in artists and poets than in the general population.[19] Like William Blake, Romney was aware of his own mental peculiarities. Following either frenzied displays of excitability or periods of gloom, he knew when he had offended others and would try to atone.

As a fashionable portraitist, Romney was to find that his shyness worsened the strain of his determination to succeed, since the demands of his London sitters were in themselves quite an ordeal. Though tall, well-built and physically strong, he was constitutionally prone to the effects of cold; he also had 'aspen nerves', which rendered him incapable of enduring embarassing encounters.[20] Relationships were difficult for him and he wistfully noted that he would have had more satisfaction in life if he had 'the power of communicating [his] feelings and sentiments with facility'.[21]

His excessive nervous sensibility and 'perilously acute' feelings certainly relate to his strong aesthetic response.[22] He was all too aware of his own tendency to 'tremble at phantoms', but was equally capable of wishing to 'bend [his] bow at those that kick and tread upon [him]'; one friend said that on a field of battle he would have been capable of showing 'manly valour'.[23] Apart from his sensitivity to such 'phantoms of apprehension', he was also a melancholic, a condition that could have been triggered, in adult life, by one or more influences: a guilt-stricken marriage, professional frustration as a history painter, or the fecklessness shown by his younger brothers.

A positive aspect of the family condition was an ability to empathize with other sufferers. Peter sensitively described one melancholy neighbour as an 'eagle tethered', while George was solicitous regarding the eyesight of his friend, the poet William Hayley, and moved by William Cowper's mental decline.[24] Throughout his life he was concerned about the effects of poverty and, through his friendships with Thomas Paine and John Howard, interested in the larger radical concerns of the world.[25] In 1803 he was remembered as a 'soul of genius, honesty, generosity and petulance'.[26] The latter word, being more often used to describe a woman, might be viewed as a bizarre inclusion, but it may suggest an outward manifestation of the feminine side of his character, one usually hidden by men. Gentler elements of his personality would partly explain his success as a portraitist, especially with women and children.

Among friends Romney showed 'real politeness and delicacy of behaviour', stemming from his naturally friendly disposition.[27] He also had a strain of eloquent conversation, coupled with sensitivity, which was attractive to his literary friends and delightful to ladies.[28] He was generally a quiet man, but when in company with his intimates:

> he would sit for a length of time absorbed in thought, and absent from the matter in discourse, till on a sudden, starting from his seat, he would give vent to the effusions of his fancy, and harangue in the most animated manner upon the subject of his art, with a sublimity of idea, and a peculiarity of expressive language that was entirely his own, and in which education or reading had no share. These sallies of natural genius, clothed in natural eloquence, were perfectly original, very highly edifying and entertaining in the extreme. They were uttered in a hurried accent, an elevated tone, and very commonly accompanied by tears, to which he was constitutionally prone.[29]

Reading or being read passages of sentiment in literature was another frequent source of Romney's tears, taken as 'the mark of true sensibility', but his friends tended to avoid raising subjects of this sort as they elicited his manic side, agitating him 'like a man possessed'.[30] This powerful simile gives a clue to the difficulties he experienced even when with his friends, and which progressively contributed to his isolation. On one occasion William Hayley was to describe his outbursts as 'seriously alarming' and emanating from 'a powerful and sometimes a rough spirit' which could be 'as wild as the Wind of the Equinox'.[31] His depressive phases are well documented, especially later in life, but the more positive aspects of his cycle less so. Mania, as distinct from depression, is closer to behaviour that is generally regarded as normal, and such manifestations as the 'uncommon vivacity' of his conversation, being less remarkable, remained unrecorded.[32] There is also a clinical correlation between his mania and the speed of his painting, again a wonderful rather than a threatening symptom. Observers tend to perceive some artists as depressives when actually they are manic depressives.[33] However, it is appropriate to attribute to Romney a lesser form of the positive phase of the condition, 'hypomanic excitability' rather than mania, although even in his dark moods he could show fits of spleen which 'burst out in rapid and transient flashes like the explosion of a rocket'.[34]

A recent analysis of the links between art and mental instability lists Romney among sufferers from cyclothymia, a milder form of manic depression.[35] Few manic depressives are hospitalized, as most of the time they are effectively psychologically 'normal'.[36] Cyclothymics and their siblings often experience repeated conjugal or romantic failure and the condition is more frequent in men who, like Romney, have experienced a rise in social position.[37] Romney has also been described as one who was able to make art a stronghold of sanity amidst the chaos of melancholia, whose art came not from the mental condition but as a foil to it.[38] This may be more true of his portraiture than his imaginative work, as portraiture, which the artist himself termed 'drudgery', has been viewed as 'a steadying force . . . traditional and sane'.[39] His drawings reflect less restraint, but were a necessary outlet for the emotional energy bottled up during the day. Together the two provided the needful balance to enable a disciplined output amidst his lifelong struggle with depression.[40]

When George was eight years old, he began to experience one of the most positive influences on his subsequent work and personality. In 1742 his grandmother, Bridget Simpson, died leaving her leased house, garden and meadow in Dalton to be divided among her children, including Ann. John Romney and his brothers George and Thomas soon afterwards sold the Beckside property and, with this share together with Ann's capital, John purchased for £147 some land at High Cocken, near the hamlet of Hawcoat, now part of the shipbuilding town of Barrow-in-Furness.[41] Here he built a new farmhouse, sometimes to be known as 'Quarrys' from its proximity to an area of huge red sandstone cliffs which for centuries had been a source of building stone.[42] A more significant aspect was its panoramic view across the sand dunes of Walney island and over the Duddon estuary to the Lakeland fells. Romney experienced the 'poetic fervour and almost magical influence' of this environment, and in the words of his friend the sculptor John Flaxman:

> the rainbow, the purple distance or the silver lake, taught him colouring; the various actions and passions of the human figure, with the forms of clouds, woods, mountains or valleys afforded him studies of composition. Indeed his genius bore a strong resemblance to the scenes he was born in; like them it partook of the grand and the beautiful and like them also, the bright sunshine and enchanting prospects of his fancy were occasionally overspread with mist and gloom.[43]

In 1742 George followed his elder brother William to the local village grammar school at Dendron, where for five shillings a quarter he attended lessons in the chilly nave of St Matthew's church. For something under £5 a year he boarded meanwhile with Mrs Gardner, a family friend and a cultivated woman, who in her leisure hours made architectural drawings.[44] At Dendron Romney was not instructed in Latin or Greek, but the imaginative part of his education did feature tales from the Bible and classical literature. Also, his 'contemplative mind was employed in observing carefully, inquiring minutely into, and refecting continually on the objects around him, and thus by comparing and adding the results of his own observation, with the little he was taught, he gained perhaps as much useful knowledge as is commonly acquired, in the ordinary way, with greater assistance from books and masters'.[45] At the age of ten he was called home by his father to begin an apprenticeship as a cabinetmaker. Academic ineptitude has been stated as one cause of George's curtailed education, but the local effects of the Young Pretender's march south in 1745 may have presented a more pressing reason. At any rate, the boy's acute powers of observation coupled with his manual dexterity now recommended him. Certainly, considering this meagre three-year education, his eventual achievement is astonishing. Under his father's supervision, Romney learned to wield gouges and chisels and to carve chair legs and picture frames. In time, he began to supervise the men both in the workshop and on the farm. He was also sent to work in Church Street, Lancaster, with David Wright, a cabinetmaker and an associate of the Gillow family of furniture makers.[46] His surrogate master came to observe with fascination whenever young George sketched his fellow workmen's faces as a recreation from his training.[47]

Several influences on the young Romney as an artist were personal ones. Among the earliest was a watchmaker called John Williamson, who arrived in Dalton some time after 1748 from the port of Whitehaven. A man fascinated by mathematics and alchemy, this 'universal sage and referee of the village' would tell the tale against himself of the disastrous explosion of his crucible, which had destroyed a great deal in his workshop – a story which, with its allegorical resonance, Romney was never to forget.[48] Williamson explained to the boy the workings of a camera obscura, and together they also went up the coast to Whitehaven, then rapidly growing, to hear the virtuoso violinist Felice Giardini, whose performance for Romney was a new inspiration.[49] This led Williamson, himself a masterly player, to give George violin lessons and John Romney to assist him in making stringed instruments, one of which has recently been located.[50] Williamson, as Romney's first real mentor, may be the figure depicted beside a cello and a violin in *Unknown Man in a Landscape* (New Haven, Yale Center for British Art; Pl. I).[51] In his maturity, Romney was to find that playing his instrument while surrounded by paintings helped him to resolve problems of composition, which was a 'singular coincidence of the arts' in one man.[52] His dual expertise meanwhile placed him in the dilemma of having to choose between music and art.[53]

Later, he forbade his brother Peter to scribble verses whilst under his tutelage, being aware of the dangers of dissipating energy in the sister arts.

Two of the Romney brothers, George and Peter, enjoyed drawing. Before graduating to the more expensive support of paper, George would draw likenesses of men and women in chalk on workshop doors and gather a 'crowd of idlers' to admire him.[54] Peter was nine years younger and thus benefited from the example of his creative brother. As George developed this recreation he made a striking impression by drawing from memory the 'singular countenance' of a man seen at church.[55] Two small heads, possibly dating from this period, survive in a private collection in Cumbria, which may give credence to the tradition in the Duddon valley that Romney had drawn likenesses of local farmers before he went to Kendal.[56]

In this boyhood period Romney copied woodcuts from the *Universal Magazine* and engravings from another series lent by his father's employee, Sam Knight. Several more affluent neighbours had modest libraries to which Romney had access, and the Romney family owned several books themselves, including *Art's Masterpiece* (1697), which gave practical instruction in painting.[57] Romney himself also owned, by 1754, a copy of Leonardo da Vinci's *Treatise on Painting*, a compilation of texts which provided another source of engravings and gave practical instruction in painting and drawing, discussing the perennial questions of perspective, colour, light, shadow and form.[58] The text of the *Treatise* is closely linked with Leonardo's drawings of grotesque heads, which show numerous variations of the human face from the beautiful to the ugly. By 1755 Romney also owned a copy of Charles Le Brun's *Passions*, which codified the expressions of the human face.[59] Le Brun (1619–98), an early physiognomist, was a founder member of the French Academy and its Director from 1675; his book was to be the basis of Romney's delineation of human emotions for the rest of the artist's life.

One early likeness by Romney was that of the artistic Mrs Gardner. She had maintained contact with her young lodger and, seeing his teenage drawings at High Cocken, asked to sit to him for her portrait (untraced). Pleased with the result, she urged John Romney to release his son from his apprenticeship and to find him a new master.[60] In this she was supported by his mother's cousin, William Lewthwaite at Kirkby Hall, and David Wright at Lancaster, which suggests the discussions were protracted.[61] As the young man had only used his powers of invention so far upon 'designs for carvings and embellishments for models that existed only in his own imagination, the construction of all which did not add one corner cupboard to his father's stock and brought in only visionary custom and employ for palaces and castles in the air', his hitherto reluctant father now began to find a change of trade appropriate.[62] Mrs Gardner's prompting led eventually to the choice as master of the Kendal-based itinerant portraitist Christopher

Steele, who had executed a number of portraits for her family.[63] She must be credited with acute aesthetic perception: without her timely intervention, the artist may have remained a competent violin-playing cabinetmaker.[64]

It might appear that Romney could have had no artistic training prior to arriving in Kendal in 1755. However, a tradition holds in the village of Urswick, three miles from Dalton, that the young cabinetmaker 'learned colouring' from James Cranke the Elder (1707–80) after the older artist returned from London in 1752.[65] Indeed, Romney's portraits sometimes have anatomical similarities with Cranke's; for example in Romney's *Leigh Family* (Melbourne, National Gallery of Victoria; Pl. 8) and Cranke's *How Family* (Whitehaven, The Beacon Museum), the children have box-like skulls. Cranke's maturity, and his success in London, would certainly have made him a more prudent choice of master than the mercurial Steele.

Christopher Steele (1733–67), the son of a tallow chandler of Egremont in Cumbria, had established a bohemian lifestyle in France. On his return, his adoption of fashionable dress and deportment earned him the nickname 'Count'. Following a brief association with Richard Wright (*c*.1720–*c*.1775) in Liverpool, Steele is said to have 'received some instructions' in Paris from Carle van Loo (1705–65), who from 1762 was to be Painter to Louis XV.[66] Whatever the truth of this, descriptions of Steele as a mere itinerant dauber are misrepresentations of a talented portraitist who certainly studied in Paris, and whose painting techniques had enabled him to enjoy considerable success on his return to the Lake District. His technical expertise is evident in the freshness of colour and skilful satin sheen of his drapery in several identified works. A typical strong example is *John Knubley Wilson* (England, private collection), which confirms his ability to give the young Romney a sufficient grounding in his new profession.[67]

The 'old grey town' of Kendal, twenty miles distant from Dalton, had been for several centuries a thriving centre of the wool, leather and horn trades in the Lake counties. In addition to the landed gentry, there were a number of wealthy merchant families and affluent professionals in the area for portrait painters to depend upon. The site of Steele's studio is off Stricklandgate in Redman's Yard, whose entrance is located almost opposite the market place, and which was named after Alderman Christopher Redman, the brother of Mrs Gardner. Surviving photographs show the buildings in the yard as modest cottages, albeit with the windows of Steele's studio duly facing north.[68] It is always assumed that this building was the studio used by Romney until he left Kendal in 1762.

Steele needed an apprentice in dealing with commissions and, apart from John Romney's fee of twenty guineas, a further incentive for hiring George was the prospect of the young man's aptitude for making beautifully carved frames. Though shy, Romney had considerable muscular strength, yet another asset in an assistant.[69] The apprenticeship indenture (Kendal Town Hall) was signed on 20 March 1755 by Christopher Steele and George Romney, stating that Steele would instruct his apprentice 'in the art or science of a painter'.[70] The flamboyant personality of Romney's new master shines from the very curlicues of his signature.

Romney was only a year younger than Steele, and the disparity of their temperaments must rapidly have become obvious as his master 'followed painting as a calling but pleasure as his choice'.[71] Nonetheless, Romney generously acknowledged his master's appeal as a companion and his skill as an artist.[72] During a relatively beneficial co-existence of two years, Steele demonstrated grinding dry pigments supplied from the apothecary, mixing them with oil and preparing canvases; eventually his instruction culminated in the finer points of painting. Steele's sound training in well-tried techniques and his tendency to avoid experimentation, once passed on to Romney, enabled his pupil to paint portraits which would endure the passage of time. The toil at Redman's Yard, coupled with Romney's native ability, laid the foundations of his later success, but the finishing of many of Steele's incomplete canvases was a great trial and he resented his master treating him more as a servant than a pupil.[73]

To boost his income, Steele gave drawing lessons to young ladies. A corollary aim was to catch a wealthy heiress and, after a series of amatory exploits, he eloped with the young Amy Grundy.[74] Acting as his accomplice, Romney caught a severe chill and was cared for by Mary Abbot, the daughter of his widowed landlady. Some months later Romney, having been 'lured into a romantic liaison', had to marry his nurse, who by then was five months pregnant.[75] She was no beauty, as is clear from surviving drawings such as *Mary Romney* (Cambridge, Fitzwilliam Museum), and even her son refers to her 'symmetry of form' rather than her 'regularity of features'.[76] Mary (always known as Molly) was the daughter of John Abbot of Crosthwaite-cum-Lyth, near Kendal; the record of her baptism in August 1725 shows her to have been the artist's senior by nine years, a fact Romney may not have known.[77] Her father had died of 'a lingering and expensive illness' when both she and her sister Esther were children, leaving the family in 'impoverished circumstances'.[78] Now, nearing thirty, she had secured an attractive and elegible young man who appeared not only to have prosperous relatives but to be making a good start in the world.

Hearing of the match, Romney's parents were horrified that he should consider marriage before completing his apprenticeship. Portrait painting, for all its glamour, did not have the steady potential of cabinetmaking. But he wrote to them saying rather disingenuously that it would be 'a spur to my application' and 'the best thing that ever happened to me'.[79] So Molly and George were married in Kendal parish church on 14 October 1756, the artist being described in the marriage allegation as a 'face painter'.[80] The hasty wedding was also brought about in part by Steele's call for Romney to travel to York to assist with commissions there. This the new bridegroom did after a very short honeymoon in Kendal, leaving Molly with her mother and thus prefiguring his later role as an absentee husband. Notwithstanding his attempt to reassure his parents, his premature marriage was causing him mixed feelings of satisfaction and anxiety, so going to York may have been a blessed retreat from the 'excruciating conflict'.[81]

Among Steele's sitters in York was the writer Laurence Sterne, contact with whom prompted Romney to illustrate four subjects from *Tristram Shandy*. The figures in *The Introduction of Dr Slop into the Parlour of Mr Shandy* (Pl. 1), which only survives as an engraving, are crude even by the standards of Romney's earliest known works, while the grimace of Dr Slop, the man-midwife, derives from Romney's familiarity with Le Brun. Sterne's character of Dr Slop was taken from the eminent Dr John Burton of York, whose book *Towards a Complete New System of Midwifery* (1751) had been illustrated by George Stubbs.[82] Representations of contemporary literary subjects, such as Highmore's scenes from Richardson's *Pamela* or Hogarth's from Gay's *The Beggar's Opera,* were popular by the middle of the eighteenth century as an acceptable alternative to stereotyped classical subjects. As Sterne's novel was not published until after 1759, it seems certain that Steele and Romney were treated to readings at a draft stage. Sterne's serious aspect was effectively rendered in Romney's *The Death of Le Fèvre* (untraced), described at the time as 'wonderfully expressive'.[83] This choice of both comic and tragic subjects anticipates the duality of feeling expressed throughout Romney's work. Paradoxically, the author urges his readers to approach the book as if it were a picture, while the artist's son's description of the lost *Le Fèvre* composition is longer than Sterne's original text.[84] Although never used in an edition of Sterne, Romney's illustrations must be, with Hogarth's, among the earliest of their kind.[85] The figures, painted eighteen inches high, were even smaller than those in his early portrait full-lengths and, though rather wooden, are important as 'curious specimens of uninstructed genius'.[86]

While in York, Romney found himself irked by Steele's habitual reluctance to provide food and clothing as he was contracted to do; he also tended to borrow from Romney.[87] This reneging upon the terms of his indentures necessitated Molly sending her husband part of her wages, half a guinea at a time, secreted under the wax seal of her letters.[88] Inevitably, Steele's debts soon accumulated, necessitating his rapid departure. Following altercations between them, Romney was instructed to stay behind to complete several of his master's pictures, and with the proceeds to settle the outstanding accounts.[89] Steele's ebullience never forsook him, even when he was skulking

1 *Dr Slop Entering Mr Shandy's Parlour* (engraving by W. Haines), from William Hayley, *The Life of George Romney* (1809), 19 × 15.5 cm (7.5 × 6.1 in). This crude early work demonstrates Romney's interest in depicting emotion.

to avoid the 'unwelcome gripe of the unrelenting bailiff', but the son of 'Honest' John Romney remained exasperated by such antics.[90]

At last, in July 1757, Romney was able to return home. Terminally frustrated by his master's cavalier attitude to the apprenticeship, he arranged to break the indentures in exchange for the cancellation of a ten pound debt. Having declared sincerely that Romney would 'do wonders', Steele immediately fled to Dublin.[91] Whatever relief George felt at his departure, it curtailed the apprenticeship at a time when his father's other responsibilities were significant. Although 'Honest' John's eldest son William was now twenty-six years old, there were still five sons who had not yet reached their majority, of whom George was the most reliable; little Thomas was only seven.

Free of the erratic Steele, Romney was now able to pursue his own career, but he too had the responsibilities of a family. His son John, named after his versatile grandfather, who was to become an Anglican priest and one of his father's biographers, had been born and baptised in George's absence: another mouth to feed. Whatever Romney's own anxiety about the incomplete apprenticeship, he was ambitious and used to long hours and he settled down to work with great assiduity. Although he still had a great deal to learn, he had absorbed enough skills to establish an independent practice in the Kendal area. His first commission, for Hugh Holme the postmaster, was a sign for the postbox at the King's Arms: *A Hand Posting a Letter* (Kendal Town Hall).[92] Because the ancillary tasks Steele had set him had been so numerous, the people of Kendal on seeing this sign, expressed astonishment that 'so ingenious a carver should turn painter'.[93]

Early in his Kendal days Romney made friends with William Cockin (1736–1801) and Adam Walker (1730–1821), both schoolmasters in Lancaster at different periods, whose interests ranged over both the arts and the sciences. 'The ingenious Mr Cockin' later assisted Father Thomas West in the preparation of his *Guide to the Lakes* of 1778, and among his own verse is an 'Ode to the Genius of the Lakes'.[94] Adam Walker, who was to be one of the new breed of natural philosophers or scientists, was the son of a Troutbeck woollen weaver. While in Lancaster he and the artist shared lodgings, where they and other friends held musical evenings with Romney joining the ensemble on his violin.[95] Though Romney was not memorable for his liveliness, his sense of humour is apparent in a surviving early letter to Walker – on the evidence of his own correspondence an entertaining friend – where he relives an encounter between them in the street:

> Good God! (say I to myself) who can this be? I certainly must know the person but he seems so disguised with that importance and gravity, which look so like burlesque, I can scarcely forbear smiling.[96]

Initially, Romney achieved recognition in Kendal among middle-class patrons who were not remote from him socially. The resultant portraits included *Alderman Thomas Wilson* (Kendal Town Hall), who was mayor of the town in 1763–4, and *The Reverend Dr Thomas Symonds* (untraced), the vicar who had officiated at his wedding to Molly.

Romney's reputation in the Lake District was made, however, when he painted various members of two prominent county families: the Wilsons of Dallam Tower and the Stricklands of Sizergh Castle. Walter Strickland was his first major patron and the artist eventually painted at least five portraits for his family. Of these, the best are Strickland's sister-in-law *Cecilia Towneley* (Sizergh Castle, National Trust), dressed as a shepherdess, and the small-scale portrait *The Reverend William Strickland SJ* (Sizergh Castle, The National Trust; Pl. II).[97] This, the most detailed interior Romney ever produced, depicts its subject in his study with his globe and books. In 1759 Colonel George Wilson sat to Romney soon after the building of Abbot Hall, his new house on the River Kent.[98] *Colonel George Wilson* (England, private collection; Pl. III), also a small-scale portrait, includes the Colonel's three dogs, and gives the surrounding landscape as much prominence as the sitter. A second Wilson portrait, *The Reverend Daniel Wilson* (Wakefield Art Gallery), was also painted in 1759–60, perhaps in Lancaster, where the Wilsons had a town house in Church Street. The interest shown by the Stricklands and the Wilsons, the latter family being also patrons of Cranke, firmly established Romney in the town of Kendal.

Other small-scale full-lengths of the Kendal period were *Jacob Morland of Capplethwaite Hall* (London, Tate Gallery) and *John Postlethwaite* (private collection, Abbot Hall Art Gallery), likenesses of a Killington landowner and a solicitor of Kendal.[99] Such attractive, 'less overbearing' portraits, the best early pictures, bear fine detailing and finish of the kind usually seen as hallmarks of Arthur Devis of Preston (1711?–1787), whom Romney could have met.[100] The carved rococo frame of *John Postlethwaite*, with its swept, pierced outer rails, is similar to Joseph Wright's frames dating from the 1760s and may be a surviving Romney original.[101]

Sitters did not stay in the studio longer than was essential to establish the composition and to take a likeness. This necessitated the completion of each canvas while they were not present. Artists such as Devis employed life-sized mannekins, or lay figures, which had flexible joints and could, if large enough, wear a sitter's clothing arranged to adopt the chosen attitude. In this way the folds of drapery could be accurately modelled, though sometimes the effect was stiff and doll-like.[102]

The artist's brother Peter, who had by sixteen years of age developed a flair for pastels, joined him in the studio shortly after their mother had died, aged fifty-five, in April 1759. This had been the family's second death within a few months, little Thomas having died the previous year. Peter despaired of ever attaining his brother's dexterity, and experienced great frustration. Though he had some success, he was to lead a life of caprice and recklessness, featuring a series of traumatic and disastrous relationships founded on the inherited melancholia he shared with his brother George.[103] Another newcomer was Mrs Gardner's young son Daniel, later a popular pastellist himself, who at nine years old began to take an interest in the processes of portraiture and was allowed to amuse himself in the studio at Redman's Yard.[104] An indication of how the artist's status was rising appears meanwhile in the parish records for 1760, when Molly's second child was baptised Ann, after the artist's mother. In noting this event, the parish clerk makes the point of describing the father as 'Mr' Romney, an unusual distinction.

Having secured sitters in and around Kendal, and being familiar with Lancaster and its greater mercantile wealth, Romney began to build upon family and personal contacts in that town also. The resulting works, though modest in scale, were creditable but not always immediately paid for. The elderly 'Mr B.', who lived near Lancaster, rejected his portrait, only changing his mind when he discovered that the artist's fame was increasing.[105] Romney was ambitious enough to desire more taxing commissions, more appreciative and discriminating patrons and the challenge of competition. These, he knew, could only be found in London. His better-known Lancaster paintings were produced during his visits to the north after he had moved to London.

At this stage of his career, following his experiments with subjects from the fictions of Laurence Sterne, Romney was determined to broaden his scope beyond that of face painting. Like many painters of the period, he copied in oils from other artists' works, in his case landscape engravings after Berchem, Poussin and Wouwerman which he had purchased in York.[106] Other work from this time also included two 'war pieces', Dutch genre subjects and a Holy Family.

Keen to vie with the best artists in Britain, Romney nonetheless experienced agonies of indecision. The incentives to stay included his respectable income in the north, his family responsibilities and his anxiety regarding the risk of trying his luck in London. Incentives to leave were his keenness to improve his art, and the likely future shortage of sitters in the north. After considerable family debate he determined to go south.

It was a move requiring capital, principally to fund the venture but also to provide some security for his wife and two children, John and Ann. In 1762 he decided to hold a lottery of his stock of twenty historical and landscape pictures in Kendal Town Hall, for which he managed to sell eighty-two tickets at half a guinea each. These pictures demonstrate the considerable breadth of his experimentation in little more than four years of independence, as they include biblical and genre subjects, portrayals of saints and scenes from Shakespeare and Sterne.[107] Clearly he was laying claim to

2 *Memories of Windermere, c.*1761, 81 × 126.5 cm (32 × 50 in). This rare landscape achieves subtle reflections and a sense of distance.

an involvement in a wider British culture. The first two lottery prizes, valued at eight guineas each, were *King Lear Awakened by his Daughter* (untraced), for which Molly had sat as Cordelia, and *King Lear in the Storm Tearing off his Robes* (Kendal Town Hall), both subjects from his favourite Shakespeare play.

Memories of Windermere (sold Christie's, 18 June 1971; Pl. 2), another lottery picture, is Romney's only surviving landscape in oils. Depicting the artist, Molly, Adam Walker, his wife Eleanor and brother Tom crossing the lake for a picnic party, is dated *c.*1761. It is thus a very early example of Lakeland landscape art and pre-dates by ten years the earliest significant topographical writing about the region.[108] Its composition relates to an illustration by William Kent for *The Faerie Queene* of 1751; in it Romney has 'distilled something of the fête galante' of Watteau, and it has a sophistication 'very far beyond what might have been expected of so young and inexperienced an artist'.[109] His other lottery subjects include a landscape in oils entitled *Coalbrookdale* (untraced).[110] This lost work is the earliest recorded oil painting executed of this valley, the strategic setting for the most prominent iron industry of the era, in the years before the building of the first Iron Bridge.[111]

Throughout his life, Romney, familiar with dramatic lighting effects from his father's small forge, experimented with the effects of candlelight upon both human subjects and plaster casts of sculpture. In about 1759 he painted the delightful portrait of his small brother, *James Romney Holding a Candle* (Kendal, Abbot Hall Art Gallery), where the soft light enables the young face to glow and the light behind the hand gives a transparency to the fingers.[112] This North European use of chiaroscuro had impinged upon his imagination via Dutch engravings after Schalken, Terbrugghen and Honthorst. A more dramatic torchlit subject was offered by *King Lear in the Storm Tearing off his Robes* (Pl. IV) which carried, in the frenzied unbuttoning of the King, a foreshadowing of Romney's own mental frailty. As well as drawing attention to the relationship between costume and status, so fundamental to portraiture, the painting also parallels his professional vulnerability soon after he had parted from Steele. Beside these autobiographical vestiges, the potent elements of the storm – the lightning, the torchlight, the disguise of Kent, the anxiety of Gloucester, shortly to have his eyes plucked out, the feigned madness of 'Poor Tom' and the madness of the King himself as he identifies with suffering humanity – are collectively an early, representative demonstration of the vocabulary of protoromanticism, and the painting is also a very early example of an artist's creative response to Shakespeare in oils on canvas. Later in his career Romney was to develop this interest, and the text of *King Lear* was to provide him with sources of drawings and paintings for the next forty years. Since one of the witnesses of the signing of Romney's apprenticeship indenture was Thomas Ashburner, the founder of the theatre in the market place in Kendal, Steele and his pupil had close links with local drama at a time when Shakespeare was, once again, becoming popular.[113]

Two of the other lottery paintings were Dutch-style genre candlelight subjects: *A Droll Scene in an Ale House* and *A Tooth – Drawing by Candlelight* (both untraced). These choices demonstrate Romney's further awareness of the potential of lighthearted and grotesque themes as exploited by Hogarth in *Night* (Upton House, The National Trust). With Joseph Wright of Derby, Romney was one of the first in England to follow Hogarth in producing such 'nocturnes', but his output was far less extensive than Wright's.[114] In later life he sketched *The Corinthian Maid* (Princeton, University Art Gallery), in which a girl traces the shadow of her sleeping lover's features on a wall, a subject also chosen by Wright and sometimes entitled *The Origin of Painting* (Washington, DC, National Gallery of Art).[115] Though Romney did not use this technique himself to obtain accurate profiles, several of his contemporaries, such as Nathaniel Marchant, did.[116] Privately, in later life, he experimented with various ways of illuminating his casts of antique sculptures, and he created dramatic effects of light and dark in works like *Serena*

Reading (Dunrobin Castle) and *Susannah and the Elders* (unfinished and untraced), depicting candlelight and lamplight respectively.

Having divided with Molly the lottery money and other savings, Romney left Kendal with two companions on 14 March 1762 and rode south with his share of the capital in his saddlebags. Eleven-year-old Daniel Gardner felt totally bereft, and during the following months wrote 'London' numerous times in his school books. In a few years he was to follow his mother's protégé and his own first master to the metropolis.[117] In the same year three of Romney's brothers also left the north-west of England: John for London and William and Lawrence for the West Indies, in search of advancement as agents for Samuel Bradford of Lancaster on his sugar-cane plantations.[118] John, who was indolent and debauched, made continual demands for money and was an embarassment to all his family. The artist could ill afford this further drain on his purse, and having lived with Steele was all too conscious of the disadvantages of an irregular life. A letter from their brother Peter refers to 'his Release', which suggests John's imprisonment for debt, an unhappy echo of Hogarth's idle apprentice. To no avail, however, did Peter urge his brother to be forceful with John, while even their father threatened to come south to help. This reprobate sibling eventually died in 1782, aged only forty-five.[119] Hints of the personalities of William and Lawrence arise in the same letter from Peter, where the melancholic Lawrence is described as 'carrying too much sail' and being bullied by William.[120] In one of his last letters home, which proved prophetic in several respects, Lawrence wrote: 'I sometimes hear of my brother George's performances in such a manner as gives me great pleasure, I suppose he is one of the first painters in England. I hope he may enjoy his health to make a fortune.'[121] Though George's aspirations were realized, those of William and Lawrence were not and they both perished in the islands as young men: William in Antigua in 1768 and Lawrence in Dominica in 1772.[122] In his concern for his older brothers, the youthful Peter's perception and eloquence quite transcend his imperfect legibility.

En route for London, Romney broke his journey in Manchester to meet Steele, who had returned from Dublin. As restless as ever and recovering from his wife's recent death, Steele himself sailed to the West Indies in December 1762. Adam Walker, Romney's friend from his days in both Kendal and Lancaster, agreed to settle Steele's affairs. His correspondence described the 'general wreck' of the Manchester studio and how he dealt with creditors and a bevy of distressed damsels: 'some in want of a pair of stays, others of gauze handkerchiefs . . . and many, no doubt, of their most precious maidenheads'.[123] In 1767 Steele returned to die in his native Egremont, success having eluded him abroad.[124] Whatever the failings of his professional and private life he must be acknowledged for his crucial role in Romney's development and be accorded a share in his pupil's achievement.

It is unclear whether at this point the artist intended to abandon his family.[125] Molly wanted to visit London in 1762 and still hoped to do so in 1773. At the latter date Romney angrily forbade her, writing that if she did come she would 'regret it'.[126] Their relationship had already deteriorated and the tone of this draft letter recalls the emotional turmoil he experienced in 1756 on discovering Molly to be pregnant. He did the decent thing and married her, but however much he assured his parents of his happiness at this point, he must have been apprehensive about his future responsibilities and the effect these would have upon his art. Such apprehension may well have bred resentment. This feeling is likely to have increased during his Kendal years as Molly's lack of intellectual pretension became more evident. Once in London, Romney was probably apprehensive of introducing an unattractive country wife to his educated new associates, while the geographical separation led to them drifting further apart emotionally.[127] His familial psychology undoubtedly exacerbated the situation, and this unfortunate experience may have contributed both to his inability to engage emotionally with other women and to his voyeuristic tendencies. He continued, however, to support Molly financially, while only seeing her two or three times in the next thirty-six years, an exaggerated variant upon a not uncommon arrangement during this period.[128] The artist probably experienced some guilt, but he may not have been alone in this as Molly could conceivably have felt some remorse for what appears to have been her seduction of a younger man. Having experienced his coldness, she remained with her friends and sister in Kendal, where her social position was more secure than in London. By being in the north she enjoyed a relative independence, with her husband out of reach, and as his reputation grew she probably enjoyed a little reflected glory. Her encouragement of their son John led eventually to his academic success at Cambridge; otherwise little is known of her life. When Romney returned permanently to Kendal in 1798, he was nonetheless fortunate to receive from her a positive welcome.

In London: architect of his own fortune 1762–4

After seven days' travel on horseback, Romney arrived in London on 21 March, taking a room at the Castle Inn, probably on the east side of Wood Street, near Cheapside, where the Nottingham carrier left the city for the turnpike north.[1] Here for two weeks he used this 'noisy receptacle of comers and goers' as a base while he located suitable sources of materials and considered how he might attract his first sitters.[2]

London at this time was overcrowded and growing rapidly, with a confusion of wealth and indigence on all sides. Much of the West End was impressive, with its streets and squares laid out on a grid pattern. So too were the clean stone spires of new churches, the graceful façades of pilastered terraces, the innovations of streetlamps and pavements, the immaculately painted carriages, the larger book and print shops, the elegant costumes and elaborate entertainments by the river at Vauxhall and Ranelagh Gardens. The Thames, forested with masts, was itself a marvel, where a profusion of foodstuffs and colourful cargoes were traded: furs from the American colonies, Chinese porcelain, Mediterranean citrus fruits, Indian spices, slaves from Africa to become exotic servants, Italian marbles and Baltic timber. The city nonetheless held areas of unparalleled poverty and squalor, as a place whose rewards and penalties could both be extreme.

In early-eighteenth-century Britain, there was no significant native visual art. The nobility preferred to commission the work of Italians or Frenchmen, whose work had a greater cachet, based upon perceived cultural continuities in Europe. The Reformation's virtual ousting of Catholicism had destroyed the British market for sacred art and for two centuries the country's artistic potential had had few outlets. By the time of Romney's arrival in London, however, British talent had been asserting itself for several decades and was gradually displacing the work of foreign artists.[3] Among prominent older artists, Thomas Hudson (1701–79) and Joseph Highmore (1692–1780) had retired, George Knapton (1698–1778) had virtually ceased work, William Hogarth (1697–1764) was still active, but Allan Ramsay (1713–92) was largely restricted to royal commissions. Of Romney's own generation, Thomas Gainsborough (1727–88) was still in Bath and although Joshua Reynolds (1723–92) was a rising star, he was being seriously challenged by Francis Cotes (*c.*1725–70).[4]

These were the major players, but estimates vary regarding the number of portrait painters in the city. There were certainly more than a hundred and, although demand was rising, there was insufficient work to go round so that the task of achieving a reputation in this savagely competitive world was immense.

Following the Peace of Paris in February 1763, the economic situation was to improve, however, and travel in Europe on the Grand Tour again became easier. Gentlemen, and rather fewer ladies, travelled to see continental architecture, old masters and antique sculpture, partly in order to establish their credentials as persons of taste. This, coupled with increased prosperity, led to a demand from the aristocracy and, increasingly, from the middle class for a wider variety of art. There was a tension between artists and connoisseurs who envisaged the development of elevated genres and the commercial values of those who preferred to commission portraiture of people, dogs, horses or property. A particularly British predilection, domestic portraits were visible evidence of wealth and prestige, apart from being a record of absent family and friends.[5] As artists' incomes rose, following those of their patrons, so did their status and independence. This in turn generated a stronger sense of professionalism, enhanced in the 1760s by the founding of the Society of Artists and subsequently the Royal Academy. Artists were no longer viewed merely as craftsmen, but they continued to be frustrated by a shortage of ambitious commissions. Romney himself took an optimistic view, observing by 1773 that 'true taste is growing up; that kind which inspired the Italian schools'.[6] In the meantime, as a northerner with few contacts, his achievement was considerable in the short space of his first years in London.

Writing to his wife ten days after his arrival, Romney expressed satisfaction with his move south and asked her to send two history pictures: another *King Lear* (untraced) and *Elfrida* (untraced) 'rolled up in a box by the first waggon'.[7] The dramatic tale of Elfrida probably relates to the poem of this title published by William Mason in 1752 and eventually dramatized for performance at Covent Garden in 1772. It recalls the fate of one who falsely reported the beauty of Elfrida, the mother of Ethelred 'the Unready' – an object lesson for portraitists which was also painted by Angelica Kauffmann in the 1770s.[8] Romney's resolve to have these works adorning a very modest studio was of a piece with his ambition to paint more intellectually and technically challenging work than portraits. Although they exchanged letters, Molly's side of the correspondence had to be written by Peter Romney as Molly was illiterate.[9]

After a few weeks in town, Romney moved to lodgings at Dove Court, Old Jewry, near the Mansion House. Here, determined to strike a major blow, he started a large-scale history piece, *The Death of David Rizzio* (destroyed), depicting Mary Queen of Scots in the act of protecting her unfortunate secretary from his assassins. This canvas was one of Romney's early favourites and he referred to it in later life 'in warmer terms of self-approbation than he was apt to employ when speaking of one of his own productions'.[10] Considering the difficulties of the market and his financial obligations to his wife, children and demanding brothers, it is remarkable that he made such a committed start with time-consuming histories. Gradually, he was driven to expend most of his time on the more lucrative work of portraiture, but he still maintained an ambition to succeed as a history painter. In these early London paintings, as in his previous career, Romney once again staked his claim to a wider historical and literary culture, but this time before a larger and more demanding audience.

On his arrival in London, Romney was not totally without connections. His acquaintance included the wealthy banker Rowland Stephenson, son-in-law of a Kendal alderman and nephew of a former Governor of Bengal.[11] A chance meeting with Daniel Braithwaite, a clerk with the Post Office, introduced him to many of the principal works of art in the city.[12] Items on view included works by Hogarth and Richard Wilson (among others) at Captain Coram's Foundlings Hospital. In the supper boxes at Vauxhall Gardens hung Francis Hayman's canvases depicting children's games, rural festivals and Shakespearean drama. There were also the more accessible private collections, together with the contents of print shops, including that of the energetic and successful John Boydell. Braithwaite, a fellow northerner, was soon to become Secretary to the Postmaster General; by 1790, he was Controller of the Foreign Department. A man of broad interests, he was universally liked, 'associated with many of the wits of the age' and from 1782 was a Fellow of the Royal Society.[13] Romney used to dine regularly at his house. At the time he was establishing himself in London, the artist was himself an attractive man, as Hayley attests, with broad strong features, a look of vigour in the eyes and an acute mind.

Since the seventeenth century, history painting had been regarded as the most prestigious genre. This blanket term included biblical, literary, mythological and allegorical subjects and, from the 1760s, contemporary events. Romney, by the end of his career, had tackled all these categories.[14] As with Reynolds and others, he aspired to history painting as Gainsborough did to landscape art, but it was virtually impossible to survive without painting portraits too. Though portraiture was 'theoretically and idealogically . . . an inferior genre, actually it was the dominant art form'.[15] Romney's talent, as established in Kendal, was in the precise representation of facial features and drapery rather than in the invention of poses, so that he was in fact best suited to portraiture. Prestige apart, he nonetheless gained more pleasure from the imaginative work required for history painting. As he matured, he worked at the skills necessary in more complex composition, by producing a huge body of wash drawings which are often viewed as preparatory work.[16] Hence he faced a frustrating dilemma as his reputation grew, leaving him increasingly 'shackled' to portraiture.[17]

Many creative men in London struggled to success from similar provincial backgrounds: the writer Samuel Johnson; the actor David Garrick; the composer William Boyce. By mixing increasingly with his well-educated middle-class sitters and the young professionals of Braithwaite's circle, Romney was able to develop his social, intellectual and aesthetic skills. This was essential in order to be acceptable to the more fastidious members of society. Such a process of self-improvement and identification with the values of wealthier sitters had its dangers. James Northcote (1746–1831), the artist son of a watchmaker, after a life of aspiration ended up isolated both from his own class and the one he had aimed to join.[18] Romney's more modest social aspirations spared him such indignity, as he tended to spend more time with professional friends, not necessarily artists, with whom he could relax more easily.[19]

Once Romney was familiar with the significant personalities of the metropolis, his two main objects were to find further professional instruction and a means of exhibiting his work. These were aims he shared with numerous others. Training facilities for British artists had developed more slowly than those on the continent, and Hogarth's St Martin's Lane Academy was for many years, from 1734, the only school available to them.[20] Romney was, however, able to make use of access to the young Duke of Richmond's cast collection at Richmond House in Whitehall, a rare source of antique and Renaissance models, including casts after the *Borghese Gladiator* and Michelangelo's *Bacchus*. Here he improved his ability to draw drapery, and established friendships with artists including Ozias Humphry (1742–1810), the son of a peruke maker from Honiton in Devonshire and one of the best miniaturists of the period.[21]

Praised by Horace Walpole, the great connoisseur, as 'a very grand seigneurial design', the collection was housed in a large room in the Duke's garden and supervised by the sculptor Joseph Wilton, who had recently carved the state coach for George III. Its casts enabled students to acquire 'a purer taste in the knowledge of human forms' than was otherwise possible at this time without travelling to Italy.[22] Romney responded hungrily to this great feast of beauty, making the most of the opportunity it offered and eventually meeting the Duke, his exact contemporary, who was in time to become an important patron in a relationship which endured for more than thirty years.

The foundation of the Society of Artists in 1760 provided a further place of instruction and it began to organize public exhibitions. Until 1768 these exhibitions were the best way a new artist from the provinces could make himself known.[23] Early successes there inevitably bred dissension and a splinter group formed, the Free Society of Artists, in 1761, partly through the intervention of Hogarth. As an early sign of his identification with movements of protest, in 1763 Romney signed the Free Society deed with a hundred others and subsequently exhibited with them for seven years.[24] Predictably, two of his early exhibits were history paintings.

The reluctance of patrons of art to purchase history pictures had caused a dearth of opportunity, offset since 1760 by prizes offered by the Society for the Encouragement of Arts, Manufactures and Commerce, for subjects taken from British history.[25] The lack of history commissions is illustrated by Hogarth's satirical drawing, printed as the tailpiece to the 1761 exhibition catalogue, in which a monkey is shown watering exotic dead plants.[26] Although the market was still limited, the availability of new prizes resulted in 'an explosion of subject matter' as fresh subjects were sought and exploited.[27] In 1763 Romney entered for the prize an adventurous composition entitled *The Death of General Wolfe* (untraced and probably destroyed).

Major-General James Wolfe, an officer of the Duke of Richmond's own regiment, had died in the act of leading the British to victory against the French at the battle of Quebec on 13 September 1759.[28] This major piece of national news inspired pride and patriotism through its 'bright lesson of heroic death'.[29] In painting such a recent event, Romney courageously chose to violate a basic principle by rejecting the established convention of depicting great men in classical robes and adopting the historical accuracy of contemporary military dress.[30] By now, Braithwaite had found Romney a slightly better studio in Bearbinder's Lane, south-east of the Mansion House at the historic spot where the great plague of 1665 had made its first appearance in the city.[31] Here John Hamilton Mortimer (1740–79), who had already won prizes at St Martin's Lane Academy, came to view the progress of *The Death of General Wolfe* 'in a room so small that he could not examine the effect of the whole at a single view and at a proper distance and [observed] that under this disadvantage [Romney's] performance was surprising'.[32]

The use of modern dress was familiar enough on the theatre stage and in painting, Francis Hayman (1708?–76) had set a precedent in his *Surrender of Montreal*, which had hung at Vauxhall Gardens from 1761. Nonetheless, Romney's innovative production was regarded as a shocking attack upon convention.[33] It may not have helped that, to the exhibition's sophisticated metropolitan visitors, Romney was a presumptuous young artist from the north country.[34] However, one observer recalled this 'nobly pathetic scene' as the 'dawning effort' of Romney's ability. Horace Walpole was sufficiently taken to record a lengthy description of Wolfe 'leaning against and supported by two officers', and effectively confirmed Romney's growing ability to follow Le Brun, in capturing the emotion on the face of an officer 'greatly struck with Surprize'.[35] But Walpole did also record the general criticism that Wolfe's countenance was 'more like a Dead than a dying man's', and not only did others dislike the use of modern dress but they also quibbled over regimental details.

Despite the somewhat mixed response, it was an artistic event of importance. Romney had shown the hero in the poignant pose of a dying saint and attempted 'a shift of emotional allegiance from religion to nationalism', a tendency later manifest in his radical politics.[36] On 1 April the Society for the Encouragement of the Arts, Manufactures and Commerce awarded first prize to Robert Edge Pine for his *Canute Reproving his Flattering Courtiers* (untraced), while Romney was awarded the second prize of fifty guineas. Tradition holds that Joshua Reynolds intervened in favour of Mortimer's *Edward the Confessor Stripping his Mother of her Effects* (San Marino, Huntington Art Collections), the committee then presenting Romney with twenty-five guineas in consolation.[37] This event is usually offered as the root of the antipathy between Romney and Reynolds, who had not yet painted any histories.[38] However, Reynolds hardly knew who Romney was and the future President of the Academy was still in the process of attaining his position of pre-eminence. Though the decision is said to have fixed 'a lasting impression of disgust' upon the mind of Romney against Reynolds, it is probable that the tale has grown in the retelling.[39]

The stir caused by *The Death of General Wolfe* undoubtedly raised the young artist's profile and increased his portrait business, while he experienced for the first time the unpleasant aspects of the jostling world of public exhibitions. Romney did not enjoy, at any stage in his life, the agonies of exhibition, and although he continued to exhibit regularly until 1772, after his visit to Italy he had no need of the exposure and was glad to avoid the skirmishes attendant on exhibiting his work. In 1794, following his marginally more positive experience of exhibiting at the Boydell Shakespeare Gallery, he was still of the same view, writing: 'My nerves are too weak for supporting anything in public.'[40]

The Death of General Wolfe was bought for twenty-five guineas by Romney's friend Rowland Stephenson for Harry Verelst, soon to be Governor of Bengal, and the grandson of Cornelius Verelst the flower painter, who hung it in the Council Chamber in Calcutta. This was the highest price Romney had yet received for any painting. If the painting was shipped out to Verelst in 1763, this was the year of the victory at Buxar and only seven years after the notorious incident of the 'Black Hole'. Bengal was still in a state of some confusion and *The Death of General Wolfe* was being sent to a somewhat vulnerable future. Certainly, enquiries in this and the last century have failed to locate this picture.[41]

Romney's work anticipated by a year *The Death of General Wolfe* by the Cheshire portraitist Edward Penny (Oxford, Ashmolean Museum), and a more famous treatment of the subject in 1770 by the American Benjamin West (Ottawa, National Gallery of Canada). According to a later suggestion by Romney's friend, the dramatist Richard Cumberland, Romney's version, exhibited in the year of West's arrival from Rome, was an important influence upon its more familiar counterpart.[42] The West picture, which involved even the Archbishop of Canterbury in an intense debate about the propriety of modern dress in history paintings, was to achieve a revolution in art which sent history painting on a new course.[43]

Later in 1763 Romney moved to a larger studio at Charing Cross, near the Mews Gate, and shortly afterwards to James Street, Covent Garden.[44] This was an area where many artists lived and where potential sitters would tend to seek a painter for their portrait. Mortimer also lived in Covent Garden and Reynolds in his new house nearby in Leicester Fields.[45] Also in 1763 Francis Cotes refurbished the house in Cavendish Square which was eventually to become Romney's own. The younger artist's awareness of the success of Cotes appears to have influenced the style of *Mrs Wilbraham Bootle* (sold Christie's, 18 June 1976; Pl. 3), a portrait perhaps identical with the one exhibited in 1764. This sitter was a close friend of Mrs George Wilson of Abbot Hall, Kendal, so it seems Romney continued to find work through his links with the north-west of England.

Romney also continued to exhibit varied and complex history subjects, including an unfinished religious subject, *Samson and Delilah* (untraced), the design of which may relate to his later series of drawings *Samson Overpowered* (New Haven, Yale Center for British Art; Pl. 4). In the same year he visited Benjamin West in his studio to see his fellow artist's *General Robert Monckton*. Under unusual and secure conditions of royal patronage, West was soon able to produce large numbers of history paintings.

In 1765 Romney exhibited *The Death of King Edmund* (untraced), which demonstrated his enthusiasm for the growing fashion for depicting violent death, and which this time won a second premium without unnecessary argument.[46] Many other artists followed, exploring the scope of violent literary and historical death scenes which eventually led, via David's *The Death of Marat* (Brussels) and several depictions by others of the death of Lord Nelson, to Delacroix's *Death of Sardanapalus* (Paris, Musée du Louvre).[47]

3 *Mrs Wilbraham Bootle*, *c.*1764, 126.5 × 101.2 cm (50 × 40 in). The mask-like face of the wife of the MP for Chester.

4 *Samson Overpowered*, 1777–80, 49.7 × 39.7 cm (19.7 × 15.6 in). Betrayed by Delilah, the strong man, now shorn, is easily defeated.

After Romney had been two years in London, his friend Thomas Greene (1737–1810) suggested that they should go abroad to France. Greene had been a close friend since the late 1740s, following Saturday visits to High Cocken from Dendron School with Romney's younger brother Lawrence.[48] Greene's parents lived at Slyne Hall near Lancaster, and their son was to be the artist's legal and financial adviser over many years. His portrait now hangs at Abbot Hall Art Gallery. Europe had been in Romney's sights since youth, and certainly since hearing Steele's tales of travel on the continent. He knew such experience would enhance his professional standing with his sitters and enable him to talk on more equal terms with those who had completed the Grand Tour. He had been 'frequently mortified' to have to admit that he had not travelled abroad, so Greene very generously sold all his stocks to raise the cash for their journey.[49] It was an important step towards the artist's goal of seeing Italy, an aspiration he would have to nurse for another nine years.

On 30 August 1764 they sailed to Dunkirk from Horsely Downs, a wharf at Southwark, on the London sloop *Earl Godwin* in the company of William Dickinson, probably the engraver of that name.[50] Of their arrival in Paris, Romney wrote, 'I was very struck by the strange appearance of things at the first sight. The degeneracy of taste which runs through everything is farther gone here than in London. The ridiculous and the fantastical are the only points they seem to aim at.'[51] They looked at paintings in Notre Dame, but a mass was in progress and their companion Dickinson, unfamiliar with ritual details, was seized by the collar by the priest and forced to kneel to the host.[52] Romney spoke no French, and a whiff of xenophobia runs both through his own comments and the diary kept by Greene. At the French Royal Academy they enjoyed the casts after the antique, but contemporary painting elicited their disapproval and they seem to have preferred work from the time of Louis XIV. Romney felt overwhelmed by the vast collections and found he had 'no inclination either for designing or writing'.[53] Encountering Louis XV on the way to mass, they were stared at by the King as the only strangers present. They noted that the Queen and her ladies were 'all elegantly dressed (but) . . . all painted very much'. Having seen the King they were well entertained by a mountebank and his monkey. Greene wrote that the creature's sagacity and drollery gave it 'much more the appearance of the human species than many strutting Frenchmen we had seen'.[54] Like travellers anywhere Romney and his companions also commented upon the services they received including a *perruquier* who 'scraped us tolerably and dressed our wigs etc miserably'.[55] Admiring the statues at Versailles, they thought a copy of the Laocoön 'very fine' but complained of the extravagant demands made for money upon Englishmen.

Many works of art seen by Romney and his friends were, however, to find correspondences in his own work. Meeting Mark Parker, the antiquary and father-in-law of Claude-Joseph Vernet (1714–89), in the Luxembourg Palace, they were escorted round the magnificent Rubens Gallery.[56] Parker introduced them to Vernet, one of the greatest French landscapists of the day, who showed Romney round his painting room. This contained a landscape being completed for the Marquis of Tavistock, a work which showed the influence of Salvator Rosa and Vernet's own protoromantic 'sacred sense of horror'.[57] Another high point of the tour was the meeting with Jean-Baptiste Greuze (1725–1805), who was just emerging as a celebrity with such works as *L'Accordée du Village* (Paris, Musée du Louvre) and whose portraiture, in its cloying sweetness, has some similarities with Romney's later work.[58]

Access to the Orléans collection in the Palais Royal was next procured and they hired a coach to view the paintings at the palace of St Cloud. At the church of the Carmelites they saw Guido Reni's *Salutation* and Le Brun's *Magdalen* and, shortly afterwards, admired six paintings by Eustache Le Sueur (1616–55), the 'French Raphael', at St Gervais St Protais. The classicized element of these works and their tendency to strong gesture were a contrast to what Romney regarded as the degenerate frivolity of French popular taste. Echoing his preference, in 1766, Horace Walpole said that he was 'almost tempted to prefer Le Soeur [*sic*] to every painter I know'.[59]

In common with other travellers, Romney and Greene 'surveyed that dreadful building the Bastille, where no strangers are admitted out of curiosity and few out of choice'.[60] By now becoming short of cash, at Poissy the friends refused to give something for St Sebastian. Immediately they became lost and muddy and Greene, a convivial companion throughout, in jest attributed this plight to their slighting of the saint. At Louviers, en route for home, they endured some of the usual hazards for contemporary travellers in the form of 'damp sheets and plenty of fleas'.[61]

Upon their return to London, the friendship between Romney and Greene continued to grow. To be nearer to his friend at No. 2 Coney Court, Gray's Inn, Romney moved into rooms at No. 5, and Greene introduced him to a number of sitters from the legal profession, and their wives, including Sir Joseph Yates, a Justice of the King's Bench, and Mr Secondary Barnes. This professional group, as with many of Romney's Kendal sitters, was not socially remote from him and helped contribute to his confidence as he continued to establish himself in the metropolis. The artist maintained close links with the Inns of Court, and even in the mid 1780s would walk to Gray's Inn for breakfast with Greene, or to Barnard's Inn with the witty and eloquent preacher Dr John Warner (1736–1800). Friendship apart, the astute Greene's legal and financial advice was invaluable to Romney, as the artist tended to forget 'all the lower concerns of worldly discretions'.[62] Romney was sometimes generous, and even careless with his money; but it is an exaggeration to say that he 'threw money away as rapidly as he acquired it'.[63] He is elsewhere described as avaricious and although that also is a misrepresentation, he could not have accumulated the fortune he eventually did by squandering cash at a significant rate.

By this stage of his career, he had attained considerable social and professional contact with his peers in various other arts. The multi-talented John Henderson (1747–85) was to come into Romney's orbit in 1767, when he won a premium at the Society of Artists. Henderson became the greatest actor of his age after the death of Garrick and was much admired by the King. He was a small man with remarkable elocution, whom Romney heard perform on at least one occasion with the actor Thomas Sheridan, in a public reading 'exquisite beyond conception', from popular authors such as Sterne. The duo were nicknamed 'Shandy' and 'Sherry'.[64] In Bath, Henderson was known as 'the Bath Roscius' after playing Hamlet there, and at the Haymarket in London he triumphed as Shylock and created the role of Edward Atheling in *The Battle of Hastings* for another of Romney's new friends, the dramatist Richard Cumberland.[65] Later he became a tireless promoter of Sarah Siddons, who played Beatrice to his Benedick. Well aware of his own abilities, he described the keeping of over fifty characters in his memory as 'no trifling business'.[66] From time to time he and Romney would dine together and, though not keen on a hectic social life, Romney was to find that his contact with such creative men of other professions sustained him over many years.

Shortly after his journey to France, Romney twice visited the north: the first time in 1765, the second two years later. He did so partly at Molly's behest, also because continued business in Lancaster, in this transitional period of his life, was useful in raising the capital needed for a bigger studio. Following the relative triumph of his award for *The Death of General Wolfe* in 1763, the dreadful news had arrived that his 'beautiful and interesting' three-year-old daughter Ann had died.[67] In Kendal the crushing sadness of this event 'threw all into disorder and confusion', which was partly assuaged by Molly and five-year-old John moving to High Cocken to look after old John Romney who by then had been alone for four years.

Crossing the sands into Furness to see his family, Romney also agreed to requests from sitters in Kendal, for example the local doctor *James Ainslie* (Bradford Art Gallery; Pl. 5). He also contacted Dr Wynne Bateman, the headmaster of Sedbergh School, whose fee for his portrait was overdue. When Bateman refused to pay the modest two guineas, Romney sent him a solicitor's letter, an indication of his new businesslike approach, very distinct from his father's.[68] The portrait, showing the headmaster in wig and clerical bands, still hangs in the school today.

His contacts in Lancaster enabled him in 1765 to paint *Thomas Hutton Rawlinson* (Lancaster, Judges Lodgings Museum) and his wife. Rawlinson was a mahogany importer for Gillows and another likely business associate of John Romney. He also produced portraits for other Lancaster merchants such as *Mrs Salisbury and Child* (Sadeville, Canada, Mount Allison University, c.1767).[69] Later still he painted *Mr and Mrs Lindow* (London, Tate Gallery, Pl. 6). Both of these are strong examples of his slightly hard early style; the latter particularly demonstrates his preference for bright colours. *Mr and Mrs*

5 *Dr James Ainslie*, c.1765, 145 × 121 cm (57 × 47.5 in). The father of Dr Henry Ainslie, the Reverend John Romney's friend.

6 *Mr and Mrs Lindow*, 1772, 139.2 × 113.9 cm (55 × 45 in). A record of the dynastic marriage of two Lancaster merchant families.

Lindow is a record of a dynastic marriage: William Lindow was the partner of Romney's earlier sitter Thomas Hutton Rawlinson, while his wife Abigail was Rawlinson's daughter. Between them, the two men controlled a large proportion of the mercantile business in Lancaster.[70]

On his return to London in 1765 Romney brought with him his younger brother Peter, who proved, however, to be lazy, extravagant and unable to earn a living as a pastellist.[71] It was also about this time that Romney painted the superior young shot, *Peter Woodhouse* (sold Christie's, 20 April 1990; Pl. 7), which shows a considerable development in sophistication beyond the earlier shooting portrait *Jacob Morland* (London, Tate Gallery).

Individual sitters and acquaintances aside, Romney also sought advancement through membership of the appropriate professional organizations. Thus, he was much closer to the activities of academies in his first few years in London than in his maturity. In 1765, in Mr Moreing's Great Room in Covent Garden, George III presented a royal charter of incorporation to the Society of Artists, which thus became the first organization of its kind to be so recognized. In 1766, Hayman, a great promoter of history painting, was President and Cotes a director of the Society, whose 211 members included Reynolds and Gainsborough. Romney, who was already a member of the Free Society, hedged his bets by signing the roll of this organization too.[72] Over the years that followed, covering nearly a decade between his journey to France and his departure for Italy, Romney's advancement as an artist brought not only greater financial rewards, but involvement with the politics of his profession's official bodies. The quality of his work in due course was also to provoke the envy of one of the foremost artists: Joshua Reynolds, who in 1768 became first President of the Royal Academy.

7 *Peter Woodhouse*, c.1765–8, 192.3 × 126.5 cm (76 × 50 in). A strong diagonal composition with the sitter's head in one corner.

3

Great Newport Street 1764–73

Whatever the rivalries that success was to impose on Romney, by the mid 1760s it had other effects. The status of his profession was beginning to rise, and as his horizons expanded, the range of fellow artists and craftsmen among his acquaintance offered elements of a cultural panorama over eighteenth-century London. In Great Newport Street, Long Acre, at the sign of the Golden Head, stood the house of John Augustus Richter the engraver and scagliolist. Late in 1767, after his second return visit to Kendal, Romney took lodgings here, where the golden sign would advertise his presence among other skilled craftsmen.[1] Richter and his partner Bartoli were currently producing artificial marbles as components of pillars and panels in fashionable interior design.[2] In 1772 Richter appears to have sat to Romney.[3] Occupying neighbouring rooms was Ozias Humphry, his fellow student from the Duke of Richmond's cast gallery. Over several months they became intimate friends.[4] Humphry not only painted miniatures such as *Queen Charlotte* (London, Royal Collection) but life-size portraits, including *George Stubbs* (Liverpool, Walker Art Gallery).[5] Following their close association, Humphry's work has occasionally been confused with Romney's, as was the case with his full-size canvas *The Waldegrave Sisters* (sold Sotheby's, 15 July 1992).[6] The rivalry provoked by Humphry's success on this larger scale may have been the source of Romney's later withdrawal from the relationship.

Another valued friend and contemporary was Jeremiah Meyer (1735–89), a fellow member of the Society of Artists. The son of the court painter to the Duke of Württemberg at Tübingen in Germany, Meyer was a pupil of the enamelist Christian Friedrich Zincke (1683/4–1767) and had designed the head of George III for the new coinage.[7] He was the first to realize fully the potential of miniature painting on ivory, and the Royal Collection contains several of his miniatures, notably one of the young King, set in diamonds and given as a betrothal present to his future queen, Charlotte.

Meyer's relationship with the royal family resulted in the King and Queen both being sponsors at the baptism of his son George, who eventually became Superintendant of Opium Manufacture to the Honourable East India Company in Calcutta.[8]

During these early years in London Romney purchased casts from the 'plaister cast' workshop of John Flaxman Senior in Covent Garden.[9] Here he gave encouragement to the younger John Flaxman (1755–1826) when the boy's father was completing work for Scheemakers and Roubiliac, who met with much success as sculptors of sepulchral monuments and garden statuary. Flaxman Junior later wrote: 'I was a little boy and as he frequently found me employed in modelling, he would stand by me a long while together giving me encouragement in a manner so obliging and affectionate that he won my heart and confirmed my determination in the pursuit of sculpture.'[10] After Romney's death Flaxman still extolled the benefit of their acquaintance, recalling the artist's 'original and striking conversation [and] his masterly, grand and feeling compositions'.[11]

Romney's generosity as an adviser was also felt by Daniel Gardner, his young pupil from Kendal, who had continued to benefit from this contact on the artist's visits north. It seems likely that in 1767 they travelled to London together. Gardner, who eventually received tuition at the Royal Academy, preferred to work in pastel and gouache, and, like Romney, painted small-scale full-lengths. Though he exhibited at the Academy only once, from 1772 he achieved a successful portrait practice of his own, as exemplified by *Archbishop John Moore, his Wife and Children* (London, Tate Gallery).[12]

One of Romney's own early supporters, who had 'a marked effect upon the painter's fortunes', was the dramatist Richard Cumberland, whose comedies were celebrated for their 'deftness and lightness of tread'.[13] Cumberland was the nephew of Richard Bentley, who had made numerous designs for Horace Walpole's Strawberry Hill. The playwright was also an art critic and one of the first 'to see the promotion and improvement of British art as a matter of national concern'.[14] Cumberland became a valuable ally, in particular urging Romney to increase the price of his portraits.[15] Early in 1768 Cumberland brought David Garrick to the studio while the artist was finishing his portrait of the family of Jarret Leigh, a proctor in the courts of Doctors' Commons, who was also an active amateur marine artist and had exhibited at the Free Society.[16] His kind gesture backfired rather painfully when Garrick, a friend of Reynolds, observed that Mr Leigh was 'doubtless a very excellent subject to the state, I mean (if all these are his children) but not for your art, Mr Romney' and by referring to a 'well-rubbed mahogany table' made an oblique swipe at Romney's artisan background.[17] Following the visit, Romney turned *The Leigh Family* (Melbourne, National Gallery of Victoria; Pl. 8) to the wall. Fortunately, however, he knew it was one of his

8 *The Leigh Family*, 1767–8, 185.8 × 202 cm (73.4 × 79.8 in). An important early group portrait demonstrating variety in the orientations of the heads.

greatest performances to date and it was duly completed and exhibited soon afterwards.

Undeterred by Garrick's rudeness to his new friend, Cumberland, who was much given to versifying, praised Romney in the *Public Advertiser* as a 'pensive artist . . . as pure and patient as his art' and concluded with the exhortation to this 'blushing, backward candidate for fame': '*Romney*, advance! be known and be admir'd.'[18]

Whether this recommendation pleased or annoyed Romney, he continued to be reluctant to step into the limelight. However, as an important figure in the literary world, Cumberland did enhance the artist's reputation. The verse prompted Dr Johnson, another of Reynolds's friends, to say that the verse 'would go well by itself but twice as well with Romney's name attached to it'.[19]

Cumberland sat to Romney for four portraits between 1768 and 1786. One of these is now in the Huntington Art Collections, San Marino, and another is in the collection of the National Portrait Gallery, London (Pl. 9). His daughters' portrait, *The Misses Cumberland* (Boston, Museum of Fine Arts) shows them reading one of his plays; a portrait of his wife Eliza (London, Tate Gallery) was anticipated by the dramatist in another verse, urging Romney to use his 'chastest tints' to paint her face.[20] In 1771 Cumberland's greatest dramatic success, for which Romney drew a vignette, was *The West Indian*. Earning his salary as Secretary to the Board of Trade, the playwright suffered by being satirized as Sir Fretful Plagiary by R.B. Sheridan and was also described by Garrick as 'a man without a skin'.[21] This latter jibe conveys a similarity of character with Romney, which may have been a source of the empathy between them.[22] Garrick described Romney to Reynolds as the playwright's 'second Correggio', notwithstanding that he also disparaged Cumberland's plays, saying 'Damn his dish-clout face; his plays would never do for the stage if I did not cook them up . . . so that they go down with the public.'[23]

It was also Cumberland who introduced Romney before 1771 to his first major aristocratic patrons, the Earl of Warwick and Charles Greville, the Earl's brother, both notable connoisseurs. The Earl, who gave his name to the huge Warwick Vase (Glasgow, Burrell Collection), arranged for Georgiana, his first wife, to sit to Romney.[24] Greville's position in the most cultured circles is manifest by his presence in Zoffany's *Charles Townley in his Library* (Burnley, Townley Hall) and in Reynolds's *Members of the Society of Dilettanti* (London, The Society of Dilettanti). That such men took Romney seriously even before he had visited Italy is a significant tribute, not only to his growing ability in the 1760s and early 1770s, but also to his assimilation of the repertoire of connoisseurship.

Already by 1768, *The Leigh Family* was 'a combination of the conversation piece and the most avant-garde neo-classical linearity [that] was as ambitious, if not more so, than anything Reynolds had produced to date'.[25] Indeed, its appearance in this year undoubtedly increased Reynolds's anxiety about his rival from the north, who was now on the hanging committee of the Free Society.[26] This was a year rent with the manoeuverings of cabals, as members of the Royal Incorporated Society of Artists battled over whether directors should be elected for life and whether there were too many members as a consequence of undemanding entry criteria. At this point in a noisy democratic process, Reynolds, by now a prominent figure, contributed to the clandestine selection of the foundation members of the new, smaller and more exclusive Royal Academy, so ostracizing four dangerous competitors: Romney, Robert Edge Pine, Benjamin Wilson (the Serjeant Painter, who had been a serious threat to Reynolds in the 1750s) and Allan Ramsay, who was

9 *Richard Cumberland*, c.1772, 124 × 98.7 cm (49 × 39 in). The sea view recalls the dramatist sitter's use of shipwreck in the theatre.

Painter to the King.[27] At the same time, as an indication that membership was based more upon the membership of such cliques than upon artistic ability, even Peter Toms, a drapery painter much used by Reynolds, was included. It seems possible that Romney's northern origins contributed to the prejudice he encountered, rather as Dr Johnson was derided for his Staffordshire accent. His friend Meyer, meanwhile, was the only miniaturist to be welcomed as a foundation member; his likeness appears in Zoffany's *Members of the Royal Academy* (London, Royal Collection). Meyer's inclusion created an awkwardness between him and Romney, happily one which did not alienate them.[28] Romney's independence of outlook helped make him a greater artist than all the RA's foundation members apart from Reynolds, Gainsborough and Richard Wilson; it was also at odds with the elitism which gave membership to a mere forty members and appointed a President for life.

Romney was content to remain loyal to the Society of Artists for the present and his subsequent career shows that non-election to the RA did not hinder him.[29] Indeed, he continued to exhibit with the Free Society in 1769 and with the Incorporated Society in 1770–72, right up to his departure for Italy in 1773. On his return, he wanted to show himself strong enough to stand alone, without the publicity of exhibition. He consequently remained aloof for twenty years, both from the Academy and its rivals, although his name was one of the most prominent in the metropolis and his non-membership of the Academy was a remarkable exception. The foundation of the RA assured the professional status of the new academicians and, as dual membership was proscribed, the original societies immediately lost a large group of members.[30] The King's inconsistency, in having given a royal warrant to two art societies within three years, was criticized anonymously by 'Fresnoy' in the *Middlesex Journal* in May 1770, and soon afterwards the Royal Incorporated Society of Artists reverted and became once more simply the Society of Artists.[31]

In 1769 Romney had made a successful application to attend the Society's drawing academy in Maiden Lane, an implicitly humble gesture which contrasted with his new standing. By 1770 he was on the committee whose members took it in turns to pose the models and to keep order among unruly students. In January 1772 he was elected a Director of the Society.[32] The previous year, the Society of Artists had bought a plot of land in a more convenient, central position on which to erect their own academy and exhibition room to rival the new Royal Academy. The building committee raised £5,000 for the completion of this room, near the Exeter Exchange in the Strand, to a handsome design by the then President, the architect James Paine (1725–89).[33]

No expense was spared at the opening of the rooms on 11 May 1772, which featured an orchestra and singers, and the members were proud to have an exhibition room larger and better lit than their usual venue at Spring Gardens near the King's Mews at Charing Cross. Disaster struck later in the summer when Paine withdrew his financial guarantees; by October, when George Stubbs was elected President, the Society was obliged to let the new academy to the auctioneer Mr Christie and mortgage the building. This caused considerable worry for all the members, especially the Directors. Their new building became the Lyceum Theatre, the scene of numerous triumphs of Sir Henry Irving.

That year Romney exhibited for the last time, with his portrait *Ozias Humphry* (England, private collection) which was bought by the Duke of Dorset. Romney detested conflict and acrimony and his withdrawal from exhibitions after this date may also have signalled his rapid dissociation from the disastrous financial circumstances surrounding the Exeter Exchange project.[34]

Initially, most of his commissions had come from members of the professions and their families. Other sitters in exhibited portraits were anonymous or Romney's own next of kin. His exhibits in 1764 had raised little apparent interest, though his *Lady's Head in the Character of a Saint* (untraced) in 1765 elicited the waspish comment in the *Public Advertiser* that 'this saint is likely to have few votaries.'[35] The conversation piece *Peter and James Romney* (New Haven, Yale Center for British Art; Pl. 10) of 1766, with its references to gentlemanly pursuits and classical learning, demonstrates the artist's desire to ally his brothers, and by reflection himself, with the tastes of the educated bourgeoisie.

Sadly, this statement of social aspiration did not square with the conduct of Peter, who had a weakness for alcohol, and even less with that of their unfortunate brother John, who was to find himself in prison. In 1767 the *Morning Chronicle* opined that another Romney double portrait, this time of two sisters, was 'a fine picture in the style of Reynolds'. This was probably *Two Sisters Contemplating Mortality* (untraced, but engraved by Dunkarton for Boydell) which, in responding to a melancholic preoccupation with death, gives an early hint of Romney's interest in esoteric subjects. It also demonstrates his growing ability with drapery, architectural detail and antique sculpture: his delayed studies were bearing fruit.

A great Lakeland eccentric who first sat to Romney in 1769 was Bishop Richard Watson (1737–1816) (portrait now in Trinity College, Cambridge), an ambitious collector of sinecures. As Professor of Chemistry at the University he invented the black bulb thermometer. Subsequently he took holy orders, becoming Professor of Divinity at Cambridge, and then Bishop of Llandaff. He retired early to a life of cultivating his estate at Calgarth Park,

10 *Peter and James Romney*, 1766, 92.3 × 91 cm (36.5 × 36 in). Strong family aspirations, both intellectual and aesthetic, are evident here.

near Ambleside, where years later he sought in vain to invite Romney as his guest.[36]

As Romney's reputation grew, his sitters came increasingly from the higher social strata. The best picture before his trip to Italy was *The Warren Family* (private collection; Pl. V), exhibited in 1769. Sir George Warren was the wealthy and aristocratic MP for Lancaster. In Romney's portrait he stands pointing towards the distant Colosseum, a setting evoking the Grand Tour and reflecting Romney's own aspirations to study in Rome himself. As the most recognizable building in Rome, the Colosseum appears in several portraits by Pompeo Batoni, such as *James Caulfield* (New Haven, Yale Center for British Art; 1753–5), which has given rise to the observation that *The Warren Family* is 'like Batoni before he could have experienced him'.[37] In an informal, affectionate pose, Lady Warren is seated with her arms round the neck of her small daughter Elizabeth, while the girl caresses a bullfinch, a tender motif reminiscent of Raphael's *Madonna del Cardellino* (Florence, Uffizi).[38]

In 1770 the artist exhibited with the Incorporated Society at Spring Gardens, near Charing Cross, two full-length personifications entitled *Mirth* (Pl. 11) and *Melancholy* (Pl. 12), taken from Milton's poems *L'Allegro* and *Il Penseroso*. Melancholy posturing was fashionable; in the later 1770s, when Drury Lane Theatre was being re-modelled, figures of Mirth and Melancholy were painted on either side of the proscenium.[39] Romney's own fluctuating moods of joy and gloom also drew him to these subjects, which evoke the duality of life and derive from such contrasts as the Comic Muse, Euphrosyne, and the Tragic Muse, Melpomene.[40] Romney discussed the titles of these works with Cumberland, who suggested 'Mirth' and 'Meditation' as alternatives, his friend urging that he should not use Milton's 'modern, barbarous and affected' titles as they would 'rob your ideas of their originality'.[41]

The more than usually mask-like faces of *Mirth* and *Melancholy* seem to be derived from Le Brun; the superb sculptural folds of drapery are evidence of a developing skill with costume. *Mirth* has links with the Renaissance bacchanal, and depicts a dance of celebration, whereas *Melancholy* reflects an introspective Renaissance cult, more familiar in Dürer's allegory of that name. The iconography of melancholy was to repeat itself in Romney's work and life nearly twenty years later, as he designed a dual composition called *Mirth and Melancholy* (Petworth, National Trust); he also owned casts after antique sculptures of both *Euphrosyne* and *Melpomene*, ironically later sold to the Royal Academy.[42]

Romney's contribution to the fashion for sublime portraiture included, in 1771, the stately *Mrs Mary Ann Yates as the Tragic Muse* (Brisbane, Queensland Art Gallery), depicting the fine tragic actress who rose to fame after the

11 *Mirth*, 1770, 234.7 × 142.9 cm (92.7 × 56.5 in). This figure of a bacchante may be compared with that of Lady Anne Gower (Pl. IX).

12 *Melancholy*, 1770, 234.7 × 142.9 cm (92.7 × 56.5 in). A study of antique sculpture enhanced the morbid aspect of this allegory.

death of Mrs Cibber. This portrait, one of six paintings he exhibited that year with the Society of Artists, relates to Cotes's *Mrs Yates as Electra* of 1769. The uncluttered composition, with incense burner and simple drapery, anticipates much of Romney's later achievement in ladies' full-length portraiture, while the dagger foreshadows his interest in Lady Macbeth and the horror of his later cartoon *Medea* (Liverpool, Walker Art Gallery). Whether or not in response to an antique convention, the muse appears to be inspired herself, rather than being the fount of inspiration.[43] This work indicated to Reynolds that Romney was a force to be reckoned with, and may have moved the President to paint his *Mrs Hartley as Jane Shore* later in 1771, which has been viewed as 'a deliberate attempt at doing a Romney one better'.[44] Romney's painting was bought by John Boydell, the major print publisher, who was thus associated with two of Romney's significant early works, having already sold engravings after the artist's *Two Sisters Contemplating Mortality*. Maintaining her prominence in melancholy roles, in 1779 Mrs Yates was to recite R.B. Sheridan's *Monody on the Death of Garrick* beside a funeral pyre in a setting of cypresses at Drury Lane.[45] As an early essay in the sublime, Mrs Yates's portrait anticipated Reynolds's more familiar *Mrs Siddons as the Tragic Muse* (San Marino, Huntington Art Collections) by thirteen years.

A more complex portrait executed in 1771, and admired by Horace Walpole, was *Major Thomas Peirson Conversing with a Brahmin* (destroyed; fragment at Akron, Stan Hywet Hall and Gardens).[46] In this, the eponymous 'cultivated soldier' stands under a 'spreading palm' accompanied by the figure of a black servant, for which a precedent may be found in, for example, Knapton's *Hon. John Spencer* (untraced).[47] Romney and Peirson, who came from Cockin's birthplace at Burton-in-Kendal in Westmorland, were close friends: the artist habitually used a seal which bore the Major's profile.[48]

Romney's portraits in the 1760s were rather stiff, but by the early 1770s his drapery was becoming much more fluid. *Mrs Anne Verelst* (Rotherham, Clifton Park Museum; Pl. VI), depicting Governor Verelst's lovely wife, painted in 1772, the year after their marriage, demonstrates this in the 'felicitous disposition of the folds in the wrapping gown, emphasised by the dignified motion down the steps'. The similarities are worth noting between this portrait and the *Mattei Ceres* (Rome, Vatican Museum), which Romney could have known from a cast.[49]

As neighbours, Romney and Humphry had for some time discussed their mutual plans of travelling for a couple of years in Europe.[50] They had enquired of the gem engraver Nathaniel Marchant, already established in Rome, the best route to take, and Charles Greville gave them an introduction to his uncle, Sir William Hamilton, Envoy Extraordinary to the Kingdom of the Two Sicilies. This erudite diplomat, connoisseur and vulcanologist was based in Naples.[51] With such arrangements completed, for the next few months they savoured the anticipation of their much-delayed expedition. Adam Walker, Romney's friend from his Kendal days, regretted he was not able to travel with them but hoped to read an account of the journey.[52] Romney's actual decision to depart was not an easy one: he was now thirty-eight years old and had built up a lucrative practice of around £1,200 a year. He knew, however, that his lack of European experience was the main obstacle in realizing his full artistic potential. Intellectual, aesthetic and social snobbery demanded a familiarity with Italy; but Romney also sought to transform his work through studying the painterly skills of the old masters and the sculpture of antiquity. In this he had the encouragement of the Duke of Richmond and he and Humphry had also obtained an introduction to Pope Clement XIV from the Duke of Gloucester.[53]

Before departing for Italy, Romney left £200 with his bankers for his wife. He also wrote to his father, in justification of his departure, 'I do not doubt but you think my leaving England a very imprudent thing . . . I assure you I shall never take any steps but what I think will tend to advance either my reputation or fortune . . . take care of Molly and John and keep him at a good lattin scool'.[54] This last adjuration reflects Romney's appreciation of the importance of instruction in classical languages and how his own scant education had left him with a hatred of writing, poor spelling and a sense of being the educational inferior of most of his present associates, especially Greville, Cumberland and Greene.

News of his imminent departure for Italy brought even more sitters to the studio, but Romney and Humphry finally set off on 20 March 1773. They had hoped to leave in the previous year, but, apart from the backlog of work, delays had arisen from Romney suffering a fever and Humphry falling from his horse. En route they visited their mutual patron, the Duke of Dorset, at Knole in Kent. The treasures in the Duke's great house included several van Dycks, which whetted the travellers' appetites for their adventure. Romney's own portrait of Humphry, commissioned the previous year by the Duke, was now part of this fine collection.

4

'Egad George, we're bit!' Italy and neo-classicism 1773–5

As Romney was already a mature artist by the time of his Italian travels, these were not destined to be crucially formative for his portraiture.[1] His tour, as a rite of passage, was important mainly for his professional credibility back in England, though the influence of one recent movement would be seen in his drawing and his imaginative work. He was in any case fortunate to be visiting Italy during the 'golden age of the British Grand Tour'.[2] Italy, and Rome in particular, was more than usually thronged with British visitors: connoisseurs, collectors, aspirant lovers of art and groups of gifted European artists. There was a fashion for tourist-portraits, and for the pastimes of exporting excavated antiquities and acquiring old masters. Intending to keep a journal for a friend, probably Walker or Greene, Romney began immediately to write his 'Cursory Observations and Reflections Made during a Journey from England to Genoa'.[3]

On the way, Romney and Humphry stayed three weeks in Paris at the Hotel de York.[4] Here for his second visit, he was 'very much pleased with the polite manners of the people, their public buildings and fine collections of pictures', but complained:

> The taste for painting, and the art itself are at the lowest ebb; simplicity they call vulgar and pure elegance passes for gravity and heaviness; every thing must have the air of a dancer or actor, the colour of a painted beauty, and the dress recommended by the barber, tailor and mantua-maker. I think there is no better criterion whereby to judge of the minds of a people, than by their general taste; the correspondence certainly holds good with respect to the French. They are a people that have no idea of simplicity, and are totally void of character and feeling. Nothing can be a greater proof of their degeneracy of taste, than the indifference with which they treat every thing produced by those great masters, who have held the first rank for so many ages; viz., Raphael, Michel Angelo, Titian etc. They say their works are too dark, gloomy and heavy. With them every thing must be light, false, fantastical and full of flutter and extravagance – like themselves. Happily

for us, we have to return to a country where manly sense and feeling still remain . . . We have no reason hitherto, from what we have seen, to repent of our journey; but on the contrary, to be inspired with double ardour to pursue the plan we have formed.[5]

Travelling on to Lyons he noted that the landscape on the banks of the Yonne was 'the finest champaign you can imagine'. They did not cross the Alps, as Romney developed a sore throat, but continued south to Avignon and the Pont du Gard, which he viewed as 'perhaps the most beautiful specimen of that kind of architecture in the world'. At Nîmes, having seen the 'Maison Quarré' (Carrée), he knowledgeably described numerous details of the portico, architrave and cornice, concluding that it was 'the most chaste and beautiful building imaginable'.[6] During a week in Marseilles he recorded the 'striking view' of the town and harbour and delighted in the variety of landcape as he and Humphry continued east.[7] They surveyed the Roman remains at Fréjus and in Nice admired groups of girls dancing round maypoles, 'like *The Hours of Guido*'. The air of antiquity the girls conveyed 'had the most enchanting effect. I thought myself removed two thousand years back and a spectator of scenes in Arcady.'[8]

Strong winds prevented their sailing to Leghorn so they accepted the hospitality of Mr Aubert, a Genoese merchant. In his company they relished watching further rustic dancing to the music of a violin, eventually sailing to Genoa in a felucca on 27 May. Here, amongst the 'dazzling half-amphitheatre of marble palaces', Romney described the opulence of the city's architectural fabric and visited buildings including the Durazzo Palace, where he marvelled at Veronese's *Magdalen Washing the Feet of Christ*.[9] Sailing on towards Leghorn, they met a great storm in the Gulf of Pisa which persuaded them to continue afterwards on land.[10] In Leghorn they admired the colossal slaves by Giambologna, with their exaggerated expressions, gestures and musculature, which gave the two travellers an exposure to mannerism in three dimensions.[11] Initially taking the route north to Pisa where they sought out some works of Giotto, they travelled east to Florence, then south via Siena and Viterbo to Rome, arriving on 18 June.[12]

The diary of Thomas Banks (1735–1805), the erudite expatriate sculptor, records their arrival, upon which they were introduced to other British artists frequenting the English Coffee House in the Piazza di Spagna, almost opposite the Spanish Steps.[13] This, the principal meeting point for Grand Tourists, artists, dealers and *ciceroni*, was 'a filthy vaulted room' decorated with 'capricious designs of Piranesi' in the Egyptian taste, which would have been lost had Piranesi not engraved them himself.[14] The Piazza di Spagna was also one of the favourite arenas for the Italians to show off their magnificent carriages and equipages by driving up and down.[15] Romney had no appetite for the kind of gossip exchanged in such a place, but he did come here to collect his post.[16]

The two friends were soon to occupy separate lodgings, apparently because Humphry was less keen than Romney to study.[17] Following the assistance given them by the Duke of Gloucester, Humphry busied himself in copying Titian's *Danäe* at Capodimonte for their patron.[18] Prince Charles Stuart, the pretender to the British throne currently living in Rome, also sat to Humphry (drawing, Edinburgh, National Portrait Gallery) as did his wife, the Countess of Albany.[19] Humphry was having to convert his skills from miniature work to full-scale painting, as his eyes were deteriorating, a transition recorded in the verses of an admirer, who wrote of his paintings:

> May their distinguish'd merit still prevail
> And shine with lustre on the larger scale.[20]

Romney, perhaps through his contact with a former sitter, the Reverend William Strickland SJ (Pl. II), was able to occupy 'appartments' in the Jesuit College, which had an attractive colonnaded court.[21] It was, however, an awkward time to be associated with the Jesuits, since on 16 August Pope Clement XIV published his *Dominus ac Redemptor Noster*, decreeing the order's abolition.[22] Oblivious to this development, Romney attempted to leave the college on the day that the building was 'surrounded by a military guard and all egress prohibited'. The newly posted soldier at the gate cautioned him not to proceed, but Romney, preoccupied with his own thoughts and unfamiliar with the Italian language, ignored him. This angered the guard who levelled his musket at Romney's chest. In the nick of time Romney realized the danger he was in, and hastily shouted 'Anglese!', a 'mystic word [which] operated like a charm' and saved his life.[23] This was the most vivid moment of crisis arising from his lack of French or Italian; as Humphry noted, 'people who speak a little of our own language . . . afford you no small consolation, I believe'.[24]

Although Romney's studies were largely 'sequestered', he 'did not altogether relinquish society'.[25] His stay overlapped with those of Nathaniel Marchant (1739–1816), Thomas Banks (1735–1805), Joseph Wright of Derby (1734–97), the Reverend Matthew Peters (1742–1814), Henry Fuseli (1741–1825), Edward Edwards (1738–1806) and George Carter (1737–94). His well-developed taste made him determined to absorb the variety of 'counsels of perfection' in both ancient and modern painting and sculpture.[26] Many artists visiting the city were jostling for commissions, but Romney had sufficient resources to be free of this constraint. His aim in Rome was anything but spending time on portraiture, or copying old masters for sale, although he had been asked to obtain some old masters for the Earl of

Warwick. Jealousy of his relative financial independence may be partly to blame for some of the negative reports that were to follow him home.

Humphry described his friend while in Rome as 'a man of uncommon concealment; in no way communicative', who refused to let his studies be seen.[27] This was confirmed by the antiquarian Father John Thorpe, a picture agent to Lord Arundel for over thirty years, who added spitefully that 'Romney's work is weak and feeble like himself.'[28] Romney's tendency had always been to work rather than play; amid the professional opportunities of Italy, when Humphry proved 'a gossip and an idler', Romney did feel he had reason to draw back from the relationship.[29] Rather as he had withdrawn from his apprenticeship with the incompatible Steele, he found that close daily contact with Humphry during their three-month journey had exposed the flaws in their friendship. They were, however, to remain on relatively amicable terms into the 1790s.

Romney's acquaintance in Rome included a variety of foreign visitors and expatriates, brought there by every kind of motive. Thomas Jenkins (1722–98), an artist and former pupil of Hudson, through whom Romney drew his money from Greene in London, had become the unofficial British diplomatic representative in Rome. He was, however, more active as a banker, cicerone and excavator. He was also a dealer in antique marbles, in which capacity he made the notable sale of the caryatids from the Triopion of Herodes Atticus (London, British Museum, and Rome, Vatican Museum), and in 1774 he was involved in dredging the Tiber to search for antiquities.[30] There was a lively market in such items, recycled or restored, via such outlets as the so-called 'Museo Cavaceppi', a 'superstore of antiquities' and a factory where copies and restorations were made.[31] Such renovated marbles, which were often sold as largely authentic, were to be satirized along with their optimistic buyers by the dramatist Richard Cumberland, who wrote:

> Virtu however is to be purchased, like other superfluities, and in the end their Cicerone lays them in for a bargain, perhaps a patch-work head of Trajan set upon a modern pair of shoulders, and made up with Caracalla's nose and Nero's ears . . . Thus equipt with these imperial reliques, with a veritable daubing of Raffaelle, copied from the very print which is given to prove its originality, and a huge cameo on the little finger, home they come priviledged Virtuosi, qualified to condemn every thing that their own countrymen can produce; and thus having contributed all that in them lies to disgrace their native land, they conclude their career by affecting to despise it.[32]

Romney and Humphry extended their acquaintance with Nathaniel Marchant, the gem engraver, whose route they had followed from Paris.[33] A Fellow of the Society of Artists, Marchant was a bachelor connoisseur and one of the artists and wits who later frequented the Devil's Tavern in Fleet Street. He made several state seals for George III and his gems appealed to

Romney as a 'remarkable testimony to Neo-classical taste'.[34] Over the years that he lived in Italy, he became a specialist in making miniature copies of ancient sculpture in fine intaglio. Romney used one of the seals fashioned by Marchant after his own portrait of his friend Major Peirson. Eventually they had several patrons in common, including Sir William Hamilton who commissioned from Marchant an intaglio of Emma, Lady Hamilton (New York, Metropolitan Museum).[35]

Romney's exact contemporary Joseph Wright of Derby was another successful artist working in Rome in the mid 1770s. Wright, with whom Peter Romney had had to compete in Liverpool in 1769, produced his *Grand Fireworks at Castel Sant' Angelo* (Birmingham, City Art Gallery), which typifies the joyous reaction of northern artists to displays of the Catholic exuberance that had been lost from religious festivals in Protestant Europe since the Reformation.[36] Romney and Ozias Humphry may have witnessed one such display, for the festival of St Peter and St Paul took place a few days after their arrival in Rome.[37] Wright's own subject, *The Captive*, based on *The Sentimental Journey* by Laurence Sterne, was completed in Rome in 1774 and may have interested Romney in the depiction of prison scenes, influencing his own later series on John Howard the prison reformer.[38]

An influential acquaintance in Rome was Richard Payne Knight (1750–1824), aesthete, critic and refiner of the notion of the picturesque, who was to correspond with Romney after they had returned to England.[39] Knight, whose fortune came from ironworks in Shropshire, was a young man of precocious intellect; he wrote to Romney upon such esoteric matters as the false sublime in considerable detail. That he did so is a tribute to the impression Romney had made upon him in Rome. Their correspondence also provides a relatively rare, concrete indication of the artist's intellectual capability, for, despite his cerebral power, Romney was known as a man who hated to write.[40]

Another contact in Rome was the Yorkshireman Thomas Harrison (1744–1829), an architect who was likewise a carpenter's son. Harrison's 'spark divine' caused a stir at the papal court when he redesigned the Piazza del Popolo.[41] He later rebuilt Chester and Lancaster Castles as jails, following the reforming doctrines of John Howard, and built the first level bridge in England, over the river Lune. Richard Cumberland, who also knew Harrison, had predicted his success before he arrived in Italy.

The most significant figure for Romney among English-speaking artists in Rome was the erudite Swiss, Henry Fuseli (1741–1825), who had come late to painting from literature, where he had been formed by the 'Sturm und Drang' movement.[42] Fuseli's reputation in 1773 was founded upon his 1765 translation of some of the art historical writing of Johann Joachim Winckelmann (1717–68), regarded by many as the founding father of the modern discipline of classical archaeology and whose teaching was influential upon Romney.[43] Fuseli, Romney, Humphry and Banks all came to share motifs, themes and mannerisms, contributing within a short space of time to what was essentially a new artistic style, one that heightened the emotional and dramatic content of their designs through exaggerated gestures and simplified forms.[44] In Romney's drawings can be found the elements of pathos and horror which are more familiar in Fuseli's oil paintings. Unlike Romney's effectively private creativity, much of the long-lived Swiss artist's imaginative work was realized in this more publicly accessible medium. His chilling depictions of Shakespeare's tragic characters, such as Lady Macbeth, strike similar chords to Romney's delineations of this subject and they both rejected Winckelmann's insistence on restrained representations of the passions. In many ways Romney's spontaneous drawings convey more effectively the power of the ideas behind them, but Fuseli's influence on their development in Italy was crucial.[45]

An enigmatic sketch made by Fuseli in 1778, after Romney's return to London, entitled *Caricature of the Artist Leaving Italy* (Zürich, Kunsthaus), shows Romney, Humphry and West as mice, endeavouring to divide England between them.[46] This satire was meant to be teasing rather than derogatory; Fuseli was later to write about Romney: 'If he had not genius to lead, he had too much originality to follow and whenever he chose was nearer to the first than the last of his competitors . . . Romney as artist and man is entitled to commendation and esteem.'[47]

In the artistic crucible of Rome, Romney spent some of the pleasantest hours of his life, exploring the city's art collections and sculpture. It was a period for him of 'strenuous labour and high intellectual delight'.[48] The artist's diligence shines from his exhortation in 1775 to George Carter: 'do not leave a stone unturned that is classical; do not leave a form unsought that is beautiful'.[49]

Old masters and sculpture were accessible in the Villa Borghese and, to a lesser extent, in the depleted collections of the Villa Albani (now the Villa Torlonia), outside the Aurelian walls. This collection also featured the fine *Parnassus*, a ceiling painting by Anton Raffael Mengs (1728–79). This work, which played a part in the genesis of Romney's later drawing *The Ghost of Clytemnestra* (Cambridge, Fitzwilliam Museum), reflected the influence of Winckelmann, formerly Cardinal Albani's librarian.[50] Alessandro Albani himself, now an elderly man, had greatly encouraged the fashion for the Grand Tour, and was a major patron of Mengs, one of the pioneers in Italy of neo-classicism in painting. Romney had already adopted some elements of this fashion in London; he was to develop it with great success in England upon his return, having Mengs's writings read aloud to him in his studio.[51] Similarities with the work of Pompeo Batoni (1708–87), the principal portraitist resident in Rome, were already apparent in the portraiture of Romney, who may have first encountered Batoni in the flesh in his capacity as Curator of the Papal Collections. On his return from Rome, Romney was to assimilate a more vital element of Batoni's striking ability in portraying the nonchalance of wealth, which he later used in *William Beckford* (Upton House, The National Trust; Pl. VII).

Romney furthered his study of antiquity with an excursion to Tivoli, where he drew the Grotto of Neptune, the Cascatelli and the Temple of the Tiburtine Sibyl (untraced).[52] The rural contrast of this experience with the bustle of Rome is effectively evoked by Jacob More's *Self Portrait* (Florence, Uffizi Gallery); while the grandeur of the water-filled grotto was captured by Louis Ducros in his *Grand Duke Paul at Tivoli* (Pavlovsk Palace Museum, Russia).[53] The appeal of the ruin of the Temple of the Sibyl (now known as the Temple of Vesta) has been conveyed by numerous artists including Francis Towne (London, British Museum).

Romney was conscious all his life of his poor mastery of anatomy, which had stemmed from his curtailed training and from the limited demands portraiture generally made upon his invention of poses. This deficiency is apparent in the limbs of Lady Warren, in *The Warren Family* (Pl. V).[54] In Rome, his anatomical accuracy improved through intensive study, and he was fortunate to be able to hire a nude female model, giving him a greater familiarity with the female form 'in all its diversities of attitude'.[55] Such private female models were not widely available, but Romney appears to have had her exclusive use for a time, as the drawings are all taken from the principal viewpoint.[56] Although John Romney later prudishly asserted that she was always chaperoned, one drawing, in which she proffers her breast, is 'remarkable for its candour' and has 'much in common with the sensuality of Boucher's nudes'.[57] A similar physical directness is present in his remarkable mid-1770s painting *A Wood Nymph* (untraced; engraving, England, private collection; Pl. 13), where the figure is lying recumbent on her side with her back to the viewer, for which the same woman may well also have been the model.

Ecorché figures, small models of the human figure with the skin stripped down to expose the musculature, were another useful aid to the study of anatomy, derived partly from the studies of Vesalius and Michelangelo.[58] William Hunter's flayed felon, cast first in wax and then in bronze by Michael Henry Spang and Nathaniel Marchant's master, Edward Burch, was available in London by 1775. Mason Chamberlin's portrait of Hunter includes an écorché bronze, as does Zoffany's *William Hunter Giving a Lecture* (London, Royal College of Physicians).[59] Romney's own *Art Instruction* (England, private collection), in which a tutor and his pupil closely examine a small écorché bronze, shows him sharing this interest with the two people who

13 *A Wood Nymph* (engraving by Valentine Green), 1778, 59.5 × 41.7 cm (23.5 × 16.5 in). Braided hair adds to the appeal of the fine form of this young model.

were his sitters.[60] In 1775 in Bologna Academy, en route for Venice, Romney was to see several fine, coloured, wax anatomical figures, which may have been the source of some of his own écorché drawings.[61] He may also, in Florence, have encountered the waxworks of dissected bodies in the Gabinetto Fiscino.[62] The stylized musculature is comparable to that seen in Fuseli's work and in Romney's *Charon and Psyche* (Cambridge, Fitzwilliam Museum); the influence of both is traceable in the later work of Flaxman and Blake. As another source of anatomical truth, Romney did own a human skeleton.[63] Criticism of his anatomical ability is not, in fact, supported by the bulk of his work, and certainly after the visit to Rome he gained in confidence in portraying the human form.[64]

Sensitive to 'a pure grace of line', Romney is noted for the harmonious fluidity of his drapery. This was based upon a love for the intricacies of antique sculpture, and the direct experience of masters such as Raphael. It also reflected the importance given by received opinion to the handling of draperies; Walpole believed that this was the surest guide to a great artist.[65] The amalgamation of these influences raised his portraiture into the realm of history painting. An important early canon of perfection for Romney had been the sculpture and casts after the antique at Richmond House. In Rome he was able to scrutinize the marbles on view in the spectacular rooms of the public museums, the Museo Capitolino and the Museo Clementino. He also drew the Medici Venus, and the statues on the Monte Cavallo, partly depicted in *The Horseman of Montecavallo* (New Haven, Yale Center for British Art). Among the antique sarcophagi in the Villa Pamphili, he made sculptural studies whose traces can be seen in later works such as *Alope* (untraced; engraving, London, British Museum).[66]

Many of his Roman drawings confirmed rather than enhanced the development of his sophisticated sculptural drapery, which was already of superb quality in Lady Warren's dress in *The Warren Family*. Flaxman, whose own mastery of drapery was admirable, held that Romney's drapery was 'well-understood, either forming the figure into a mass with one or two deep folds only', as is evident in *Melancholy*, 'or by its adhesion and transparency discovering the form of the figure', as in *Emma Hart as Circe*.[67] Benjamin West stated that the broad drapery of Romney's *Melancholy* was 'equal to Raphael', and two centuries later the painstaking excellence of the drapery of *Mrs Scott Jackson* (Washington DC, National Gallery of Art) has been called 'marble geology', so exquisitely carved are its ridged folds in contrast to the erotic hint of the sitter's rounded body beneath.[68] This straightforward contrast was recommended by Winckelmann, which may partly explain the artist's preference for light rather than robust cloth.[69] Neither was he slow to exploit the appeal of a peeping toe, as in *Mrs Bankes* (Kingston Lacy, The National Trust; front jacket) or even that of a naked foot as in *Emma Hart as Circe*.

In *Dr James Ainslie* (Bradford, Cartwright Hall, Pl. 5) Romney included the bust of a philosopher to enhance the sitter's intellectual status, and he had featured a sculpted plinth in *Melancholy*, but it was not until after his return from Italy that his works depicted larger, full-length and more detailed sculpture. The lovely The Hon. Mrs Trevor was painted standing beside a fine sculpted urn (Pittsburgh, Carnegie Institute; Pl. VIII), and the subjects of *Dr Allen* (Dulwich Gallery) and *Lady Augusta Murray* (sold Sotheby's, 15 March 1967) sit respectively by a statue of Aesculapius, to symbolize the medical vocation, and Minerva, goddess of wisdom. Other forms of sculpture had their uses too. For the posthumous portrait of Isaac Newton, Romney used a death mask as his source of the scientist's likeness.[70]

With his near contemporary Edward Edwards, an amateur violinist and a fellow student at the Duke of Richmond's gallery, Romney visited several Roman churches. Unlike Romney, Edwards had quitted the Society of Artists and the Free Society and had exhibited at the Royal Academy from 1771. Much employed by Horace Walpole, Edwards painted a portrait of Sir Edward Walpole, the connoisseur's brother, and in 1788 was to be elected as Professor of Perspective at the Royal Academy.[71] Many churches contained works by Michelangelo and Raphael, and when Edwards and Romney went for the first time to see the Sistine Chapel, they were exhilarated by Michelangelo's mastery of the nude figure. Totally elated, the diminutive Edwards turned to Romney and said: 'Egad George, we're bit!'[72] The uplifted mood he shared with Romney in this city was not unique; Humphry made reference to his own state of 'continual ecstasy'.[73]

In the Sistine Chapel, Romney made an especial study of the anatomy and drapery of the prophets and sibyls, whilst several figures in Michelangelo's *Last Judgement* influenced his Medea series and his own drawings of devils.[74] In *Providence Brooding over Chaos* or *The Spirit of God moving on the Face of the Waters* (untraced; drawing, Cambridge, Fitzwilliam Museum), a bearded figure with arms outstretched is flying over water.[75] This can be related to the figure of God in Michelangelo's *The Separation of the Earth from the Waters* in the Sistine Chapel, though the canvas was re-named *Jupiter Pluvius* by the fastidious John Romney, who was appalled that his father had attempted to depict the Creator.[76]

Romney also sought the grace and expressiveness of Raphael, and had been greatly beguiled by the colours and finish of the *Judith and Holofernes* which he had seen in Genoa, perceiving 'great spirit and strength in the eye'.[77] Using the Duke of Gloucester's introduction, he sought the Pope's permission to erect scaffolding to copy several heads of *The Expulsion of Heliodorus from the Temple* in the Vatican.[78] Between November 1774 and the following spring he also copied, to scale, the lower half of Raphael's *Transfiguration*, then in the church of San Pietro in Montorio, observing that in this work 'all the excellencies of that master are united'.[79] His technique here was to first trace the outlines in chiaroscuro on several sheets and then transfer them to a single canvas.[80] As he painted this 'spirited copy', which hung for years in the hall of his subsequent home at Cavendish Square, the monks came to pray undisturbed below his scaffolding. Another Raphael copy he made was of a group of figures, including Bramante, from *The School of Athens* in the Stanza della Segnatura, also in the Vatican.[81]

Romney was also 'under the spell' of Correggio, and in Parma he had described the angels in this master's *Assumption of the Virgin* (Parma Cathedral) as 'divine beyond conception or imitation'.[82] He was to comment in Bologna on the influence Correggio had had upon the Carracci, and his consciousness of the earlier master's potency was still alive in 1793 when he described two of his own pictures as 'Correggiesque'.[83] By saying this he was probably drawing attention to elements of sensual elegance and glowing colour, achieved through the use of lighting effects.

To a lesser degree Guido Reni was important to Romney, especially his use of billowing drapery, which Reni had adopted from antique mosaics.

Reni's ceiling painting *Aurora* in the Palazzo Rospigliosi depicts the deity encircled by swags of creamy cloth which enhance her energy and sensuality, increasing the illusion of motion. Numerous Romney portraits after his journey to Italy, for example *The Cornewall Children* (England, private collection), show this motif fully developed.

Visiting Thomas Jenkins' house in Rome, he described with technical detail his impression of a van Dyck, a dominant master in the imaginations of eighteenth-century portraitists. He noted 'an exceeding tenderness between flesh and hair', identified the subtle use of 'ultramarine in the lights' and added that on the woman's face 'the colour that sparkles through is of a reddish hue'.[84] As 'the most magnificent examples of the English cult of ancestor worship', van Dyck's designs made a great impact upon Romney, who had seen examples at Versailles as well as at Knole in Kent.[85] Van Dyck's *Lucy, Countess of Carlisle* is echoed in Romney's *Lady Milnes* (New York, Frick Collection) and the earlier artist's *Marchesa Brignole-Sale and Son* inspired *Lady Warwick and her Children* (New York, Frick Collection).[86] Keen on simplicity, Romney rarely dressed his subjects in the style of van Dyck's time, though a characteristic lace collar appears on Sir George Warren in *The Warren Family* (Pl. V).[87]

Romney reacted strongly in Rome to two artistic movements: neo-classicism and protoromanticism. As manifestations of the fundamental bipolar elements of the human psyche, these reflect two principles of Greek thinking: the reason of the Apollonian principle and the passion of the Dionysian principle.[88] This polarity, evident in many periods, was described for his era by Winckelmann and is witnessed in Romney's own work in the division between his essentially neo-classical portraiture and his more romantic imaginative works. Back in England he became an important progressive figure, not only 'one of the founding fathers of the neo-classical movement in England' but also, with Fuseli, 'a harbinger of romanticism'.[89]

Though this theoretical field is complex, the contrast between the two poles can be powerfully evident. One need only contrast the simplicity of line and absence of ornamentation in the neo-classical cartoon *Venus Commanding Psyche to Fetch the Waters of the Styx* (Liverpool, Walker Art Gallery; Pl. 14), with the dramatic use of light and shade, jagged line and harrowing expression on the witch's face in Romney's protoromantic studies for *The Lapland Witch* (Cambridge, Fitzwilliam Museum; Pl. 50). Rarely, however, did Romney's protoromantic mood reach the canvas. To some extent this had occurred in the 1750s with *King Lear in the Storm Tearing off his Robes*, but now he had an intellectual apparatus with which to focus such an emotional response. Aside from hints in numerous portrait backgrounds, the protoromantic impulse is more overt than before in *John, Lord Somers* (Eastnor Castle, Hervey-Bathurst Collection; Pl. 47), where the sitter holds a

14 *Venus Commanding Psyche to Fetch the Waters of the Styx*, c.1777–83, 101.6 × 124 cm (40.2 × 49 in). Swirling sculptural lines relate to the development of Romney's neo-classicism.

lock of his dead brother's hair. Among Romney's portraits of women, *Miss Warren as Hebe* (on loan to National Museum of Wales, private collection; Pl. 18) is a magnificent example of a classicized work that is also protoromantic, where the sitter's vulnerability is enhanced by a background of steep cliffs, crashing cataract and eagle's wings. However, most of his portraits painted on his return home can be described as neo-classical, for example *The Gower Children* (Kendal, Abbot Hall Art Gallery; Pl. IX), in which the austerity of current fashion coincides with his own desire for simplicity.[90]

In later life, and notably in *The Tempest* (Pl. 42), Romney strove, as 'a closet Romantic bedevilled by Neo-classicism', to merge both traditions, as did Fuseli in *The Nightmare* (Frankfurt, Goethe Museum).[91] It is unsurprising that he found the process difficult, as these concepts are not evenly matched; neo-classicism is a style, whereas romanticism is an attitude of mind. Thomas Banks has been viewed as achieving this synthesis, in works like *The Falling Titan* (London, Royal Academy), but most other artists kept the two movements distinct in their work.[92] Flaxman, for example, is better known for his flowing neo-classical designs for Wedgwood, but his protoromantic *Chatterton Receiving Poison from the Spirit of Despair* (London, British Museum) surprises by its utter contrast of style. This powerful depiction of 'the archetype of the Romantic tragic genius', who was only valued after his death in 1770, reflects the anguish of many creative artists in an indifferent society and indicates the poignancy for his contemporaries of the young poet's death.[93] With Romney, the dual artistic movements can be aligned with his own cyclical personality. His adherence to both also contributed to his isolation from the group allegiances of the contemporary art world, and offer an early manifestation of the romantic notion of the artist as a social outsider.

A related paradox in Romney's work is his alternate rejection and adoption of classicism. With *The Death of General Wolfe* he shocked society by spurning the convention of classical dress, whereas ten years later as a neo-classicist he was meticulous in following sculptural designs of rigorous severity. In both, he was in the vanguard of fashion and his work demonstrates in a microcosm the interaction between the classical and anti-classical movements of taste.[94]

While at High Cocken, Romney had owned a copy of Le Brun's *Passions*, and in 1769 William Cockin, the artist's schoolmaster friend from his Kendal days, wrote in verse of his friend's 'nicest knowledge of th'impassion'd face'.[95] In Italy he admired Raphael's tormented physiognomy of the boy in the *Transfiguration*, also Masaccio's exaggerated depictions of emotion in a church in Florence, probably the Brancacci Chapel, demonstrating a taste ahead of his time as fresco painting of the quattrocento was generally disliked in the eighteenth century.[96] In Rome, meanwhile, Fuseli had produced designs for the next generation's sourcebook, Johann Kaspar Lavater's *Physiognomy*, which aroused extraordinary interest in the peculiar manifestations of human diversity.[97] Fuseli's involvement in the book is reflected in the exaggerated expressions of his subjects in pictures like *Macbeth and the Witches* (Petworth, The National Trust). It seems likely that similarities in Romney's drawings derive from his contact with Fuseli and access to the Lavater designs in Italy – a source of the admiration felt for him by Blake.[98]

Observing and recording exotic and picturesque characters in the street was one of Romney's pleasures in Italy; John Romney was to possess three such heads by him (untraced). The first was of a dwarf called Baiocco, 'a savage looking man with black hair and beard', who had also been captured by Philip Wickstead's brush *c.*1772 (Burton Constable, Leeds Museums and Galleries). Others included a professional assassin, 'handsome and fierce', whom Romney thought an excellent model for Brutus, and an 'exquisitely painted' old Jew with bald head and grey locks.[99] Goya's palace dwarfs, parallels of Baiocco, have been described as the basis of his essential modernity; the proximity of subject in Romney is worth noting.[100]

At length, Romney considered he had learnt enough to return home. While in Italy he had not only studied the established canon but had been exposed to the development of new movements in art, which would lead to his close involvement with their gestation and birth in Britain. After a sojourn of nineteen months, he left the city on 10 January 1775, 'almost lost in sorrow'.[101] Soon after his departure he wrote to George Carter that, for him, Rome was the place where 'the rays of Apollo shone . . . with greater lustre than on any other spot on this terrestrial globe', and where the recollection of all the places visited brought him 'a thousand tender sensations'.[102] He added that 'a thousand hopes and fears were pushing my mind for some weeks before I left Rome', which suggests a severe bout of melancholy. This new friend, apart from having a dual interest in history painting and the theatre, had a sympathy that Romney much appreciated.[103]

While in Rome, Ozias Humphry had received a letter from England which said: 'forty artists send their best respects to you and will be glad to know how soon they may expect to see Humphry and Romney back again in London'.[104] Cumberland also wrote to his friend assuring him that 'you are not forgot; on the contrary, your fame rises as the expectations of your country increase, and we shall demand great things of you on your return'.[105] Despite their divergence, Romney and his former travelling companion kept in touch in Italy: Humphry also assisted Jenkins in shipping home Romney's possessions, not returning to London himself until 1777.[106]

Reaching Florence, Romney found the collector Lord Cowper and the British envoy Sir Horace Mann keen to serve him. The Grand Duke of Tuscany refused to allow his pictures to be taken down, however, so in order to view them Romney had to content himself with climbing a ladder.[107] In his attempts here to purchase old masters for the Earl of Warwick, he was in touch with Johann Zoffany (1734/5–1810), who, at the same time that his splendid representation of *La Tribuna degli Uffizi* (London, Royal Collection) was nearing completion, doubled as a picture dealer.[108] During his three weeks in this city, Romney made drawings after Cimabue and Masaccio, before crossing the Appennines to Venice via Bologna with John Udney (1722–1802), the British Consul in Florence.[109] Udney was 'a socially adept man of considerable connoisseurship', a shrewd agent for British collectors and a dealer in old masters. He must have been an agreeable companion and guide.[110]

In Bologna Romney admired the drawing school; of the members of the Carracci family he preferred the work of Lodovico, saying it was 'well-adapted to the pathetic and the terrible'.[111] Romney's son records that his father was offered the presidency of the Academy of Painting in Bologna, although Romney only stayed two weeks.[112] There are several precedents of academy membership by Englishmen, but there is no record in Bologna of such an offer being made to Romney.[113] As he was not in favour of academies, this tale may be his son's elaboration of his refusal merely of membership.

Arriving in the 'Merry World of Water' that was Venice, during the carnival on 25 February, Romney, amid the masks, colourful costumes and decorated gondolas of the festivity, became 'almost lost to everything in the world but Titian'.[114] Encountering multiple examples of this great master's work at last, he enthused about his 'amazingly fine pictures, in invention, composition, character, expression and colour'.[115] Though many of the canvases were damaged, the lighting was poor and the scaffolding had to be taken down each night, he managed to make studies of a number of subjects including *John the Baptist* and *Antiope*, one of the paramours of Zeus.[116] There was so much to respond to that he stayed here for almost two months, and several of his surviving drawings, such as *Diana Bathing* (New Haven, Yale Center for British Art) relate to Venetian material.[117]

Here too he met the eccentric Edward Wortley Montagu, who had just returned from the middle east. Brought up in Constantinople, Montagu had converted to Islam and had adopted Turkish garb. His mother, the extraordinary Lady Mary Wortley Montagu, had had her poetical works edited by Romney's friend Isaac Reed in 1768. Montagu himself had known the great Winckelmann. Sitting to Romney, Montagu cut a dramatic figure and the resulting *Edward Wortley Montagu* (private collection, on loan to the Metropolitan Museum, New York) indicates the artist's response to Venetian *colore*, while the composition relates to Titian's *Cardinal Ippolito dei Medici* (Florence, Palazzo Pitti).[118] Though very different in character, the two men became friends; on one occasion Montagu showed Romney how to prepare Turkish coffee. To the latter's great sadness, Montagu died the following year of septicaemia, having swallowed a tiny ortolan bone.[119]

Romney had now visited three of Italy's four major cultural foci: Rome, Florence and Venice. Though Greville had given him an introduction to Sir William Hamilton, he would only ever visit Naples vicariously, in the person of Hamilton's second wife Emma. Leaving Venice, he appears to have started towards Genoa, staying two weeks in Parma, where he had been given English-speaking introductions by Matthew William Peters.[120] Here he was again captivated by the graceful forms and rosy beauty of the Correggios, which had some later effect upon his painting of women and children.[121]

Possibly in consideration of the near shipwreck on his outward journey, he changed his plans, accepted a cheaper offer and travelled overland, crossing the Alps in a heavily loaded carriage which he shared with an Italian fencing master and his wife. The journey was uncomfortable and the horses tended to hurry downhill. Once the carriage overturned, but Romney had luckily taken the precaution of walking. Reaching the point of the accident, he noted the fencing master's face looking so forlorn that the more prudent Romney could not resist transferring its expression to his sketch-book. He was often obliged to share a room with the couple, which caused him some embarassment, but the journey was brightened by the young wife singing to him when bribed with chocolate.[122] Eventually, with his funds running perilously low, he journeyed alone from Lyons to Paris. Here he managed to borrow money for the Channel crossing from Henry Peirse, MP for Northallerton. Peirse was later repaid by being given the portrait *Miss Charlotte Beresford Peirse* (England, private collection; Pl. X), a delightful representation of his young daughter holding the dangling ribbons of her enormous hat.

Romney arrived back in London on 1 July, the return trip from Rome having taken five and a half months. Once again he found accommodation near Greene, in Gray's Inn. The next six months were evidently an unsettled time of low artistic output for Romney, during which he apparently endured a further bout of severe depression caused by mounting financial pressure from his extended family, looming queues of sitters and the end of this period of relative freedom.[123] Though he still aspired to history painting, lack of money now obliged him to return to virtually full-time portraiture. Society would now view him as being well-travelled and experienced, and his studio as a desirable place of resort. Now, in company with many of his sitters, 'the memory of the classics [would be] like a shared religion'.[124]

The same awareness of the antique world was also to be heightened, through Romney, in the work of others. That the twenty-year-old John Flaxman was appointed, in 1775, as Wedgwood's principal designer was in no small measure the result of Romney's encouragement. Flaxman was soon to enlarge the scope of Wedgwood's business, producing many unsurpassed designs including *The Dancing Hours*. He admired the monumental, classically inspired series of cartoons that Romney embarked upon soon after his return from Italy, and the 'melodious sculptural flowing line' of his drapery; furthermore, both artists shared a preference for a shallow spatial field. It was through this relationship that the essential element of stylized, two-dimensional figures of the kind which evolved in Rome during the 1770s was conveyed, not only to Flaxman himself but also to William Blake.[125]

5

Growing reputation and 'The Hermit of Eartham' 1775–86

The fifteen years that followed Romney's return from Italy in 1775 were the period of his greatest success. They overlapped with a time of increased prosperity for many, as the industrial revolution and related shifts in population away from the countryside contributed to the rise of the urban middle class. It was a time when numerous pictures were bought to enhance the fashionable houses built by the newly affluent generation.[1] Gainsborough had moved to London from Bath, perhaps to take advantage of Romney's absence, and Romney's other major metropolitan rival as a portraitist was Reynolds. Zoffany, West, John Singleton Copley (1737–1815) and Nathaniel Holland (1735–1811) must also have given him moments of unease. It was a commonplace that a portrait painter required an impressive studio if he wanted to be in vogue, so Romney made the sound choice of a north-facing house, No. 24 (now 32) Cavendish Square, between the entrances to Holles Street and John Prince's Street.[2] Built by Anthony Collins, the freethinker, the house was well known to society through its most recent occupant, Francis Cotes.[3] Had this rival lived, Romney might not have been so successful, as Cotes's pastels and brilliant full-length oils, such as *Princess Louisa* (London, Royal Collection), were justly celebrated. However, in 1770 Cotes had died, aged forty-four, of a cure for the stone.

The house, which Romney occupied shortly before Christmas 1775, was a powerful sign of confidence in his own ability. It was eminently suitable for an artist of his achievements and ambitions, and by being newly resident there he was, in a sense, perpetuating Cotes's own challenge to Reynolds. Romney's ground landlord at Cavendish Square was Lord Edward Hartley, with whom the settlement of the lease represented a considerable coup as studios were difficult to find, and although the rent was high it represented only a quarter of his income in the period before his stay in Italy.[4] The square was composed of opulent houses of different sizes. In its centre was a garden landscaped by Charles Bridgman, with an equestrian statue, ironically in modern dress, of the Duke of Cumberland by John Cheere. In 1775 an additional advantage for the artist was the proximity of open country. Neighbouring households during Romney's tenure included those of Lord Somers, the Earl of Bessborough, Viscount Barrington and the 'lively mischief-making' Princess Amelia.[5] Collectively these were the reasons for his decision, but this was only made 'after much persuasion' from Thomas Greene and other supportive friends.[6] By 1783 sixteen portraitists exhibiting at the Royal Academy were to give their addresses as Cavendish Square; Romney's occupancy had made the address even more desirable, speeding the drift of artists westwards.[7]

Having endured cramped conditions in the past, Romney now had possession of a large painting room, 'big enough to entertain a crowd of guests', in which he was to produce much of his best work.[8] There was also a gallery in which visitors and prospective sitters could view completed works and collections of engravings, to assist in the negotiation of a powerful, elegant or appealing pose.[9] Elsewhere in the house could be seen Romney's *Providence Brooding over Chaos* and his copy of Raphael's *Transfiguration*. Like many contemporaries, he collected copies of old masters, in his case works after Rembrandt, Raphael, Titian, Veronese, Poussin, Murillo, Rubens and van Dyck.[10] Sometimes visitors came just to see the paintings, such as Lady Spencer in 1787 and James Tate, a Yorkshire schoolmaster, who called in January 1792 when the artist was not at home and was shown the pictures by Romney's 'very civil' valet. In 1795 Mrs Flaxman brought Miss Flaxman and the daughter of John Wilkes to the gallery.[11]

As Romney's rooms were often thronged by wealthy sitters and their families, many sittings were turned into a performance, made dramatic by his speed of execution.[12] Sitters frequently brought friends with them, a social tendency which Romney encouraged in order to animate his sitters' features and also to keep them entertained.[13] Lady Newdigate, for example, recorded how in March 1792 Lady Templetown sat with her for two and a half hours to provide conversation.[14] Romney needed to be adept at playing the courtier while working; it is, however, notoriously difficult to paint and talk at the same time. His sitters also may have found his studio rather uncomfortable as Romney, who was later plagued by vascular disorders, prefered to paint in rooms 'immoderately hot'. Such pressures from his daily schedule increased his determination to spend the evenings quietly.

On Romney's return to England, he had met with support both personal and professional. To offset one of his attacks of melancholia, his friend Adam Walker, who had regretted not being able to travel to Italy himself, requested that he 'scrawl an outline' of his tour in a light-hearted letter which refers satirically to the travel writers Smollett and Sharpe as 'Smelfungus and

I *Unknown Man in a Landscape (perhaps John Williamson)*, 1758-60, 64.1 x 56.8 cm (25.2 x 22.4 in). A hint of music in a lakeland setting: two major influences juxtaposed.

II *The Reverend William Strickland SJ*, c.1760, 102.5 x 86 cm (40.5 x 34 in). The library of this scholarly Jesuit inspired Romney's most detailed interior.

III *Colonel George Wilson*, c.1760, 102.5 x 87.5 cm (41 x 35 in). A meticulous portrait of one of Romney's most important early patrons.

IV *King Lear in the Storm*, c.1758, 102 x 103 cm (40.8 x 41.2 in). The earliest example of Romney's lifelong preoccupation with *King Lear*.

V *The Warren Family*, c.1769, 240.4 x 182.2 cm (95 x 72 in). Sir George Warren MP, his wife Frances (née Bisshopp of Parham Park) and his daughter Elizabeth Harriet.

VI *Mrs. Anne Verelst*, c.1771, 242.9 x 141.7 cm (96 x 56 in). The daughter of Josiah Wordsworth of Wadworth Hall, near Doncaster.

VII *William Beckford*, 1781, 236 x 170 cm (93 x 67 in). The Gothic novelist, art collector and builder of Fonthill Abbey.

VIII *The Honourable Mrs. Trevor (later 2nd Viscountess Hampden),* 1779, 237.9 x 148.9 cm (93.5 x 58.5 in). The beautiful, accomplished daughter of General David Graeme.

Mundungus'.[15] Also, at the prompting of Cumberland, the Earl of Warwick offered Romney rooms in a tower at Warwick Castle, there to paint a companion to a van Dyck. The artist however politely declined this flattering offer.[16] He valued his relative independence and knew it was imperative that he should channel his energies towards re-establishing himself in London.[17] The Earl was evidently not offended by this refusal and soon afterwards bought *Edward Wortley Montagu*. By 1779 he had also purchased *Joseph Brant* (Ottawa; National Gallery of Canada, Pl. 15), an early painting from the next phase of Romney's work. Known as 'the father of the Six Nations', Brant was a Mohawk chief, named in his own tongue Thayendanegea. He had fought for the British in North America and sat to Romney wearing his gorget of rank, presented by the King.[18] Once he had resettled his people in Canada, he spent much time translating the gospels into Mohawk. These two works, with their exotic subject matter, demonstrate the Earl's taste for mirabilia, a new fashion in painting. *Joseph Brant* can be related to Reynolds's *Omai* (Castle Howard), and *Penn's Treaty with the Indians* by West which, for Romney, may have held a resonance of the figure of a brahmin in his portrait of Major Peirson.

In 1776 Cumberland published his *Ode to the Sun*, which was dedicated to Romney in a further effort to catalyse his friend's business. With the Earl of Warwick he had travelled to the Lake District in 1775 and the title was a wry reference to the heavy rain they had endured.[19] The panoramas of this region were now being placed on a par with the great views of continental Europe, and Cumberland's celebratory ode followed Edmund Burke's paper, *A Philosophical Enquiry into the Origins of our Ideas of the Sublime and Beautiful*, of 1756 and Thomas Gray's popular journal of 1769 (published 1775). Cumberland explicitly recognizes Romney as a native of this recently discovered 'region of wonder', with its newly fashionable associations.[20] Indeed, the inspiration of the liminal zones of Lakeland, the interfaces between the elements of earth, air and water, is a phenomenon he shares with many literary and artistic residents and visitors to the region. Unlike Wordsworth's 'spots of time', Romney's own childhood-derived inspiration sustained him at a distance. He was not a regular landscape artist; nonetheless the elemental themes of rocks (earth), skies (air) and cascades (water) pervade many of his landscape backgrounds and imaginative drawings. The elusive fourth element, fire, is implicit too in his cartoons of Odin and Orpheus descending to the underworld (Liverpool, Walker Art Gallery) and explicit in his drawings from Dante's *Inferno* (Oxford, Ashmolean Museum).

Despite Cumberland's support and an enduring public memory of his former success, Romney was painfully aware of how fickle sitters could be. Fortunately the Duke of Richmond came to sit from 24 April 1776; the resulting portrait (Goodwood House) shows him seated, wearing the star of

15 *Joseph Brant (Thayendanegea)*, 1776, 127 × 101.6 cm (49 × 39 in). Commended for valour during the American War of Independence, Brant also translated the New Testament.

his order and reading a book. It was copied by Romney for the Duke's friends in slightly differing versions, one of which (London, National Portrait Gallery) includes the spire of Chichester cathedral. Other commissions from the Duke included the portrait of the statesman Edmund Burke (untraced; engraved by Jones).[21] All these portraits are modest, but they were tokens of approval which accelerated Romney's re-acceptance by society and thus guaranteed his success. Earlier sitters that year included Lord Macclesfield and the Bishop of Worcester.[22] The advent of these members of the highest echelons of society to his studio vanquished depression, re-established his name and ensured a flood of commissions, achieving what Humphry described as 'a staggering success in a short time'.[23] Another friend wrote:

> When I enter his house I tremble with what I know not! I can scarce believe my Eyes! Such pictures! and the pictures of such people! I am lost in wonder and astonishment how all these things should be! how [such] a short [period] of travel should give such Excellence to his pencil! how an almost unfriended Man should at once contract so noble and so numerous a Patronage. When I see his Shew Room filled from top to Bottom, his Painting and Drawing room crowded with Pictures of People of the first fashion, I can scarce believe the Transition from Richter's to Coates's.[24]

This change in circumstances soon enabled Romney to repay Greene an accumulated debt of £1,200.[25]

In anticipation of Garrick sitting to him on 10 June 1776, despite their earlier encounter, Romney waited unsuccessfully in the rain to see the great actor's farewell performance. Unfortunately, being particularly susceptible to the effects of damp, he caught a chill. Cumberland, who happened to call on Romney's return home, feared for his health and summoned the wealthy physician Dr Richard Jebb (1729–87), who ordered him to drink a whole bottle of madeira. Jebb made no charge, cheerfully observing that the artist might not have lived had he been delayed by half an hour. Appointed, by 1786, Physician to the King, Jebb continued to treat Romney virtually gratis.[26]

Another friend concerned to promote Romney's health and prosperity was the vivacious and generous Jeremiah Meyer (1735–89), whom Romney much enjoyed visiting at his home in the 1770s in Covent Garden and in the 1780s at Ebor House, Kew Green. In 1776 Meyer introduced Romney to the poet William Hayley (1745–1820), who had already commissioned several Meyer miniatures.[27] The meeting with Hayley was a pivotal moment in Romney's life and he soon became Romney's closest friend and confidant. Hayley, who was also a dramatist and a translator of Italian literature, addressed many subsequent letters to his friend 'Caro pittore' (Dear painter), and was to become the artist's first biographer. Ostensibly the reason for the introduction to Romney was to obtain a Ciceronian series of portraits of various friends but soon afterwards Hayley sent a characteristically florid invitation to visit his house at Eartham near Chichester in Sussex.[28] In this he urged Romney to 'exchange for a short time the busy scenes and noxious air of London, for the cheerful tranquillity and pure breezes of our Southern Coast'.[29] Hayley records that even at this relatively early phase, the artist seemed not to value life, and Hayley appears to have undertaken to dispel such thoughts as a personal challenge.[30]

Enticed from his studio, Romney made the first of many visits to Hayley's attractive house on the South Downs, which had extensive wooded gardens and sea views of the Isle of Wight. There were also tastefully ornamented walks, grottoes and a hermitage in token of Hayley's fashionable posture, having retired to the countryside, as 'The Hermit of Eartham'.[31] The poet, who was a generous host, encouraged Romney to exercise by walking in his grounds, by archery, by playing quoits and by sea bathing at his cottage on the coast.[32] Romney would revive rapidly on arrival and would, after two days, work as hard during his 'holiday' as he did in London. Indeed, Hayley was often frustrated for example by his inability to tempt his friend to swim or 'to draw the bow as regularly as I think he should do for his health'.[33]

Though virtually unknown today, Hayley's work was highly regarded in his lifetime, and his lengthy *Epistles to Romney*, written in 1777, were warmly received by his friend.[34] The second *Epistle* includes the lines:

> Ingenuous Romney, whom thy merits raise
> To the pure summits of unclouded praise.[35]

Other artists ignored Hayley's effusions, with their tendency to flatter, but Romney responded to the poet's attention and during thirteen sittings between 1777 and 1779 produced several portraits, including *William Hayley* (London, Dulwich Picture Gallery), in which the poet leans upon an upended tome. Gradually the artist became 'in thrall' to Hayley.[36] John Romney believed that the poet monopolized his father, drew him away from society, encouraged his indifference to other artists and dissuaded him from exhibiting at the RA. He also deeply resented Hayley being 'a shrewd gleaner of inconsidered trifles' in his father's studio.[37] Whether or not these charges are exaggerated, it is probable that in the second half of Romney's working life he would have benefited from the regular company of congenial artists. It is certainly true that the poet accumulated numerous pictures and drawings.[38]

Although Hayley considered himself to be a playwright and was moderately successful with his *Lord Russel*, he did not earn much from his plays.[39] In contrast, his verse was popular and earned him the offer, which he turned down, of the King's laureateship upon the death of Thomas Warton.[40] Walpole remarked that his vast corpus of prose and verse, including more than a hundred epitaphs, contained 'no genius, no fire and not a grain of originality'.[41] Yet this 'sociable and well-intentioned being', who also negotiated a pension for William Cowper, gave Romney consistent support for twenty years.[42] In his retirement in Sussex he cut a colourful local figure on horseback, wearing spurs and carrying an umbrella.

The poet came to terms with his limited success as a writer only at the cost of considerable frustration, which helped him to empathize with Romney's melancholia. Hayley also suffered from the effects of the mental peculiarities of his wife Eliza, daughter of the Dean of Chichester, the Reverend Thomas Ball, who eventually had to be cared for in distant Derbyshire. His failed marriage led to several sexual liaisons with female servants, one of whom, Sarah Betts, became the mother of his only son Tom. Mrs Hayley, who was childless, generously acknowledged the boy as her own. As both Hayley and Romney had to deal with their wives at a distance, the shared difficulties of coping with Eliza and Molly served to cement their growing friendship.

Hayley particularly liked the company of other creative men and women, and in adopting the cult for figures of genius became a 'collector of people'.[43] His relations with other artists were 'a mix of generosity and a suffocating desire to control their work', but his gifts as a friend were not insignificant: among his intimates, apart from Meyer and Romney, he numbered Edward Gibbon, Joseph Wright of Derby and William Blake.[44] He frequently invited such prominent people to be temporary members of the Eartham set and also welcomed Romney's own friends, including Thomas Carwardine, Joseph Flaxman and Adam Walker. Lavish with his hospitality, Hayley was described by the latter, using a watchmaker's metaphor, as 'our master spring of joy'.[45]

Edward Gibbon (1737–94), author of *The Decline and Fall of the Roman Empire*, had been at school with Hayley. In 1783 Gibbon sat to Romney and invited the artist and the poet to dinner several times in Bentinck Street.[46] Romney relished painting the odd-looking, corpulent 'Roman Eagle', whose resulting portrait *Edward Gibbon* (England, private collection), one of many Hayley obtained gratis, does not flatter, showing the mouth 'like a round hole in his visage'.[47]

One member of the Eartham set in the 1780s was the poet Anna Seward (1747–1809), the 'Swan of Lichfield', who lived in the city's cathedral close with her father, Canon Thomas Seward, a co-editor of the plays of Francis Beaumont and John Fletcher. Visiting Eartham in 1782, Anna Seward met Romney, to whom she sat. *Anna Seward* (Burlington, Vermont, Robert Hull Fleming Museum), in which the poetess is posed with her index finger against her cheek, was hung at Eartham beside a bust of Pope. Her novel *Louisa* is her best-known work; she also wrote a memoir of Erasmus Darwin. Her verse includes a poem to 'her beloved and honoured Titiano', praising both Romney's soul and pencil, which:

Glows with bold lines, original and strong.[48]

Seward's letters contain reiterated descriptions of Romney's work as standing among 'the finest Delphic ornaments of the eighteenth-century'.[49] She was friendly with Thomas Day, an advocate of Rousseau's educational theories and a critic of industrial pollution. She also knew John Howard and she bequeathed her poetical works and letters to Walter Scott, some of which he edited.[50] Hayley's support of Anna Seward and later of Charlotte Smith, at a time when few women were educated and women writers were largely disregarded, was an expression of his advanced radical thinking, though he could be conventionally insensitive, as in his *Essay on Old Maids*.[51]

In 1781 Romney introduced Flaxman to Hayley, who commissioned him to design a memorial in Chichester Cathedral to his father-in-law, Dean Ball. Flaxman also modelled a bust of Hayley, a sculpture commemorated by Romney in a much later work, *John Flaxman Modelling Hayley's Bust* (New Haven, Yale Center for British Art; Pl. 16), which represents Hayley's image presiding over the creativity of two great artists. Subsequently Flaxman wrote how he had 'the happiness of living such a fortnight at Eartham as many of my fellow creatures go out of this world without enjoying', and it was he who eventually introduced Hayley to Blake.[52]

Hayley's aims in his friendship with Romney were by no means all selfish, and though he was often infuriated by Romney's reluctance to write, he wrote himself to the artist in 1787: 'You are an enchanting rogue and however out of humour I am with you, I am always solicitous for your glory.'[53] Romney appreciated his hospitality and wrote of the poet's 'great kindness to me in your paradise'.[54] His journeys to Eartham were effectively substitutes for the family visits he was unable or unwilling to make. In return, Hayley stayed regularly with him at the house in Cavendish Square, 'a mansion where I have passed so many pleasant and sociable hours'.[55] Although it was not a house of lavish entertainment – 'a little broth or tea' usually sufficing for the artist, who was certainly not a gourmet – Hayley was often sweetened by gifts of paintings.[56] Their relationship is complex. While the poet benefited more in a material sense, Romney undoubtedly gained psychologically from their friendship. He once observed to Hayley that 'if you should go before me I should lose everything that is dear to me and the best friend I ever had'.[57]

In London, a prominent connoisseur whose criticism carried much weight was Horace Walpole. Having printed the beautiful Lady Elizabeth Craven's first play *Somnambula* on his private press, he arranged for her to sit to Romney in June 1778. *Lady Craven* (London, Tate Gallery) was displayed in Walpole's dining room at Strawberry Hill, and in 1779 it elicited some verse by him, albeit intended to flatter the sitter more than the artist:

16 *John Flaxman Modelling the Bust of William Hayley*, 1791–2, 226 × 114.7 cm (89 × 57 in). William Hayley, amidst his creative friends, dominates 'The Great Picture'.

Full many an artist has on canvas fix'd
All charms that Nature's pencil ever mix'd;
The witchery of Eyes, the Grace that tips
The inexpressible douceur of Lips.
Romney alone, in this fair image caught
Each Charm's expression and each Feature's thought;
And shows how in their sweet assemblage sit
Taste, Spirit, Softness, Sentiment and Wit.[58]

Not many artists moved Walpole to verse, although Stubbs's *A Horse Frightened by a Lion* (London, Tate Gallery, on loan from a private collection) was another exception.[59] Walpole's preference for male consorts had been common knowledge since 1764, although he enjoyed the company of both sexes, though. Among women he had a predilection for those who, like Lady Craven, had 'a shadow over their reputations'.[60] Lady Craven was renowned for both her beauty and her literary ability, which she wore 'as if they were gifts of the gods'. In 1791 she became the wife of her lover, the Margrave of Ansbach, a nephew of Queen Caroline. They both sat to Romney in 1793 and *The Margravine of Ansbach* (Ansbach, Residenz) is a fine late, full-length portrait.

While in Italy, Romney had received a letter from the Society of Artists urging him to exhibit on his return, claiming that 'peace and harmony are perfectly restored among us'.[61] Romney knew he had no need of such publicity, and declined. He steadfastly did likewise with the Royal Academy, although he did attend the Academy exhibitions from time to time.[62] According to one of his pupils he viewed the RA as 'a manufacture of lifeless mechanisms, incompatible with the glowing ebullitions of feeling'.[63] He probably took a perverse pleasure in the public and the press being aware that he was not an RA and in 'witnessing the odium which the President's party incurred by keeping an artist of his talents and fame out of their ranks'.[64] His absence also undermined Reynolds's supremacy, by demonstrating that the Academy was irrelevant to the needs of a successful British artist.[65] Walpole noted in his RA catalogue for 1780, 'Mr Romney, now in great vogue, sent none of his pictures to either of the exhibitions.'[66]

It is untrue to say that Romney was isolated professionally, since he mixed with artists, patrons and connoisseurs at exhibitions and at his own gallery at Cavendish Square. In 1781 his friend Meyer urged him, nonetheless, to contribute to the next Academy exhibition. Apparently Meyer believed that if Romney were to be elected RA at this date, after Reynolds's death he would have a chance of becoming President.[67] Whether or not this story is true, Meyer's aspiration for his friend seems a little unrealistic; even though Romney was by now a senior figure in the London art world, he would have been averse to the consequent public engagements. Though his refusal either to exhibit at the RA or to seek admission as an Academician may have deprived Romney of some professional contacts, it was probably appropriate considering his psychological frailty. Certainly he perceived the 'friendly rivalry of the exhibition room' as a form of unarmed combat, whose unnecessary 'warfare and jostling' he abhorred.[68]

As a history painter, however, Romney continued to be frustrated. In 1774 he had been listed as one of ten artists deemed capable of furnishing paintings to decorate St Paul's. This project was fated to fail and even the enticing opportunity of producing designs for the Adelphi did not materialize as several artists had hoped.[69] Romney had in any case experienced enough of the intrigue that went with such undertakings and, like James Barry, who heroically worked gratis on the latter project, was 'heartily sick of the scuffle'.[70]

A similar possibility presented itself when in November 1777 Thomas Orde, later Lord Bolton, sat to Romney. During frequent visits Orde suggested subjects for pictures and would read to the artist as he painted. One of his ideas was that of presenting an altarpiece by Romney to King's College, Cambridge. Designs for a *Mater Dolorosa* were made and discussed, but unfortunately Orde's gift was pre-empted by the Earl of Carlisle and the ambitious project foundered.[71]

The years from 1777 to *c.*1782 saw Romney undertake a monumental series of eighteen black-chalk cartoons (Liverpool, Walker Art Gallery) from the writings of Aeschylus, Apuleius, Euripides, Virgil, Shakespeare and Gray.[72] As they were unrealized in oils, it may be that they were drawn for pleasure and regarded by Romney as finished works in their own right.[73] They represent the furthest development of 'his true vocation' as a history painter, and express a desire to manifest his scholarly interests through a familiarity with the sculpture and texts of antiquity.[74]

The largest group of cartoons illustrates the story of Cupid and Psyche from Apuleius' *Golden Ass*. Of the seven in this group, the most striking is *Venus Commanding Psyche to Fetch the Waters of the Styx* (Pl. 14), whose severe yet beautiful line demonstrates Romney's neo-classical instincts. The most turbulent protoromantic design is one of two depicting *The Dream of Atossa* from Aeschylus' *The Persians*. Here the ghost of Darius, appearing to his widow Atossa in a dream, prophesies the imminent death of their son Xerxes in his chariot. A single cartoon shows one of Romney's favourite myths, that of Medea. There are also three of Orpheus and Eurydice from Virgil's *Georgics*.[75]

As part of a lifelong preoccupation with *King Lear*, there is one cartoon of *The Death of Cordelia*. There is also an early cartoon version of Romney's extensive series of designs for *The Infant Shakespeare*, taken from Thomas Gray's Pindaric ode *The Progress of Poesy* (1757). This text itself marks a shift from neo-classical lucidity to the obscure and the sublime, a development in keeping with Romney's own concerns.[76]

Classical and Shakespearean sources aside, it is intriguing to see Romney's response in cartoon form to another work by Gray, namely a 1768 retelling of the Norse tale *The Descent of Odin*. Romney's work shows the eponymous hero descending to the underworld in search of his son Baldur, where he is confronted by the fearsome earth mother.

The subject of another single cartoon shows the fate of Prometheus, who stole fire from the gods, in a story taken from Aeschylus' *Prometheus Bound*. It depicts the erring Titan being attached to his rock by Jupiter's henchmen, rather than the more popular horrifying scene of his 'immortal' liver being consumed by an eagle.

Using black chalk on paper, Romney was able to achieve his very sculptural neo-classical effects quickly. Flaxman, who particularly admired the cartoons, described his friend's vigorous *The Dream of Atossa*, a subject he himself drew, as 'conducted with the fire and severity of a Greek bas relief', and referred to the series in general as 'examples of the sublime and the terrible at that time perfectly new in English art'.[77] Romney's conceptions relate strongly to the young Flaxman's Wedgwood designs and outline illustrations from Homer and Dante, with their essential grasp of form. This stylistic link is especially evident in the imposing figure of Romney's goddess in *Venus Commanding Psyche to Fetch the Waters of the Styx* (Pl. 14).[78] It is difficult for us, around the turn of the twenty-first century, to view neo-classicism as it was in the 1770s: 'a youthful fiery rebellious movement'.[79] Nonetheless, with their 'freedom and freshness of design' these studies by Romney, having the compelling simplicity of Michelangelo cartoons, stand as finished works today.[80]

Romney's knowledge of the appropriate Greek texts was largely through the translations by Dr Robert Potter (1721–1804), schoolmaster of Scarning in Norfolk and a curate of 'great merit, small preferment and large family'.[81] As the first translator of Aeschylus (1777) and Euripides (1781) into English, Potter was both attacked by Dr Johnson and praised by Walpole.[82] Romney himself was much impressed by the sublime elements of Aeschylus, which increased his interest in the supernatural. This enthusiasm was acknowledged by Potter in his second edition (1779), where he wrote 'Mr Romney . . . called Aeschylus the painter's poet' and added that he hoped his translation would give rise to 'some paintings that will do honour to our country'.[83] Following sittings in 1779, Romney presented the translator with the portrait *Dr Robert Potter* (sold Sotheby's 12 July 1995), receiving a gift of Norfolk turkeys in return.[84]

The frequency with which Romney drew the story of Psyche, an allegory of the soul in search of desire, suggests a strength of appeal to the artist, whose own psychology was turbulent. He had completed a *Cupid and Psyche* (untraced) soon after his return from Italy, just post-dating Wedgwood's use of the story as a design at his Etruria pottery.

Psyche also has a place in Romney's oeuvre as one of a number of vulnerable recumbent women, as is evident in the cartoon *Zephus Blowing at Psyche,* where the putto cheekily puffs a gust of wind.[85] Other examples include *Serena in the Boat of Apathy* (sold Sotheby's, 17 June 1966), *Iphigenia Asleep with her Maidens* (Cambridge, Fitzwilliam Museum) and *The Wood Nymph* (England, private collection, Pl. 13). The notion of the voyeur is more blatant yet in *Har and Heva Bathing with Mnetha Looking On* (Cambridge, Fitzwilliam Museum), a subject also treated by Blake. Many portraitists are licensed voyeurs and Romney spent much of his time looking intently at lightly clad young women as a professional duty; indeed his interest in drapery may even have been fetishistic. But in the absence of evidence of his keeping a regular mistress, his representation of female beauty may partly have been a process of sexual sublimation.

Elsewhere, too, Romney's reputation was large and increasing. As early as December 1777, Thomas Banks wrote from Rome to Humphry, 'I am very glad to hear of the success of Mr Romney, Sir Joshua, Gainsborough and yourself.'[86] He referred, of course, to success in the demanding world of portraiture.

6

'The man in Cavendish Square' 1775–86

Portraiture was, in the words of Dr Johnson, 'that art which is now employed in diffusing friendship, in renewing tenderness, in quickening the affections of the absent and continuing the presence of the dead'.[1] For the patrons this was understood, but the British obsession with dynastic considerations was for centuries 'the bane of many painters' lives'.[2] Sitting was an accepted part of the affluent classes' social life, and demand was constant as each generation visited the studios in turn. New portraits were then arranged to relate to the existing collection and, in the largest houses, in galleries specially built for the purpose.[3] Such demand inhibited Romney and Reynolds from fulfilling their aspirations as history painters, and Gainsborough his as a landscape painter. Their frustrations were well understood by William Hayley, who wrote in his First *Epistle to Romney*:

> Th'imperious voice of vanity and pride
> Bids him from fancy's region turn aside
> And quit the magic of her scene, to trace
> The vacant lines of some unmeaning face.[4]

Romney was well able to produce these durable manifestations of power and egoism, his success being directly related to his ability to catch in his sitters 'all those neutral qualities which are valued by society – health, youth, good looks, an air of breeding'.[5] But doing so was in each case a challenge and there was always the frisson of wondering how it would turn out. As he strove to respond to the individual energy of each sitter, the start of the process never lost its fascination for Romney. His survival at the pinnacle of popularity for this fifteen-year period following his travels in Italy was a phenomenal achievement, when patrons were so fickle and a new artist's reputation could be made overnight.[6] The pressure of his sitters was debilitating. In the season he achieved five or six sittings a day and through a combination of popularity and assiduity achieved 9000 recorded sittings in less than twenty years, with a staggering peak of 593 in 1783.[7] Sitters were often petulant, demanding and lacking in taste, but Romney persisted. He never turned a sitter away even if the face 'would have chilled the genius of Michelangelo', though he undoubtedly often wished to do so, and at one of his busiest periods he considered planting 'cannon at the door to overcome the eager crowds'.[8] His sitters books from 1776 to 1797 have survived virtually intact and demonstrate not only the volume but the social diversity that he encompassed.[9]

According to Gainsborough, 'the principle intention and beauty of a portrait' was achieving a likeness.[10] Romney always enjoyed the challenge of a new face and could catch likenesses easily. It was a skill that he shared with his master Steele and with Gainsborough himself, whereas Reynolds was sometimes criticized in this respect.[11] Catching a likeness was, moreover, a desideratum that Romney was able to achieve throughout his career.[12] The founder of Methodism, John Wesley, remarked: 'Mr Romney is a painter indeed! He struck off an exact likeness at once', and Romney's *Marquis of Lansdowne* was considered 'so very like that . . . any of his friends would know the picture'.[13] Furthermore, a comparison of the portrait *Richard Cumberland* (London, National Portrait Gallery, on loan to 10 Downing Street; Pl. 9) with another of this sitter in the Huntington Art Collections gives a strong indication of this ability.

He also managed to enhance his likenesses with a modicum of flattery, in response to demands for a fashionable ideal; faces with 'peerless complexions' were attained for many of his women sitters. Indeed, Lady Newdigate acknowledged such treatment, writing, 'I fancy I called up my good looks today; where they came from I don't know, but my picture is much improved . . . it is handsomer than I ever was in my life.'[14] Romney's liking for large umbrageous hats was a related technique of palpable deception. By having women sitters wear wide brims he was able to cast their faces in flattering, soft shadow of differing colours as he did with *Emma Hart with a Straw Hat* (San Marino, Huntington Art Gallery; Pl. 37).[15] Male sitters similarly expected their faces to 'come out of the painter's hands smooth, rosy, round, smiling; just as they expected their hair to come out of the barber's curled and powdered'.[16] Thus many of his young men are 'handsome enough for Hollywood'.[17] Although relatively few actually smile from their frames, these other requirements were generally met. Occasionally Romney was defeated by vacuous faces, and felt much 'ludicrous perplexity' when a rather simple gentleman returned his portrait asking for it to be given 'more the look of a man of sense'.[18]

Romney is sometimes criticized for painting allegedly repetitive, mask-like faces; but although many are formulaic, this was due to the contemporary fashion for idealization rather than a lack of subtlety. *Mrs Wilbraham Bootle* (1764; Pl. 3) may have been painted to a formula but her matronly portrait of 1780 (Edinburgh, National Gallery of Scotland) is far more individual, as is the modest blush on the cheek of *Mrs Jelf Powys* (Switzerland, private collection).[19] In contrast, Mrs Mary Tighe criticized her likeness for its pallor, which she said looked as if 'a young woman had wept herself sick'.[20] On the other hand, as an essay in romantic portraiture, this work (Dublin, National Gallery of Ireland) is entirely effective.

Romney obtained his effects more by delicacy in the gradation of tints on his palette than by elaborate devices of chiaroscuro. This is arguably why many of his sitters seem so youthful, and why he was so successful in portraying younger sitters.[21] Though smiles are indeed rare, a notable exception is his *Thomas Paine* (untraced; engraving London, National Portrait Gallery; Pl. 53). Occasionally, as with *Lady Stormont* (Scotland, private collection) and *Thomas Walker*, the Manchester cotton merchant (untraced), he included wrinkles.[22]

Apart from the likeness and this ideal, sitters expected their social status to be proclaimed or even enhanced by the portraits but at the same time they often wanted value for money. Romney had sufficient business acumen to charge much less than Reynolds, which gave prospective sitters an additional reason for calling at Cavendish Square. In 1786 he charged twenty guineas for a three-quarter length, while Gainsborough charged thirty guineas and Reynolds charged as much as fifty guineas. Romney also became more adept at urging sitters to settle accounts, though some of them delayed for years. Tradespeople were often made bankrupt before cash was forthcoming, as the aristocracy tended to deem such requests to be sheer effrontery and rarely saw them as urgent. In Romney's case this theme of complaint was well justified: frequently the debt was settled only when, after his father's death, John Romney became pressing.

Now that Romney was so clearly a rival, Reynolds could never bring himself to use his name, tetchily referring to 'the man in Cavendish Square' and thus disguising his jealousy with contempt.[23] Romney was indeed the more popular by the late 1770s, as his work had generated 'a more direct challenge to Reynolds' brand of elevated portraiture'.[24] This challenge is clear in his magnificent group portrait *The Gower Children* (Kendal, Abbot Hall Gallery; Pl. IX), painted in 1777. Soon he became the first choice of new patrons as his portraits were perceived as major desiderata for the completion of a fashionable interior. Furthermore, his studio was organized in a less formal manner and, unlike the President, he did not insist upon his work being exposed to public gaze on the walls of the Academy. Many merchants and professional men and their families were inclined to Romney's simplicity of design and lack of ostentatious classical reference, apart from the more obvious advantage that, whereas Reynolds's colours faded rapidly, Romney's did not. Other considerations may have included Romney's political stance and the tendency of northern sitters to be attracted to an artist who hailed from Lakeland.

James Northcote and James Barry both agreed that Reynolds lost business to his rival and there is evidence not only in the RA President's *Mrs Hartley as Jane Shore* of 1771 (private collection), but also in the more informal and elegant *Lady Elizabeth Delme* (Washington, DC, National Gallery of Art) of 1779–80 and the simple white dress of *Mrs Scott of Danesfield* of 1786 (Waddesdon Manor, The National Trust), that Reynolds had for years been following Romney.[25]

Despite this rivalry, the two men were prepared to acknowledge each other's ability.[26] Romney was happy to disseminate details of Reynolds's *Discourses* and Reynolds praised Romney's merits as a draughtsman.[27] When Reynolds's *Infant Hercules Strangling the Serpents* was adversely criticized, Romney stoutly defended him, saying 'no other man in Europe could paint such a picture'.[28] These fragmentary records suggest that the partisan nature of society exaggerated the friction between them.[29] Sir George Beaumont, for example, supported the President, saying that 'a faded picture by Reynolds is better than the best of Romney's'.[30] Oddly enough, on one occasion Sir Joshua invited Romney to dine 'in the most polite and flattering manner', saying that he 'should be happy to be acquainted with Mr Romney', but Greene was unable to 'prevail over him' to accept.[31]

Several clients sat to both artists, while the Marquis of Salisbury and his wife divided their patronage between them. A number sat to all of the triumvirate: Romney, Reynolds and Gainsborough. This was not done merely to acquire family portraits of unsurpassed quality, but also to garner increased prestige from sitting to a succession of fashionable artists. For example, William Pitt the Younger sat to Romney and Gainsborough; Sir William Hamilton sat to Romney and Reynolds; the actresses Mrs Siddons and Mrs Robinson sat to all three.

A rigorous administrative framework was essential to Romney's business. To avoid double bookings Romney kept a careful sitters book, which recorded in advance between three and six sitters daily. Each patron might eventually expect a minimum of two sittings, totalling three hours in the studio, according to his son, but in some cases the books record many more than this.[32] The disparity may reflect the many copies Romney made of his own pictures and canvases which were discarded after early false starts. Some sitters returned for minor alterations, which the artist agreed to do 'with great cheerfulness', a phrase which belies his thought.[33] He was not, however, wholly under the thumb of his sitters, as is clear from Lady Newdigate writing 'I dare not disobey him.'[34] The storage of numerous half-

IX *The Gower Children*, 1776-7, 225 x 197.5 cm (90 x 79 in). The eventual husbands of the girls were the Archbishop of York, the Duke of Beaufort, the Earl of St Germans and Lord Harrowby; young Granville became Ambassador to Russia.

X *Miss Charlotte Beresford Pierse*, 1786-7, 159.4 x 110.5 cm (63 x 47 in). Miss Pierse later married Inigo Thomas Freeman Esq. of Yapton, Sussex.

XI *Sir Christopher and Lady Sykes*, 1786, 245.4 x 184.7 cm (97 x 73 in). Sir Christopher was a scholarly man, much interested in landscape design.

XII *Mrs. John Birch*, 1777, 126.5 x 101.2 cm (50 x 40 in). The sitter was a Sussex neighbour of Romney's friend, the poet William Hayley.

XIII *Mrs. John Morris (later Lady Morris) and Child*, 1777-8, 89.8 x 69.6 cm (35.5 x 27.5 in). Henrietta, the daughter of Sir Philip Musgrave, Bart, of Eden Hall, Cumberland.

XIV *Sir John Trevelyan, Bart*, 1784-8, 240 x 150 cm (96 x 60 in). Fourth baronet of Nettlecombe, Somerset, and a considerable landowner.

XV *Lord Chancellor Thurlow*, 1782, 208.1 x 146.7 cm (82.2 x 58 in). The irascible law lord who presided over the trial of Warren Hastings.

XVI *John Milton Dictating to his Daughters*, 1793, 193.5 x 206 cm (76.2 x 81.2 in). A work painted in celebration of the great writer whom Romney had admired at Least since 1771.

finished canvases, several with undried pigment upon them, also required careful organization by his assistants. He also left a large number of paintings significantly unfinished, partly since he began too many, but also because he could never resist the challenge of a new face and never turned a sitter away.

As Romney did not exhibit for fifteen years after his journey to Italy, pictures which were not being engraved were generally sent directly to the homes of the sitters, often in the country. Efficiency was also vital, with pictures going to and from the engraver and William Saunders's picture frame workshop at 10, Great Castle Street. The details recorded in his surviving ledgers demonstrate how Romney avoided the mayhem created by Steele. *The 4th Duke of Marlborough* (Pl. 19), for example, was sent to Blenheim by carrier from The Swan at Holborn Bridge.[35] Occasionally the system failed: Lady Trevelyan's portrait was stolen in 1792 and had to be started afresh. A waiting list system is implicit in several references to sitters coming 'if there be a vacancy', and although Romney hated letter writing, he often wrote formal requests for payment in his own hand.[36]

Romney was a very rapid worker, and in the later 1770s preferred the pronounced surface texture of a twill canvas to facilitate the broad handling of pigment that he had studied in Titian and other Venetians. By contrast in his Kendal work, such as *King Lear in the Storm*, and at other times throughout his career, he employed canvas of a finer weave. As twill only became fashionable in the 1780s, it appears that he contributed to its adoption.[37] Romney also employed relatively coarse bristle brushes, evident on many canvases, whereas his major rivals used sable. These brushes were often loaded with pigment and the resulting thick impasto necessitated longer drying periods, though he speeded up the process by using oil of cloves or almonds. Crucially, as a result of his sound technical knowledge, the 'surface of his paint has stood up much better to the action of time' than that of many contemporaries.[38] His Sussex palette was preserved by Hayley's godson William Hayley Mason, and a surviving sketch (New York, Metropolitan Museum) purports to give some idea how he set his colours upon it.

Romney never made finished drawings for his paintings but frequently painted directly onto the canvas, a procedure that let him execute the details once only. This helped retain the original freedom of design, though his compositions did sometimes partly fail. At worst this demanded a new start on a fresh canvas; otherwise frequent *pentimenti* were the result. Originally Romney would have ground his own colours, and later had an assistant to do so, but by his later years they were available ready mixed. During the 1790s he bought some of his studio materials from James Poole of High Holborn, and by 1797 Griffiths the colourman was his main supplier.

It is clear that Romney did not always view toil as a disadvantage: 'in his painting room he seemed to have the highest enjoyment of life and the more he painted the greater flow of spirits he acquired'.[39] This may have been a strategy for coping with melancholy, though he found it hard to work when thoroughly depressed. It is significant that his brushwork was 'uncommonly rapid', giving a particular quality to his painting.[40]

His son confirmed this technique, writing

> I beheld his hand
> Dash on the canvas with creative might
> Visions of fancy, as by magic wand![41]

Such speed is often evident in the art of manic depressives; in Romney's case it is the main evidence we have of the manic part of his cycle.[42] When working at his best he could produce a portrait a day, and John Wesley said that he did 'more in an hour than Sir Joshua did in ten'.[43] Contemporary conservation work confirms the rapidity of his technique.[44] Though Romney may deliberately have undercut Reynolds, his prices reflect the sense of the reasonable fee which was possible when working so speedily. As a method it was incompatible with historical works, which required much more time; it suited his portraiture nonetheless.

Indeed, Romney's simplest portraits have a most summary handling of pigment, evident in *Mrs Ainslie and Child* (formerly in the Beit Collection), although the faces were always carefully rendered. Such hasty work was a considerable departure from his early meticulousness, but as evidence of his 'boldness and freedom of draughtsmanship' it does demonstrate his power as an artist.[45] This informal sketchiness has not always been appreciated, but today the loose brushwork of *Mrs Tickell* (Philadelphia, Museum of Art) of 1791 is a wholly acceptable effect.[46] In the manuscript of his unpublished 'Discourse on Art' he refers to historical pictures appearing like a 'momentary impulse', thus anticipating in his language the speed of his handling. Although critics may have described these paintings as 'unfinished', it is likely that Romney did not, and in this spontaneity he can be considered one of the 'masters of the barely finished'.[47] He may also have been influenced by observing the looser drapery in works by Titian, Raphael and Rubens.

His sitters' acceptance of Romney's more spontaneous style is not in doubt. A comparison between the portraits of the two wives of Nathaniel Lee Acton, both in the Huntington Art Collections in California, shows that the earlier portrait, *Mrs Susanna Lee Acton*, of 1787, is a sketchy work, while the later *Mrs Penelope Lee Acton* (Pl. 17), of 1791, is more finished. William Blake noted both categories in general, commenting that the true genius of Romney's work could only be realised by a combination of engravings which were 'highly finished' and 'less finished'.[48] Whether the less-finished works were produced on days of cheerfulness or gloom, or indeed to meet urgent deadlines, it is true that his portraiture anticipated in some respects the artistic movements of the next century.

Unusual poses are rare in Romney's work but, although he did not achieve the variety of poses attained by Reynolds, his portraits are not as repetitive as is sometimes believed. More innovative dispositions of figures occur occasionally, for example in *The Malmesbury Daughters* (untraced), where the sitters are both in one half of a canvas vertically divided, and in *The Willett Children* (Philadelphia, Museum of Art), where they are in one half of the canvas diagonally divided. He also had a good eye for placing the figure in the canvas space in a manner more like that of modern society photographers than that of his contemporaries, and is unusual in placing the head, for example of *Samuel Whitbread II* (Eton College), in the corner of the canvas. For more straightforward portraits he began immediately at the canvas without preparatory drawings.

Just as Renaissance artists borrowed designs from antiquity, many eighteenth-century artists borrowed from old masters and antique sculpture. Romney was no exception. *Mrs Thomas Carwardine and Child* (Pl. 40) relates to Raphael's *Madonna of the Chair*; *Lady Warwick and Children* to van Dyck's *Marchese Brignole-Sale and her Son*, both paintings being owned by the Earl of Warwick, and *Sir Christopher and Lady Sykes* (Pl. XI) to Rubens's *Self-Portrait with his Wife and Child*, then at Blenheim.[49] Romney was also a subscriber to a new edition of Cesare Ripa's *Iconologia*, another rich source of ideas.[50] Sculpture influenced numerous compositions. *Mrs Anne Verelst* (Pl. VI) relates to Matteo Mattei's *Ceres*; the figure of the boy in *The Clavering Children* (Pl. 33) to the Apollo Belvedere; and the sweeping oval shape created by the limbs in *The Boone Children* (sold Sotheby's, 16 November 1988), perhaps deriving from an antique sarcophagus, demonstrates the essence of Romney's neo-classical appeal.

Antique personifications were another inspiration, popular since the Tudor period.[51] Sitters assumed the characteristics of deities. Romney's strongest example is *Miss Warren as Hebe* (private collection, on loan to the National Museum of Wales, Cardiff; Pl. 18), in which Miss Warren, as cupbearer to the gods, is overshadowed by an eagle, the emblem of Jupiter, and depicted with a jug of nectar. This huge bird provides a contrast in scale – possibly ironic – with her likeness as a child in *The Warren Family* (Pl. V), holding a bullfinch. This painting relates to Reynolds's *Miss Mary Meyer as Hebe* (Ascott, The National Trust), which portrays the daughter of his friend Jeremiah. Painted mostly in May 1776, *Miss Warren as Hebe* anticipated Payne Knight's urging in his letter of 24 November that in such sublime portraiture, 'a single figure is more proper than a groupe'.[52] Other Romney sitters chose to personify Circe, Calypso and Psyche, in keeping with the use of classical compliments in fashionable language. At Eartham, Hayley was called

17 *Mrs Penelope Lee Acton*, 1791–3, 236.6 × 143.8 cm (93.5 × 57.5 in). The second wife of Nathaniel Lee Action beneath an umbrageous hat.

18 *Miss Elizabeth Harriet Warren (later Viscountess Bulkeley) as Hebe*, 1776, 238.5 × 148 cm (94.3 × 58.5 in). The sitter's vulnerability may be compared to that of the Bootle brothers in Pl. 21.

'Pindar', while Cumberland called Romney 'Timanthes', an artist reknowned for his shyness but who shared with Romney the subject of Medea.[53]

Cotes and Reynolds used drapery painters like Joseph van Aken and Peter Toms to finish the clothing of their sitters, rarely completing 'an atom more than the face', but Romney, like Gainsborough, was determined to paint his own.[54] Considering that many of his canvases were up to ninety-six inches high, he was forced to cover a vast acreage of twill canvas. He would have had less of a backlog if he too had employed a drapery man, but his pictures would then have lost much of their unity.[55] Since his list of tradesmen does include that of Roth, who was a drapery man, evidently he did break with this principle on occasion, presumably to meet a deadline.[56]

A secondary source of income and public exposure came from the sale of engravings. Romney had benefited from his early study of engravings after Dutch masters. Now, increasingly, his own work was in demand from engravers who sought to supply the rage for prints of contemporary portraits.[57] All men of taste had a collection, and copies were cheaply available to the public in the print shops.[58] As Romney did not exhibit after his journey to Italy, this form of advertising was useful to him. Often it was the only way connoisseurs were able to view his work once it had left his hands. The best engravers were often very busy, thus delaying the arrival of the original paintings at their purchasers' homes.

At least 58 hands engraved more than 160 of Romney's portraits. They included Valentine Green, J. Raphael Smith, Francesco Bartolozzi and Romney's friend the radical William Sharp. Their engravings, respectively, included *Mrs Yates as the Tragic Muse*, *The Gower Children*, *The Earl of Bute* and *Thomas Paine*. Another engraver, John Jones, was recommended by the literary critic George Steevens, and eventually reproduced more than twenty of Romney's works including *William Frederick, 2nd Duke of Gloucester* (Pl. 34).[59] Unlike Reynolds, Romney was not greatly concerned with posterity and often employed less fastidious engravers, so that his work is not always seen to advantage in this form. By 1801, in a position to consider his career retrospectively, he belatedly expressed concern at such variations in quality.[60] Occasionally, on a whim, he desired favourite works, such as *Lady Carlisle*, to be engraved; but although he derived some income from print sales, engravings were never his priority.

Romney preferred his women sitters to attend his studio in timeless, wrap-around gowns of white or ivory satin, the colour much in evidence in Fuseli's women and a form of simplicity also advocated by Payne Knight.[61] White was also an emblem of marriage and many of these portraits, such as *Mrs Lee Acton* (Pl. 17) were painted soon after the sitters' weddings. In the beguiling *Mrs Birch* (Phoenix Art Museum; Pl. XII), simple, coloured but unpatterned pale salmon cloth was otherwise chosen. This evokes William Collins's *Ode to Simplicity*:

> But com'st a decent maid
> In attic robe arrayed,
> O chaste, unboastful nymph, to thee I call![62]

Sometimes Romney adds a little more colour: a blue sash for *Mrs Jordan* (sold Sotheby's, 16 November 1988) or a red cloak for *Mrs Isabella Curwen* (South Africa, private collection). Reynolds often tightened the loose gowns with transverse bands, but Romney preferred free and fluid drapery. Like Winckelmann, he advised lady sitters against restraining 'stays of deadly steel', having admired such physical freedom in everyday life, for example in the dress of the women of Avignon.[63] Occasionally he was obliged to paint the lavish costume detail of a peeress's robes, as in *Lady Boston* (England, private collection). Keeping the dresses after the sittings as a matter of course, he would spend considerable time adjusting the folds on the lay figure, after which 'he looked upon [the paintings] as half done, so ready and certain was his execution'.[64] However, according to his pupil Robinson, he preferred to paint drapery from a living model and often employed both men and women for this purpose.[65]

Romney also had a mastery of the different textures of fabric and was 'unrivalled as a painter of shimmering satin'.[66] *Mary Corrance* (with Colnaghi, 1986) is a 'tour de force of brushwork', which shows 'an amazing audacity in the handling of the highlights of the blue silk. One can almost hear it rustling.'[67] Another skilled instance is *Mrs Salisbury and Child*; fine later examples include *Lady Warwick and Children*. He may also have responded to Gainsborough's interest in the play of reflected light, for example with Lady Sykes's white satin dress in *Sir Christopher and Lady Sykes* (Pl. XI), which subtly reflects the red of her husband's swallowtail coat.[68] An additional recurrent detail is in the realization of the stitches of slightly puckered seams, visible in *Mrs Roger Smith and Child* (Charleston Historic Foundation; Pl. 26), where Romney is as meticulous as van Dyck. Following his desire for simplicity, sitters seem generally to have left their jewels at home, apart from pearls, which are sometimes intriguingly draped beneath armpits. Male costume detail is usually even more restrained, but in *The 4th Duke of Marlborough* (Pl. 19) he demonstrates a sumptuous fidelity to the chain, tassel and plumage of the Order of the Garter, and at a more mundane level the men of *The Beaumont Family* (Pl. 27) display triangular clocking on their hose.

The principal glory of Romney's work is his deft deployment of colour, the result of a strong innate sense, enhanced by a feeling for the landscape of his native Cumbria and his study of Rubens and Titian. Often as fresh as the day they were painted, his canvases blazon this skill in the strong red coat of *Sir Thomas Rumbold* (Glasgow, Hunterian Art Gallery), the rich orange and yellow of *Edward Wortley Montagu* and the vivid green of *George Morewood* (USA, private collection). As a melancholic he may have found bright colours to be restorative; nonetheless he did sometimes carefully limit his palette to grey, pink and black, as for example with *The Clavering Children* (Pl. 33). Such restraint with colour evidently dates from after his visit to Italy. *The Warren Family* (*c.*1769; Pl. V), in contrast to later work, shows a far greater diversity of hue and may reflect Cotes's daring juxtapositions. In his time, Romney's subtlety of flesh tone, which encompasses a variety of complexions, was famous: in the 1760s with *Master Collingwood* (Liverpool, Walker Art Gallery) and markedly in 1777 with *Mrs John Morris and Child* (New York, Mr and Mrs Frank Schiff; Pl. XIII), hints of blue veining enhance the sitter's lifelike appearance.

Apart from *Memories of Windermere* (Pl. 2), there is little evidence of Romney's interest in landscapes, and the background painting in his portraits was often very sketchy, as in *Edward Gibbon* (England, private collection). Such 'sublime imprecision' does, however, deliberately simplify and enhance the figure.[69] More complete backgrounds survive in his early small-scale full-lengths, and later in portraits such as *Mrs Roger Smith and Child* (Pl. 26). The introduction of the backgrounds to large pictures was, to his pupil Robinson, 'something like enchantment', and although he was sometimes criticized for the 'crude and discordant colours' in the landscape backgrounds of pictures like *The Cornewall Children*, such tints are in reality fresh and invigorating, and could be related to the work of Richard Wilson.[70]

Pastoral backgrounds in the eighteenth century often allude to landed status, as in *Jacob Morland* (London, Tate Gallery). They could also reflect Rousseau's belief, fashionable in the later part of the century, that the countryside could teach social justice and morality and Romney frequently placed lady sitters like *Mrs Maxwell* (sold Christie's, 16 July 1982; Pl. 20) against a less detailed woodland background.[71] These less detailed backgrounds generally expressed his own calculated preference; alternatively, some reflect the pressure of sitters.[72] His trees are well observed, rarely standing erect and parallel but often at gentle angles, with their trunks intersecting. En route to Italy, between Fréjus and Marseilles, he had written that the scenery was 'more like that described in romance, than any I had seen before: it seemed to be a place peculiarly well suited for the study of landscape painting'.[73] Relatively few studies by Romney survive of any period, whether or not they were made in Europe; those that do are 'extraordinarily boldly washed' with careful observation of landscape forms.[74] His own advice was to 'Make the simplicity of nature your standard – beware that your fancy do not carry you beyond your good sense.'[75] Romney also

19 *The 4th Duke of Marlborough*, 1779–86, 235.3 × 144.2 cm (93 × 57 in). The pillars and the robes of the Order of the Garter underline the sitter's status.

20 *Mrs Maxwell*, 1780, 237.8 × 146.7 cm (94 × 58 in). An attractive young wife who perished in a Harley Street fire in 1789.

said that he could 'find every sentiment in the variations of colouring he observed in the clouds'.[76] His landscape backgrounds, like Gainsborough's, 'anticipate the picturesque movement with their strong use of dramatic chiaroscuro, rugged effects and a waterfall'.[77] Cascades notably enhance *Edward Wilbraham Bootle and his Brother Randle* (sold Sotheby's, New York, 2 June 1989; Pl. 21), while stormy weather enables a soldier like *Major General James Stuart* (Edinburgh, National Galleries of Scotland) to become not so much a participant in warfare as a personification of it.[78]

Threatening skies were also a useful device to accentuate the frailty of sitters, as in *Mrs Penelope Lee Acton* (Pl. 17). This was another borrowing from van Dyck, perhaps from *Princess Beatrice de Cusance* (Warwick Castle). Suggestions of water occur frequently, but the best evocation of Romney's Lakeland home is in the background of *Mrs Isabella Curwen*, which includes a stretch of Windermere and the family's round house on Belle Isle. This is a relatively rare instance of precise topography in his landscapes, though *Sir Christopher and Lady Sykes* (Pl. XI) demonstrates a view of Maramat at Sledmere, and *Mrs Jelf Powys* probably shows the view down the Severn from Berwick House in Shropshire.[79]

An unusual juxtaposition of a domestic interior and a landscape background is evident in *Richard Cumberland* (Pl. 9), possibly a development of the window view from the studio, a popular compromise for artists who 'wavered between the romantic and classicist attitudes'.[80] This effect thus echoes his own dual interests in protoromanticism and neo-classicism.[81] One of the aims of neo-classicism was to tame nature by ennobling it, and thus a plinth and trees are juxtaposed in *William Beckford* (Pl. VII). This objective is evident too in *The Gower Children* (Pl. IX), where the formal architecture is in tension with the informal foliage. A related juxtaposition of pillars and a vast expanse of sky notably enhances the ethereal beauty and manifest creativity of *The Hon. Mrs Trevor* (Pittsburgh, Carnegie Institute; Pl. VIII), so that she appears as a deity inhabiting a temple on the side of a steep mountain. Quirky horizons in *Miss Willoughby* and *The Boone Children* also increase the tension of the composition, while a dual background may also represent the watershed between youth and adulthood as in *Charles Grey* (Eton College).[82] Seldom do Romney's portraits cut the sitters off entirely from nature as in *The Reverend William Strickland SJ* (Pl. II); indeed, they are more often surrounded by it. Although his landscape detail appears at times rudimentary, he had a knowledge of botany and in his Italian journal he describes specific plants, including the bullrush. Although he included few identifiable plants in his portraits, they are usually there for a purpose. The mimosa in *Emma Hart as Sensibility* (sold Sotheby's, 8 March 1989) represents the ideal female temperament, and the foxglove in *Lady de la Pole* (Boston, Museum of Fine Art) may be an allusion to contemporary research by

21 *Edward Wilbraham Bootle and his Brother Randle*, 1786, 222.6 × 151.8 cm (88 × 60 in). The elder brother is in Eton montem dress. This was worn during a traditional celebration which involved soliciting money from passers-by in exchange for salt, to defray the School Captain's Cambridge expenses.

the physician and botanist William Withering into the medical benefits of digitalis.[83]

A glimpse of sea coast as used in *Richard Cumberland* is a reminder of Romney's childhood above the Duddon estuary and his familiarity with the moods of the shore. *The Duke of St Alban's* (sold Christie's, 23 June 1978) offers a development of this theme; in other works he hints at the presence of vessels, as in *Mr and Mrs Lindow* (London, Tate Gallery; Pl. 6); but even in *Mrs Anna Maria Crouch* (London, Kenwood House; Pl. 31), this element is tentative. More demanding commissions such as *Admiral Sir Francis Geary* (London, National Maritime Museum; Pl. 22) required Romney to hire a specialist marine artist, perhaps Dominic Serres RA (1722–93).[84]

Romney is not usually viewed as an animal painter. From his early days, however, dogs were frequently included in his portraits. Spaniels and pointers, being hunting dogs, were the prerogative of the squirearchy. Dogs such as the pointer in *Jacob Morland* (London, Tate Gallery) consequently served to raise the status of a sitter, while informality was sometimes achieved by the inclusion of a tiny puppy, as in *The Clavering Children* (San Marino, Huntington Art Collections; Pl. 33).

The various breeds are of necessity well defined, as for example the greyhound in *Mrs Wilbraham Bootle* (sold Christie's, 18 June 1976; Pl. 3), and the fluffy sketch of the long-haired fox terrier in *Miss Holbech* (Philadelphia, Museum of Art), two canine likenesses whose difference in execution parallels Romney's range of human portraiture, both sketchy and highly polished. One major achievement is the red spaniel in *Lord Charles Lennox* (Fredericton, Beaverbrook Art Gallery; Pl. 23), a composition relating to a portrait by Batoni of the 3rd Duke of Richmond (Goodwood, Duke of Richmond), and which effectively contrasts the status implied by the dog and the informality of its owner's pose.

Horses were more overt symbols of power and wealth, but were less frequently demanded and more difficult to paint. However, Sawrey Gilpin RA (1733–1807), the Carlisle-born horse painter, was involved by Romney in several collaborative projects.[85] Records of payment, combined with contemporary reports, suggest that Gilpin painted the horses in the equestrian portraits of two Lakeland sitters: *Colonel Wilson Braddyll* (Pl. 24) and *John Christian Curwen* (England, private collection).[86] He may also have painted the horse in the appealing *Master Tempest* (Sao Paulo Museum of Art). Romney's own ability with horses is clear from his *Horseman of Montecavallo* (Barrow-in-Furness, Record Office), drawn in Rome, and Odin's horse Sleipnir in one of the cartoons; but it was not sufficient to master these full-scale horses. The *Master Tempest* composition, with the horse drinking beside its standing rider, relates to an illustration showing Perseus beside Pegasus,

22 *Admiral Sir Francis Geary, Bart*, 1782–3, 235.3 × 144.2 cm (93 × 57 in). Admiral of the White who captured several French and Spanish vessels.

23 *Lord Charles Lennox (later 4th Duke of Richmond, Lennox and Aubigny)*, c.1776–7, 126.5 × 101 cm (50 × 40 in). Nephew and heir of Romney's patron, Lennox was to become Governor of Canada.

24 *Colonel Wilson Braddyll*, 1780–81, 242.9 × 142.2 cm (96 × 56 in). The owner of Conishead Priory, Ulverston, near Romney's birthplace.

in Winckelmann's *History of the Ancient Arts*, and demonstrates that Romney's sculptural research was not confined to the human form.[87]

Romney also painted several plausible sheep, as in *Bo Peep* (Philadelphia, Museum of Art), a fleecy model being recorded in his sitters book; but as the *Longus* series attests (Cambridge, Fitzwilliam Museum), he was more adept at drawing cattle. Occasionally, unexpected humour may be extracted from his sitters books, for example on 19 January 1783: 'Sheep at 9.00; Captain Williams at 12.00'.[88] Sawrey Gilpin also painted lions for *Alope* (untraced), and perhaps also the deer in *William Beckford* (Pl. VII). It had been planned that Gilpin would paint the wolves in *Emma Hart as Circe*; in the event they were allegedly executed by Romney's friend, the surgeon and amateur artist William Long.[89] The rare necessity of employing Gilpin is paralleled in Romney's work only by his likely employment of Dominic Serres for marine backgrounds with shipping; generally he preferred to deal with the whole canvas himself.

Romney's portraits are often criticized for lacking learned allusions or attributes of rank or office, but he mentioned a deliberate policy of simplicity, to avoid the 'heterogeneous and trifling'.[90] Attributes of rank are not common, though *Sir Robert Gunning* (Montreal, Museum of Fine Arts) features his new insignia of the Order of the Bath. There are also attributes of office, such as the mace in *Lord Chancellor Thurlow* (Pl. XV), while the cannon in *Admiral Sir Francis Geary* (Pl. 22) enables the subject to personify nautical power. The model of Cleopatra's Needle hints at trading activity in *David Scott* (San Francisco, Fine Arts Museum) whilst the Persian manuscript in *Captain Fitzpatrick* (England, private collection) proclaims the captain's scholarship. More esoteric allusions arise in *Lady Albemarle and her Son* (London, Kenwood House; Pl. 25), where Romney included an urn, often regarded as an emblem of fecundity, and *Mrs Sargent* (Liverpool, Sudley Art Gallery), who poses beside a large-scale version of the Marlborough gem, an indication of connoisseurship. In the delightful *The Hon. Mrs Trevor* (Pl. VIII), whose subject holds her head appealingly to one side, the lyre may either be an Orphic emblem or a token of her musical ability. Mrs Trevor elicited Romney's only known attempt at verse, although this might reasonably be regarded as a curiosity of doggerel.[91] In all of these categories of portrait, the inclusion of such accoutrements is the exception rather than the rule.

Music, despite his skill with the violin, seems to have been less important to Romney later in life, although he recorded enjoying a fiddler at Nice and being woken one morning by an Italian boy singing 'the sweetest airs I ever heard'.[92] However, he did depict several sitters with instruments. The pianoforte in *Mrs Billington* (Boston, Museum of Fine Arts) shows the musical prowess of this great singer, while the subject of *Mrs Raikes* (Adelaide Art Gallery) plays at the keyboard, and those of *The Milner Sisters* (sold Sotheby's,

25 *Lady Albemarle and her Son*, 1777–9, 235.3 × 144.2 cm (93 × 57 in). Both the magnificent drapery and the landscape setting have achieved more complexity than is usual in Romney's work.

27 June 1973) hold a mandoline. *The Spencer Sisters* (San Marino, Huntington Art Collections) is an important work in this category where the sitters display their skills in drawing and playing the harp. Music is also implicit in several works, such as the drawing of *Cordelia Waking Lear* (Cambridge, Fitzwilliam Museum), and at least one sitter requested to be painted in full voice, quite a challenge for the silent medium of the canvas.[93]

Architecture was not an important aspect of Romney's work, although he was sensitive to it. Several portraits include distant views of buildings, such as the fort near Bombay in the background of *Lieutenant Colonel James Hartley* (sold Sotheby's, 16 November 1990). In *Mrs Roger Smith and Child* (Pl. 26) he includes a domed temple, and in *Michael Russell* (illustrated in *Art News*, 30 October 1937) there appears a castle. Pillars are used as conventional emblems of power in *William Frederick, 2nd Duke of Gloucester* (Pl. 34), and a staircase enhances the elegance of *Mrs Anne Verelst* (Pl. VI); balustrades and plinths, less dramatic studio props, are ubiquitous.

Few patrons commissioned group portraits, as they were more expensive and required more hanging space.[94] There are barely a dozen in Romney's oeuvre, the earliest examples being *The Leigh Family* of 1768 (Pl. 8) and *The Warren Family* of *c.*1769 (Pl. V). After his journey to Italy, *The Gower Children* of 1776–7 (Pl. IX) was the most successful. Romney could clearly have developed further had more patrons demanded similar group portraits.[95] Such serious compositional demands were not often made on him 'but when they were, he produced a masterpiece'.[96] In the linear design of *The Beaumont Family* (London, Tate Gallery; Pl. 27) of 1777–9, by arranging the figures in a frieze he gives this informal gathering the dignity of a relief from an antique sarcophagus.[97] The funerary resonance here is carried further by the inclusion of a portrait of the late Richard Beaumont.[98]

Another important informal group is *The Johnes Family*, commissioned by Thomas Johnes, Colonel of the Carmarthen Militia. This appears to have been completed gradually in Romney's studio between 1779 and 1792 and was probably destroyed in a fire in Wales. Though all trace of it was thought to be lost, a miniature copy by another hand turned up at auction recently (sold Christie's, 9 November 1994).[99] This shows the sitters, including three family members and two friends, having their fortunes told by Mr Johnes, a notion used by Caravaggio and by Humphry for his diploma picture *Fortune Telling*.[100] In several group portraits the quality of the heads is uneven, but in *The Prescott Family* (Delaware, Nemours Foundation) the effect is consistently good. *The Egremont Family* (Petworth, The National Trust) and *The Bosanquet Family* (Scotland, private collection) were both painted in 1795 when Romney's skills were failing. However, the latter group, showing Mrs William Bosanquet and her five children, was admired by Flaxman, probably because all the figures are linked in a steep curve. As the other children

26 *Mrs Roger Smith and Child*, *c*.1786, 182.1 × 91 cm (72 × 36 in). The fine landscape setting, with a folly, underlines the status of this sitter.

27 *The Beaumont Family*, 1777–9, 242.9 × 273.2 cm (96 × 108 in). The adult children and the son-in-law of Richard Beaumont of Whitley Beaumont, near Wakefield, Yorkshire.

gather pears, Mrs Bosanquet holds her fingers to her lips to warn them that the baby is asleep.

A few sitters required double portraits. Sittings began in 1786 for *Sir Christopher and Lady Sykes* (Sledmere House, Sir Tatton Sykes; Pl. XI), a splendid neo-classical portrait which has been likened to 'Roman statues in modern dress'. That the couple touch each other enhances the delightful informality of this composition, which is sometimes called *The Evening Walk* by analogy with Gainsborough's *The Morning Walk* (London, National Gallery). *Mr and Mrs Wogan Browne* of Castle Browne (sold Sotheby's, 21 October 1987), set against the background of the sitters' library, relates to Pompeo Batoni's *Sir Thomas Gascoyne* (Leeds City Art Galleries, Hutherton Hall). Of this young couple, it was the portrait of 'Pretty Mrs Browne', daughter of the late Major Peirson, that was praised in *The World* magazine, edited by Romney's friend Charles Este, as having 'much very divine influence in her countenance'.[101] More common are Romney's paired single portraits, intended to be hung with the sitters facing each other, perhaps either side of a chimneypiece. *Mr*

Jeremiah Milles (San Marino, Huntington Art Gallery) and *Mrs Milles* (San Marino, Huntington Art Gallery) are two of the finest in this category, where the figures are as neatly balanced as their two landscape backgrounds.

Among Romney's male subjects, prime ministerial portraits include *William Pitt the Younger* (Scotland, private collection) and *The Duke of Portland* (Oxford, Christ Church College); other politicians from both sides of the House provided the artist with a steady income. He was, thus, a political chameleon, an aesthetic Vicar of Bray. There are also quantities of clerical and episcopal portraits, including *Archbishop Moore of Canterbury* (Canterbury, The Deanery), engagingly recorded in the sitters book as 'ABC'. The finest of this group is *Bishop Edmund Law of Carlisle* (Melbourne, National Gallery of Victoria; Pl. 28), depicting a native of Cartmel in Cumbria, who radiates his own benign gravitas. Romney also produced numerous other male portraits of character such as his dignified *Duke of Marlborough* (Blenheim Palace, The Duke of Marlborough; Pl. 19) and the bulky confidence of *Sir Archibald Campbell* (London, National Army Museum; Pl. 29), who had fought with Wolfe at Quebec. He captured the assured contentment of *Sir John Trevelyan, Bart* (Wallington Manor, The National Trust; Pl. XIV), the youthful energy of *Mr Bustard Greaves* (sold Sotheby's, New York, 4 June 1987; Pl. 30) and the intellectuality of *Chancellor Thurlow* (Government Art Collection, The House of Lords; Pl. XV).

It was in November 1780 that Chancellor Thurlow sat to Romney at the request of Lord Gower, who had been greatly pleased with the artist's portraits of his own family. Apart from his own superb portrait (Dunrobin Castle) and the memorable group of his younger children, *The Gower Children* (Pl. IX), Gower had asked Romney to paint the portraits of his adult children George Granville and the Countess of Carlisle. This major group of commissions indicates what an important patron Gower was; the introduction to Thurlow was a major corollary benefit.

The Chancellor was a majestic figure, likened to Vesuvius, holding his post almost continuously from 1778 to 1792. His wit, oratory and temper were legendary. After having sat to Reynolds in October 1781, Thurlow declared 'Reynolds and Romney divide the town: I am of the Romney faction.'[102] Two full-lengths resulted from the sittings to Romney. *Chancellor Thurlow* is a superb, seated portrait, where the shrewd old judge sits beside his mace of office; *Chancellor Thurlow* (London, Inner Temple) is a fine standing likeness. The seated portrait shows a kindly face that belies the Chancellor's reputation for wrath, as hinted in Peter Pindar's satirical ode:

> Indeed t'would be but charity to flatter
> Some dreadful works of seeming drunken nature
> As for example: let us suppose
> Thurlow's black scowl and Pepper Arden's nose.[103]

28 *Bishop Edmund Law of Carlisle*, 1781–3, 127.8 × 102 cm (50.5 × 40.3 in). The scholarly son of a schoolmaster from Lindale, near Cartmel, Cumbria.

29 *General Sir Archibald Campbell*, 1790, 151.8 × 121.4 cm (60 × 48 in). A remarkable career soldier, Governor of Jamaica and MP.

Discovering a mutual interest in classical subjects, Thurlow enjoyed translating Latin texts and sent Romney handwritten copies of his translation of Virgil's *Orpheus and Eurydice*.[104] In 1783 his natural daughters Maria and Catherine sat to Romney, who depicted them with beribboned hats, standing at a harpsichord (Yale, University Art Gallery). On a later occasion the Chancellor invited the artist and his friend Carwardine to dinner to discuss Shakespeare, and in 1789 he secured the living of Southery in Norfolk for the Reverend John Romney.[105] Pindar's reference to Thurlow's 'black scowl' is echoed in Romney's own description of the Chancellor's 'gloomy head', which once again indicates his sensitivity to the dark moods of fellow sufferers from depression.

One of Thurlow's wards was William Beckford of Fonthill, who sat to Romney in 1781 and commissioned subsequent portraits of his daughters and his catamite. *The Beckford Daughters* (San Marino, Huntington Art Collections) is a charming, less finished double portrait, while *William 'Kitty' Courtenay* (Delaware, Nemours Foundation) depicts one of many attractive youths. In 1797, as part of his vast collection at Fonthill, Beckford bought for 300 guineas Romney's *Indian Woman* (London, private collection), a subject from *A Midsummer Night's Dream*. In it the woman, a target of Titania's jealousy, stands on a seashore in an advanced state of pregnancy, watching the sails of a ship. In buying this late history painting, Beckford was indulging an interest in work that was very different from the work of Romney's contemporaries.

Virtually all critics today acknowledge Romney's considerable success as a painter of glamorous society portraits of women.[106] This group of sitters sought an artist who could suspend them for posterity in that elusive state known as 'grace', such that they might be taken for an 'ancient divinity who has strayed into society'.[107] Romney responded intimately and poetically to beauty in women, through the technique of idealization.[108] This is clearly most accomplished in both the enchanting *The Hon. Mrs Trevor* (Pl. VIII) and the stately *Mrs Bankes* (Kingston Lacy, The National Trust). He assessed the sensibility of his sitters via the movement of the muscles around their lips, which he held was the 'surest index of the heart'.[109] These signals were acutely developed in the artist himself, his lips quivering whenever he observed distress in others. Such sensitivity enabled him to achieve good likenesses and effectively to differentiate between sitters. There is more variety amongst his seated women than his seated men, one of the finest being the superb *Countess of Carlisle* (Dunrobin Castle). Furthermore, his women are not all gentle and tractable, as the amazonian *Lady Ducie* (sold Sotheby's, 6 December 1973) demonstrates.

One complication within the hidden anatomical structure of his women's portraits, as is evident in *Mrs Scott Jackson* (Washington, DC, National Gallery

30 *Mr Bustard Greaves*, 1786, 151.8 × 121.4 cm (60 × 48 in). A jovial young squire of Page Hall, near Sheffield, Yorkshire.

of Art), is the effect of Mannerism. Here the elongation of the femurs derives both from Romney's interest in Parmigianino, and from his involvement with the Fuseli circle.[110] His deliberate adoption of this stylized device was made partly because he knew that these portraits would be seen from below, but also to enhance the elegance of the loose gowns worn in numerous full-length female portraits of the 1770s and '80s; Reynolds too made use of it, for example in *Mrs Bouverie and Child* (England, private collection). An elongated neck, another Mannerist device, enhances the beauty of *Lady Altamount* (London, Tate Gallery). However, Romney did also show Mannerist tendencies before his travels in Italy in *Mrs Anne Verelst* (Pl. VI), who 'thrives on such anatomical impossibilities as the length of her left thigh'.[111] This suggests that apart from his access to Mannerist engravings, Romney had abstracted something from the Fontainebleau Mannerists while in France in 1764.[112]

Prominent among Romney's women sitters in the 1780s were four mistresses of two royal brothers. Mrs Robinson, attached to the Prince of Wales in 1781, had been coached by Garrick for her role as Juliet and became famous for her Perdita in *A Winter's Tale*. Her lover, who corresponded with her under the name Florizel, appears with her in Rowlandson's *Vauxhall Gardens*. Presents to her from the Prince include his miniature by Meyer, set in diamonds; among her other likenesses *Mrs Robinson* (London, Wallace Collection) is one of Romney's better-known works, and conveys a considerable sense of her strong character.

Mrs Jordan, attached to the Duke of Clarence, was popular in numerous roles, including that of Miss Hoyden in Sheridan's *Trip to Scarborough*, and in 'breeches parts' like Sir Harry Wildair in Farquhar's *The Constant Couple*. Lord Lennox described her 'silver-toned voice, her unsophisticated manner, her joyous laugh, her tenderness, her exuberant spirits'.[113] She sat to Romney twelve times in 1786–7, and *Mrs Jordan as Peggy in The Country Girl* (Waddesdon Manor, The National Trust) was one of the results. The Duke, later William IV, had ten children by her and hung this portrait, his favourite, at their home in Bushy Park.[114]

Mrs Crouch, also an actress, scored triumphs as Polly Peachum in *The Beggar's Opera*, as a singing witch in *Macbeth*, and as Adelaide in an adaptation of Walpole's *The Castle of Otranto*. Her relationship with the Prince of Wales was brief, but her faithful lover Michael Kelly described her as 'all that was exquisite and charming', an opinion borne out by the Romney portraits at Kenwood House (Pl. 31) and in Philadelphia, in both of which her fidelity is denoted by the allegorical rock of constancy upon which she leans.[115] The Prince's longer relationship with Mrs Fitzherbert was also recorded by Romney in an untraced portrait, for which she sat in 1789–90 (engraving London, British Museum).

One immortal actress who also sat to Romney, in February 1783, was Sarah Siddons. This was in the early days of her success; the previous month Romney himself had seen her as the eponymous Jane Shore in the play by Nicholas Rowe at Drury Lane. It was Siddons's portrayal of Lady Macbeth, causing women to faint in the audience, that inspired Romney's putative *Siddonian Recollections* (United States of America, private collection), an oil sketch of three heads recording guilt, insomnia and madness, reminiscent of Lavater's physiognomic formulae.

The portrayal of mothers and children, as an important area of his work, was anticipated by the portrayal of early Madonna figures including *Mrs Edward Salisbury and Child* (Sadeville, Canada, Mount Allison University, Owens Art Gallery) and *Mrs George Wilson and Child* (New Haven, Yale Center for British Art). The former demonstrates his superb colouring. In the latter the drapery enhances the proximity of mother and child, as if they were moulded out of one flesh.[116] Mrs Salisbury was formerly Miss Mary Sandys of Old Hall, Bouth, a relative of the Sandys family of Graythwaite, near Hawkshead. Mrs Wilson was the wife of Colonel George Wilson of Abbot Hall, Kendal.

Several such portraits achieve a sympathetic insight into the depth and tenderness of maternal love; *Mrs John Morris and Child* (New York, Mr and Mrs Frank Schiff; Pl. XIII) of 1777, in which the child stands on the mother's knee, is reminiscent of Titian Madonnas seen by Romney in Italy.[117] *Lady Warwick and Children* (New York, Frick Collection) of 1787 is relatively unusual in departing from the Madonna formula by having two children rather than one, perhaps alluding to Raphael's *La Belle Jardinière*.[118]

Other designs are more formal, but nonetheless effective. *Lady Albemarle and her Son* (London, Kenwood House; Pl. 25) of 1777 depicts the boy Charles with a King Charles spaniel, perhaps as a reference to his name, while *Mrs Roger Smith and Child* (Charleston Historic Foundation; Pl. 26) of 1786, remarkably, has the boy sitting on a plinth with his mother standing alongside. The most unusual achievement was *Mrs Russell and Child* (England, private collection), in which a mirror both enhances the composition and reminds the viewer of the mimetic nature of portraiture.[119] Like *Mrs Thomas Carwardine and Child* (Pl. 40), this portrait is all the more effective from Romney's intimacy with the family. His madonna portraits show women in roles 'defined by their male connections'; by contrast, his *Medea* series of drawings depicts both independence and violence.[120]

Despite Romney's limited contact with his own son during childhood, his quiet disposition rendered him especially gifted in dealing with children, whose characters were 'not yet fully formed' and who were apt to be shy yet trusting.[121] This trait also enabled him to capture the playfulness of childhood at its most beguiling, perhaps partly as compensation for having

31 *Mrs Anna Maria Crouch*, 1787, 127 × 101.2 cm (50 × 40 in). A pupil of Thomas Linley, she holds the score for one of her singing roles.

missed much of John's early life. His son acknowledges the influence of the 'graceful forms and rosy beauties' of Correggio in these portraits, while Romney's scientist friend Adam Walker, in a rare piece of verse, claimed that they were the quintessence of his art.[122] In the eighteenth century children sat for portraits more frequently than before, partly as they were now more likely to survive childhood and parents were prepared to invest greater emotion and finance in them.[123]

Contrary to the custom of previous generations, children were dressed less like miniature adults. This incipient fashion for less restrained poses and more informal clothing was a response to a number of influences, including Rousseau's *Emile*.[124] Another change was the growth of physical proximity between children and their mother, as shown in *Jane, Duchess of Gordon and her Son* (Pl. 32), or between siblings in such works as *The Clavering Children* (Pl. 33), where the boy has his arm protectively around his sister's waist.[125] Catherine Clavering's affection for the tiny puppy, which she clasps in a 'Flaxmanesque gesture', like Harriet Warren's for her chaffinch, anticipates both girls' development of maternal affection.[126] Such acute observation is also evident in *Alope* (untraced, engraving London, British Museum), where the child seeks reassurance, and in the drawing *Lovers Espied by a Child* (Kendal, Abbot Hall Art Gallery). Several young sitters appear with toys, whether or not supplied by Romney, to entertain them in the studio. *The Fazackerly Children* (Hartford, Wadsworth Atheneum) includes a yo-yo; *Lady Warwick and Children* (New York, Frick Collection) a hoop and *The Charteris Children* (Stanway, The Earl of Wemyss) a kite.

With the young men among his patrons' children, Romney was sensitive to their good looks and patrician ease, following van Dyck and Batoni in stamping a memorable image of aristocratic adolescence.[127] The bust portrait *George Capel Coningsby* (Leger, 1990) of 1781 is that of an almost girlish young man, while the sexual ambiguity of the glossy-lipped *Joseph Sidney Yorke* (untraced), midshipman on the *Formidable*, is even more remarkable set against the smoke of battle. *William Beckford* (Upton House, The National Trust; Pl. VII) of Fonthill, showing its sitter 'lounging à la Romney' in 1781, is one of the strongest of this kind, and the subject of *Prince William of Gloucester* (Cambridge, Trinity College; Pl. 34) of 1790, with his long golden locks, has a yet greater androgynous effect.[128]

During the Eton headship of Dr Barnard (1754–65), the practice had been introduced of the more wealthy pupils presenting a portrait to the headmaster upon leaving the school. Romney recorded the faces of sixteen such sitters between 1776 and 1795, five of them when he was at the peak of his popularity. These portraits including *Richard Wellesley* (Eton College), whose subject was elder brother of the later Duke of Wellington, and the 'vernally

32 *Jane, Duchess of Gordon and her Son*, 1778, 124 × 101.2 cm (49 × 40 in). Wife of the 4th Duke, who raised the regiment known as the Gordon Highlanders in 1794.

33 *The Clavering Children*, 1777, 151.8 × 121.4 cm (60 × 48 in). Thomas and Catherine Clavering were the grandchildren of the sixth Baronet.

34 *William Frederick, 2nd Duke of Gloucester*, 1790–91, 232.5 × 144.2 cm (93 × 57 in). A nephew of George III, dressed in his undergraduate gown.

delicate' *Charles Grey* (Eton College), depicting a subsequent prime minister, likewise demonstrate his 'sympathetic treatment of the growing boy'.[129]

Some sexual ambiguity was hard to avoid in painting the fashions of the time. *The Boone Children*, offspring of the governor of South Carolina, are sometimes called *The Boone Daughters*; but the sitters book clearly records Master and Miss Boone, thus revealing the child in the blue sash to be an unbreeched son.[130] Sterne's *Tristram Shandy* includes a debate about the age at which a boy was to be breeched, an important watershed in growing up. Several other boy sitters are unbreeched, for example *Master Philip Cocks* (Eastnor Castle, Hervey-Bathurst Collection). It is noteworthy that boy sitters, including Master Boone, more often have a direct gaze than girls.[131]

The range of character depicted in Romney's portraits of children is large, even without our perceptions being adjusted by hindsight. *Lord Henry Petty* (Bowood, The Marquis of Lansdowne), a son of the first marquis of Lansdowne, is one of the finest of his full-length boy portraits and a fitting study of one who was to become Chancellor of the Exchequer at the age of twenty-six. Romney's 'Blue Boy', *Master Henry Lushington* (England, private collection), the son of the chairman of the Honourable East India Company, shows determination in the way he holds his walking stick. A less finished work is *Master Hotham* (England, private collection), of a page to Queen Charlotte, whose waif-like informality, on a beach, at the watershed of adolescence, demonstrates Romnney's success with looser painting techniques.[132] This portrait is also unusual in that it is painted full-length on a small canvas, presumably by request, twenty years after the small-scale Kendal portraits.

Rustic beauty was adopted in the studio in *Miss Constable* (Pl. 35), a young girl who wears a straw hat edged with heads of corn. In *Miss Charlotte Peirse* (Pl. X) he achieved an attractive winsome quality, while the simplicity of *Miss Frances Sage* (sold Sotheby's, 15 July 1987; Pl. 36), the daughter of Lord Clive's paymaster in India, is most appealing. Despite her serious little face, Miss Sage's pose suggests that she has just looked up from smelling an armful of flowers. Her tucked up skirts are enhanced by a swinging swag of drapery, which draws attention to her left foot and shows her to be in balletic motion, her heel off the ground.[133]

In portraying infancy and youth, the finest manifestation of Romney's genius is undoubtedly *The Gower Children* (Kendal, Abbot Hall Art Gallery; Pl. IX), with its 'incomparable lyricism and sensibility'.[134] In 1776, at the beginning of his most powerful period, Romney received this challenging commission from Lord Gower, later the Marquis of Stafford, to paint several of the children of two of his three marriages on one canvas. The rare opportunity of a large group at this crucial point in his career resulted in a succinct composition, painted with tremendous force and splendour of colour. The 'sense of childish high spirits and abandonment to the dance' has delighted

35 *Miss Constable*, 1787, 76 × 64 cm (30 × 25.3 in). A Yorkshire girl then residing at Margaret Street, Cavendish Square.

36 *Miss Frances Sage*, 1779, 145 × 116.4 cm (58 × 46 in). The daughter of Isaac Sage, paymaster to Lord Clive of India.

many observers and, to the descendants of the four girls, the work was known as 'the dancing grandmothers'. There is a near-perfection of neo-classical linear design as the viewer's eye is drawn across the canvas by the linked hands, while the hard outlines are softened by the fluid swing of the drapery, extended into the flow of the dance as the children move to Lady Anne's beat on the tambourine. With her billowing drapery, she is depicted like Romney's *Mirth* (Pl. 11), beating her homage to the muse Terpsichore: a dancer in a Bacchic relief. The figures in this wonderful multiple portrait come 'nearer to the pagan spirit of the classical reliefs he so carefully observed than to any other artist of the time', and there is nothing really like them anywhere in English art.[135]

Traditionally Romney's design is related to his observations of large rings of dancers circling maypoles at Nice, which he described as being like *The Hours* of Guido Reni, 'dancing hand in hand with that glee which arises from innocence, simplicity and liveliness'.[136] Maypoles were still associated in England with popular social dancing in the eighteenth century; one appears in Romney's late work *Mirth and Melancholy* (Petworth House, The National Trust).[137] *The Gower Children* also relates in its design to Poussin's *Adoration of the Golden Calf*, although this, like Reynolds's *Daughters of Sir William Montgomery Decorating a Term of Hymen* (London, National Gallery), is really a chain, not a circle of dancers. *The Gower Children* could be more exactly compared to Poussin's *Bacchanalian Revel* (London, National Gallery) or his *Dance to the Music of Time*, where the dancers do form a circle.[138] In its turn it is possible that *The Gower Children* influenced Flaxman's *Dancing Hours*, designed for Wedgwood in 1778, although the chimneypiece from the Palazzo Borghese is held to be the more direct source.[139] Romney charged only 200 guineas for this incomparable work, a price that illustrates his freedom from rapacity and confirms his good sense of value for money. Sixty guineas were for Lady Anne, forty each for the dancing sisters and twenty for Master Granville, whom several sepia wash designs show to be an afterthought in the composition.[140]

Naked children had been painted more frequently since the seventeenth century, and Romney's work includes the natural attitude of a baby lying on its back, a difficult pose, in *Titania, Puck and the Changeling* (Dublin, National Gallery of Ireland). For several later works, including *The Infant Shakespeare with Comedy and Tragedy* (Petworth, The National Trust), his cherubic sitter was the tiny son of a guardsman. He also responded strongly to subjects involving the death of infants, as in his drawings of *Medea Contemplating the Death of her Children* (New Haven, Yale Center for British Art), a premonition of the premature death of the guardsman's diminutive child. Watching the antics of children was a pleasure he shared with Sir William Hamilton who would pay for them, as animated putti, to gambol in the waves below his Neapolitan villa at Posillipo; one of Romney's late canvases, *Boys on a Seashore* (United States of America, private collection) shows a group of naked boys playing by the sea. The two men also shared a parallel voyeuristic entertainment, delighting in the more alluring 'Attitudes' struck for the admiration of guests by the second Lady Hamilton.[141]

Romney's affinity with his more youthful sitters is nowhere more celebrated than in the series of portraits he painted of Emma Hart, later Lady Hamilton, when she was in her late teens. Emma's story has played an inordinately prominent part in Romney biographies. Although the importance of her portraits and her influence upon his portraiture has been exaggerated, she did inspire him to paint more freely and spontaneously and her emotional place in his life was particularly significant.

By 1782, Romney had known the connoisseur Charles Greville for ten years. They had corresponded while the artist was in Italy and in 1781 Romney had painted *The Hon. Charles Greville* (sold Sotheby's, 28 November 1973). Although he was MP for Warwick and Vice-President of the Royal Society, Greville had only £500 a year to indulge the good taste evident in his appearance in Zoffany's *Charles Townley and his Friends* (Burnley, Townley Hall). It is a further tribute to the artist's growing importance in the London art world that Romney was friendly with Greville, whose 'relish for ancient gems' appears in one of Reynolds's two portrait groups, *Members of the Society of Dilettanti* (London, on loan to Brooks's Club). Greville never married, but from January 1782 he had kept the young Emma as his mistress, and on 12 April he took her to Romney's studio. Now forty-seven years old, Romney had been engaged in almost unbroken labour over nearly three decades of portraiture, when this striking girl burst upon him with all her 'entrancing loveliness of person and gaiety of spirits'.[142] She had a fine figure, bright blue eyes and long auburn tresses, which sometimes grew to her heels, charms which caused one of her admirers to exclaim: 'God Almighty must have been in a glorious mood when he made you!'[143]

Born in 1765 at Neston, on the Wirral in Cheshire, Emma was the daughter of Henry Lyon, a blacksmith who died when she was a baby.[144] After a series of adventures with seducers while in domestic service, she was rescued by Greville, who established a home for her at Paddington Green and determined to give her an education. Time spent sitting in Romney's studio was part of the process, which also included piano and singing lessons.[145] There is a tradition that she posed naked as an advertisement for the Temple of Health established by Dr Graham, the successful entrepreneur and quack. This, however, is now virtually discredited, although she may have had a smaller role in the enterprise. The scandal may have arisen from a confusion of the Emma portraits with a painting of the goddess Hygeia, said to have been commissioned by Graham from Romney, or from the erroneous assumption that Rowlandson's caricature *Lady H******* Attitudes* (London, British Museum) related to absolute fact.[146]

Despite his contact with the finest of British beauty, the artist was especially engaged by Emma. Her grace, versatility, and mobile face enabled her to portray a vast range of emotions and characters: a physiognomist's dream. Thus Romney, for whom expression was central to the art of portraiture, was ambitious to portray her in as broad a variety of guises as he could and during the first four years of their association it was a luxury to have her as his model. His interest flattered her vanity, especially as it was exciting for her to see her beauty appearing on canvas, and, though he was patently in love with his model, it seems unlikely that they were lovers, despite the absence of his wife and the splenetic workings of rumour.[147] Following her earlier peccadillos, Emma was under oath not to misbehave. She was also genuinely in love with Greville, whose pride would not have countenanced polyandry, so that her numerous visits to Cavendish Square cannot have been viewed by him as a threat. It was a worshipful obsession on Romney's part, with Emma, like Dante's Beatrice, as the focus of his inspiration.

They had in common their northern origins and probable similarities of speech; also both were still somewhat out of their depth in sophisticated society, and appreciated being able to relax in each other's company. Equally dependent upon patronage, they were both highly strung, insecure and suffering from cycles of depression, while sharing an iron will and great ambition.[148] Emma acknowledged her trust in the artist, calling him 'my more than father to whom I first opened my heart'.[149] Whether or not their relationship was wholly that of father and daughter, Emma trusted Romney whose interest in her was largely aesthetic rather than sexual. A shared rural nostalgia is hinted at in *Emma Hart as the Spinstress* (London, Kenwood House), with its spinning wheel and chicken, possibly sketched at Paddington Green, although Emma's gown makes her look a little too grand for such a role.[150] The benefits for both sitter and artist in this, one of the most fruitful partnerships in British art, resulted by March 1786 in at least 150 entries in Romney's sitters books.[151] As a collaborator, rather than a passive model, Emma appears in about twenty-eight portraits, allegories and mythological paintings, many of which stand between the artist's straight portraits and his history painting.[152] There are also numerous broadly painted small heads and other portraits which are claimed to be in this group, although many attributions made in the nineteenth and twentieth centuries are doubtful.[153] The art market's subsequent mania for Emma portraits injured Romney's reputation, and the majority of this group are in any case wrongly entitled, as Emma did not become Lady Hamilton until all but one of the genuine portraits were painted.

Emma's sittings created a welcome escape from the tyranny of sitters who demanded to look like ladies or gentlemen of quality. Among the finest results are the powerful *Emma Hart as Circe* (private collection, on loan to Waddesdon Manor, The National Trust) and the rather fetching *Emma Hart in a Straw Hat* (Pl. 37), which was Greville's preferred likeness.[154] Sometimes the sittings were attended by her lover and his friends, as recorded in the wash drawing *Romney Painting the Spinstress* (London, British Museum). Sir William Hamilton also arranged for her to sit to Reynolds, but seems not to have been satisfied with the result. Following his own sittings to Romney in November 1783 she returned to Cavendish Square after a gap in her visits that was perhaps the result of Greville's domestic economies. Greville understandably found it difficult to pay for many canvases; indeed, Romney probably did not expect him to, but Sir William certainly paid for several himself.[155]

Sensibility was perceived as an essential virtue for the ideal woman in the cult of decorum, as an enemy of spleen, according to Rousseau and further developed by Hayley through his fictitious character Serena in *The Triumphs of Temper*.[156] Several paintings are more directly associated with Hayley's text, such as *Serena Reading by Candlelight* (Dunrobin Castle, The Countess of Sutherland), and *Serena in the Boat of Apathy* (sold Christie's, 17 June 1966), where the sitter is portrayed as the ideal of girlish innocence. Although associated with the Serena paintings in popular imagination, Emma's face is only truly recognizable in *Serena Reading the Gazette* (Albright Knox Museum, Buffalo). By reading *The Triumphs of Temper* she claimed that she had learned to control her bursts of powerful emotion, a restraint vital in her later relationship with Sir William Hamilton.[157] Another work, *Emma Hart as a Bacchante Leading a Goat* (England, private collection), which was owned by Sir William, was sometimes called 'Diana'. This was explicitly meant as a revival of the Petrarchan duality evident in Leonardo's *Woman with an Ermine* (Cracow, National Museum), where a courtesan is depicted as goddess of chastity.[158]

By 1786 Greville was in financial difficulties and arranged for his uncle, Sir William Hamilton, to assist with his debts. In return the fifty-six-year-old Sir William would take on his nephew's youthful mistress whom he had admired for several years.[159] Cruelly duped by the two of them, Emma believed when she departed for Naples on 13 March 1786 that she was visiting Italy merely to broaden her education. Even Sir William thought it was a temporary measure and did not realize how strong her feelings were for Greville, who by now had induced her to be constant.[160] Nonetheless they had already discussed the possibility of paying her an annuity, via Romney as her trustee. Once marooned in Naples she was shattered by Greville's duplicity and spurned the old diplomat's advances until he had promised to marry her.

37 *Emma Hart (Lady Hamilton) with a Straw Hat*, c.1782–6, 73.8 × 62 cm (29.5 × 24.5 in). One of the many alluring poses by Emma whose eyes look demurely upwards.

Greville and Sir William had turned Emma into a society beauty, but it was Romney's 'refining influence' that had contributed to her dramatic talents, which led in Naples to the first performance of her 'Attitudes'.[161] These 'poses plastiques' were also derived from her observation of Sir William's collection of antiquities and the wall paintings at Herculaneum, and became one of the prominent amusements of Neapolitan society.[162] In 1787 Goethe, seeing one of her performances, in which she used shawls to achieve fluid changes from one role to another, wrote 'that a man at last comes to think that he is dreaming'.[163] Horace Walpole was less complimentary, referring to Hamilton's 'pantomime mistress', while James Byers wrote that she would exhaust her husband 'more than all the volcanoes and antiquities in the kingdom'.[164] This aspect of Emma's versatility was drawn, in a series of simple but effective line drawings, by Friedrich Rehberg (1758–1835); more effectively it was captured in a drawing by William Locke Jr (1767–1847) of her dancing a tarantella (London, British Museum).[165]

After Emma's removal to Italy Romney missed her greatly and his periods of depression increased. Several faces he painted around this time bear a haunting likeness to his departed muse, such as Comedy in *The Infant Shakespeare with Comedy and Tragedy* (Petworth House, The National Trust).[166] He remained in touch by letter; she expressed her gratitude for his friendship, showed concern for his health, made enquiries about his painting and invited him to Naples. One of his letters looks forward to her return to England and adds, 'I have had a great number of ladies of figure sitting to me since you left England but they all fall short of The Spinstress, indeed, it is the sun of my hemisphere and they are but twinkling stars.'[167]

Romney was to see Emma again, on her return to London to be married to Sir William, in the summer of 1791, describing her as 'the divine lady'. He continued to think her 'superior to all womankind' but feared that he would not have the power to paint her again.[168] Having also doubted whether she would still hold her old friend in regard, he had her sit to him thirty-four times between June and early September, despite her current social whirl. Thus he rallied sufficiently to produce several canvases, including *Joan of Arc* (untraced; drawings Cambridge, Fitzwilliam Museum) and the relatively loosely painted *Calypso* (Waddesdon Manor, The National Trust). When the couple came to dine at Cavendish Square in July and August, Emma sang and acted a scene of the madwoman from Paisiello's *Nina* for the company, a last performance that elicited in her audience 'an agony of sorrow'.[169] Her last two sittings were as 'Mrs Hart' on 5 September and as 'Lady Hamilton' on 6 September, her wedding day, an event recorded in Romney's crabbed hand on the flyleaf of his sitters book. Despite the fact that weddings were much simpler affairs then than now, it is remarkable that Emma came to the studio after the marriage service at Marylebone Church.

The last picture was *The Ambassadress* (Austin, Archer M. Huntington Gallery), which has Vesuvius smoking in the background as an emblem of passion and in token of Sir William's enthusiasm for vulcanology. Thereafter Emma took a 'tender leave' before departing for Naples, whence she corrre-sponded with the artist:

> you was the first dear friend I open'd my heart to, you ought to know me, for you have seen and discoursed with me in my poorer days, you have known me in my poverty and prosperity . . . Rejoice with me, my dear sir, my friend, my more than father . . . Command me in anything I can do for you here; believe me I shall have a real pleasure. Come to Naples and I will be your model . . . Take care of your health for all our sakes.[170]

Romney and his muse never met again. It was seven years later in 1798 that Emma met Admiral Nelson after the battle of the Nile, so her most famous conquest entirely postdates her relationship with the artist. This remarkable woman has attained a triple immortality: as Romney's favourite sitter, as the wife of a distinguished connoisseur and as the lover of a great British hero. It was to commemorate her place in Nelson's life that the 1805 Club recently unveiled an obelisk to her memory in Calais, where she died in 1815.

7

Patterns of friendship 1775–86

Portrait painting offered one of the period's greatest opportunities for social mobility. Yet Romney in his diffidence was not a social alpinist, and is said not to have been seen 'at the tables of the great'.[1] This remark is in fact an exaggeration, for Romney did decline many invitations, as he had refused the offer of a turret at Warwick Castle. Pandering to the whims of capricious sitters during his daytime studio performances was in itself sufficiently enervating without any attempt to mix with sitters socially in the evenings, and it is not surprising that he preferred the company of his middle-class friends, with whom he could preserve some independence.[2]

During these hectic years Romney was largely occupied with his sitters and tended to relax by drawing quietly by himself in the evenings by candlelight. Rather than engage in busy social life, he had regular contact with a small informal group of friends who were more concerned with literature and drama than art. They included John Henderson (1747–85), the Irish actor; Isaac Reed (1742–1807), the editor of Shakespeare; the bookseller Thomas Evans (1742–1784) and Thomas Sheridan (1719–1788), the father of Richard Brinsley Sheridan.[3] These men effectively filled the loss made in Romney's life by the deaths of earlier friends, such as Major Thomas Peirson who died in Calcutta in 1781.

Romney painted several of these friends, including John Henderson in his role as Macbeth. *John Henderson as Macbeth with the Witches* (original untraced, engraving London, British Museum; version Windsor, Ontario, Windsor Art Gallery; Pl. 38) is another powerful instance of his interest in depicting Shakespearean tragedy in oils and there are several wonderful drawings of *John Henderson as Falstaff* (Cambridge, Fitzwilliam Museum; Pl. 39).[4] Here can be seen the natural girth of an actor who was berated by Gainsborough for his gluttony.

Isaac Reed had probably met Romney when they were next door neigh-

38 *John Henderson as Macbeth with the Witches* (engraving by John Jones), 1787, 40.7 × 50 cm, (16.1 × 19.8 in). Macbeth's figure, in contraposto, is flanked by Banquo's cropped form.

bours in Gray's Inn in the 1760s. He wrote *Biographica Dramatica* in 1782, contributed to Johnson's *Lives of the Poets* and was for many years editor of both the *European Magazine* and the *Whitehall Post*.[5] His self-effacing statement that he would 'prefer to stand in the pillory rather than put [his] name to a book' was in keeping with Romney's own temperament, and indeed, his publications often did appear anonymously.[6]

Thomas Sheridan was an influential and reforming actor-manager in Dublin and London, who laid the foundations for the strong theatrical tradition in the former city at great personal cost.[7] He had an uneasy professional relationship with Garrick, who adopted Sheridan's Dublin innovation of clearing the audience from the stage; he also lobbied successfully for a pension for Dr Johnson.[8] In his turbulent career, he was also a successful teacher of elocution capable of curing a pupil's stammer, and an orator whose influence bore fruit in the theatrical and political successes of his more famous son. Boswell wrote that his 'well informed, animated and

39 *John Henderson as Falstaff (Henry IV Part I)*, 34.3 × 56 cm (13.5 × 22 in). The old coward is shown dragging the corpse of Hotspur, his falsely claimed victim.

bustling mind, never suffered conversation to stagnate'.[9] Sheridan, like Romney, was something of a hypochondriac, and suffered from head and stomach disorders all his life. Furthermore, he shared with Romney a delicate sensibility and a hatred of criticism.[10]

The bookseller Thomas Evans kept a shop in the Strand and published volumes of old ballads, novels, editions of both Goldsmith's plays and Shakespeare's poems, and was himself 'a man of rare humour in conversation'.[11] He was also a member of the Booksellers' Club at the Grecian Coffee House at Devereux Court, also in the Strand.

After Evans's premature death in 1784, a second mortal shock to the group came in 1785 from the demise of the portly Henderson himself. Amidst much sorrow in the hearts of the theatre-going public he was justly buried in Poets' Corner, Westminster Abbey.[12] Thomas Sheridan, who was now bereft of his recitation partner, himself died in 1788. Over the next few years the group compensated for its losses by gathering new members, who in due course were confidently to reform themselves as The Unincreaseables.[13]

Official cliques and select societies were much in fashion in the late eighteenth century, serving both the maintenance of friendship and the encouragement of aesthetic interests. Romney's recreations mostly related to his profession, but in the late 1780s he was allegedly one of the eight members of this exclusive dining club, which is said to have met fortnightly at the Queen's Head, Holborn, or at the Shakespeare, Covent Garden, and sometimes at members' houses.[14] This was a colourful group, derived from a network of allegiances formed earlier in the decade.[15] There is no conclusive evidence that membership of The Unincreaseables was formally limited to a total of eight; also the diary of Isaac Reed, who was their perpetual President, records their meetings as being held irregularly rather than once a fortnight.[16] Sometimes indeed the group did include others, including Adam Walker, Richard Cumberland (1732–1811), Daniel Gardner (*c.*1750–1805) and the Anglican priest, Thomas Carwardine (1734–1824).[17] Within this able and successful group of professionals, Romney's prominence was acknowledged by Reed's tendency to place him at the head of any list of members attending meetings.[18]

The club's core membership apparently comprised Thomas Greene, Daniel Braithwaite, William Long, Isaac Reed, Charles Este, Francis Newbery and George Nicol, Bookseller to the King. Among these, Thomas Greene and William Long (1747–1818) were to become brothers-in-law, and Fellows of both the Society of Antiquaries and the Royal Society.[19] Long was elected senior surgeon of St Bartholomew's Hospital in 1791 and became the second master of the Royal College of Surgeons, where his books and instruments are preserved. His fine tomb is located in the north aisle of Salisbury Cathedral.[20]

The Reverend Charles Este (1752–1829) was described as 'perhaps the most extraordinary character of his time', becoming successively an actor, a student of medicine and, as a priest, the King's reading chaplain at Whitehall.[21] He was an early collector of landscape paintings, wrote theatre reviews and in 1787 co-founded *The World*, a daily newspaper, which throve for seven years until destroyed by a lawsuit.

George Nicol (*c.*1750–1828), who operated from his shop in Pall Mall, not far from the Boydell Gallery, was to continue selling books to George IV, having held a royal warrant as Bookseller-in-Ordinary to George III from 1780.[22]

Francis Newbery (1743–1818) was a publisher and bookseller described as 'a scholar, a poet and a lover of music'.[23] As a violin player he was 'seriously offended' by Dr Johnson, who said he should have given his fiddle to the first beggar he met. He was the son of John Newbery of The Bible and Sun in St Paul's Churchyard, publisher of Oliver Goldsmith's *The Vicar of Wakefield*, who appears as Jack Whirler in Dr Johnson's *The Idler*. The Newberys were astute businessmen who also sold patent medicines, holding the patent for James's Fever Powders, a widely known febrifuge.[24] In 1774 Francis Newbery was involved in a furore concerning the powders, which were said to have been the cause of Goldsmith's death.[25] His wife Mary was the daughter of Robert Raikes, the founder of the Sunday Schools and the couple owned a version of Romney's *The Infant Shakespeare with Comedy and Tragedy*. Several members of the family sat to Romney between 1782 and 1796, the year after Francis's election as Sheriff of London.[26]

The club's president, the bibliophile Isaac Reed, was to remain a close friend for some years after Romney's last recorded attendance as a member in 1792.[27] 'Steady' Reed, as Boswell called him, sat to the artist in November 1794 (untraced; engraving by Dickinson, London, British Museum), receiving the portrait gratis in November 1796 and reciprocating with a set of his edition of Shakespeare. He wrote, 'Every particle of vanity I am possessed of is now completely gratified and I feel great satisfaction in reflecting that my name may probably go down to posterity accompanied by yours.'[28] Reed is especially remembered for his generosity in assisting numerous writers, for his making accessible the works of others and for the posthumous sale of his vast library in 1807, which took thirty-nine days.[29]

Occasionally The Unincreaseables met at Newbery's house in St Paul's Churchyard; also at Odscombe, his country seat.[30] From time to time they gathered at more exalted venues: on 25 July 1786 they went together to Osterley Park in Middlesex. This great house was the home of Mrs Sarah Child, the widow of Romney's former banker Robert Child, who had sat to him for his portrait in 1781.[31] Mrs Child herself sat to Romney from 1781 to 1788 and again after her second marriage, to Lord Ducie. Her first husband's early death had been hastened by the dramatic elopement in 1782 of his only daughter Sarah with the Earl of Westmoreland.[32] Both the Earl and the former Miss Child had sat to Romney in the same year; both their portraits were destroyed by fire. In another such jaunt, on 23 March 1791, the members of the club went to dinner at the Mansion House, near Romney's old rooms in Bearbinder's Lane, with the Lord Mayor, John Boydell.[33]

The last reference to Romney in Reed's diary was in 1792. It appears that the artist eventually withdrew from the support and literary stimulus of The Unincreaseables, though he was still much in need of friends, being always grateful to those who helped stave off his 'melancholy malady'.[34] With the exception of Humphry, Meyer, Hodges and Flaxman, his relations with his fellow artists were generally less relaxed. It is significant that none of these four artists, two of whom were miniaturists, one a landscape artist and one a sculptor, were in direct competition with Romney. Writing in July 1795 he declared: 'Friendship is the first of human blessings, only while I can merit friendship do I wish to live.'[35] Fortunately he managed over many years to keep friends like Greene, Walker, Cockin, Carwardine and Braithwaite, whether or not he saw them regularly.[36]

Considering the length of Braithwaite's relationship with Romney, it may seem odd that there is no known portrait of him by Romney given that he sat to Angelica Kauffmann.[37] Hayley sat numerous times and through his writing over-emphasizes his own importance to Romney. But though the Hermit's actions were partly fuelled by self-interest, he did keep a beneficial eye on the restless behaviour of his prematurely ageing friend. From time to time his frustrations with Romney's reluctance to correspond come to the surface: in a letter of 1787 he chided him for his illegibility and advised him to 'trace his alphabet every day', an impertinence which the artist ignored.[38]

Another friend who began life as an artist was Thomas Carwardine (1734–1824), the son of John Carwardine of Thingehills Court, Herefordshire, who in the 1760s had exhibited with his mother Anne and sister Penelope as a miniaturist at the Society of Artists. After a few years as an artist he judiciously married an heiress and soon became both the squire and rector of Earl's Colne in Essex. Romney's portrait of this 'absolute though benevolent despot' was painted in 1772, though *Thomas Carwardine* (England, private collection) is not as fine a portrait as that of his wife in *Mrs Thomas Carwardine and Child* (England, private collection; Pl. 40).[39] Romney was godfather to their daughter Anne and is said to have been a frequent visitor to their home at Earl's Colne Priory. Like several of Romney's friends, Carwardine was an active philanthropist: in the 1780s he re-established the grammar school in his village without charging fees. He was to become a prebend of St Paul's.[40]

Lacking virtually all family life of his own, Romney was responsive to other people's children in private life as in his work. During his annual visits to Eartham in the early 1780s, his friend Hayley showed himself full of pride in the development of his natural son Tom. The boy's own talents as an artist were fostered by his doting father and on 1 February 1795 he was apprenticed as a sculptor to John Flaxman.[41] In Romney's late portrait group *The Four Friends* (Kendal, Abbot Hall Art Gallery), Tom is shown holding his own statue of Minerva. The young artist's presence at Eartham in the 1780s and 1790s added something of a family experience to Romney's life and from the surviving documentation it is almost as if Tom became more important to him than his own apparently less creative son John.

Amidst the small group of professionals comprising his close friends, Romney's lack of formal education was no barrier. He had been readily accepted into the relaxed company of Greene, Braithwaite, Henderson, Long and others and regularly celebrated with Adam Walker on his friend's birthday, 21 December.[42] He was also in the habit of dropping in on the Cumberlands at Mount Street and the family of his friend Henry Russell, sometime Chief Justice of Bengal, at Bedford Row.[43] Wittingly or not, he was following the advice of the painter Jonathan Richardson (1665–1745), whose writings on the theory of criticism advised artists to frequent the brightest company. His own table tended to be sparsely provisioned, so he would dine out at the Boar's Head at Eastcheap or at the Shakespeare in Covent

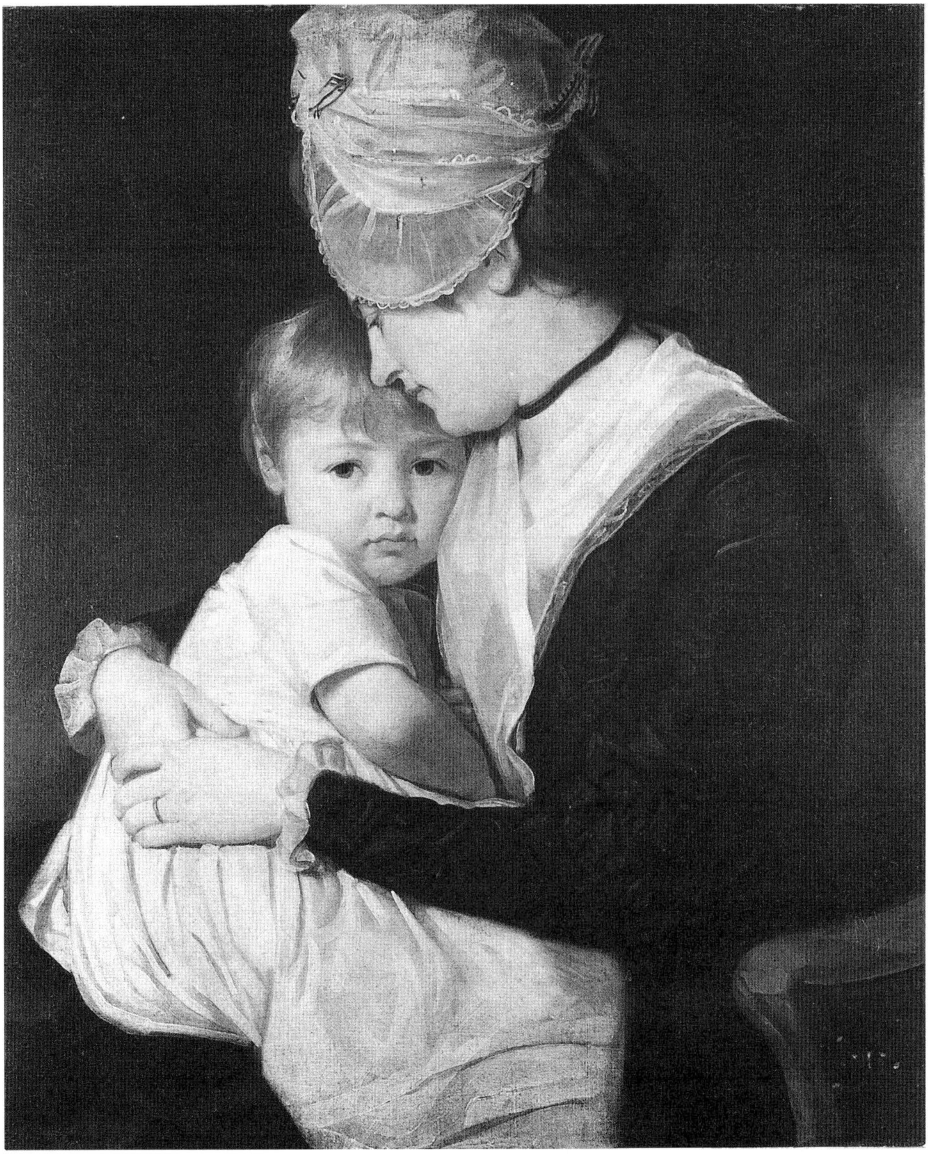

40 *Mrs Thomas Carwardine and Child*, *c*.1776, 74.6 × 62 cm (29.5 × 24.5). The heiress of Colne Priory and a descendant of Oliver Cromwell.

Garden before going to the theatre.[44] He was also familiar with the more salubrious haunts, such as Ranelagh, a building which he used in estimating the size of the amphitheatre at Nîmes.[45] Romney preferred to pass his leisure time silently on the fringe of a group, rather as he enjoyed being incognito during occasional visits to the popular spas at Kilburn and Bagnigge Wells. Here he would watch and sketch ordinary folk, as an agreeable change from his usual clients; it was on one such foray that he conceived *The Spinstress* (Kenwood House), having seen 'a cobbler's wife in a stall'.[46] As he was not under pressure to achieve a specific result, these expeditions brought him relief and much needed relaxation.

In January 1784 with his brother James, who was on leave from India, he attended 'an immense party' and met Fanny Burney, who described him as 'a very pleasing man'.[47] Their host, John Hoole, who sat to Humphry, was the principal auditor at India House, though better known for his dramas and his translation of Tasso.[48] Romney also dined with Lord Thurlow and with the Boydells. His sitters books, albeit recording only formal invitations, mention more than thirty dinners attended between 1778 and 1793. His hosts included Mr Stratford Canning, the banker, and Mrs Anne St George of Headford Castle.[49] As late as 4 February 1792 he wrote that he had dined out often and had had people to dinner, so he was certainly not a total recluse even in the later years of his practice.[50]

Commercial galleries periodically refer to a 'Studio' or 'School' of Romney. This is strictly inaccurate, since the artist had few pupils, never allowed them to work on his canvases and was unusual in not having permanent assistance in his studio other than from his servants, whose help was largely domestic and administrative. Some references to Romney's domestic arrangements survive: Joseph Barker periodically signed receipts; Richard Williams, his tidy book-keeper whose name occurs frequently in the accounts books of the 1790s, lent his master cash and recorded the dispatch of pictures including *John Milton Dictating to his Daughters* (England, private collection; Pl. XVI).[51] Another studio assistant, John Watson, who wrote up appointments and memoranda in the sitters books, ran errands and took messages.[52] One of these men, or Romney's valet, seems to have been the servant Hayley described as the 'black Gentleman in the service of our dear Magician' (Romney).[53] The household records include writing in different hands with references to 'Mr Romney' and 'Master', suggestive of senior and junior staff; among his women servants was Lydia Garrod.[54]

A chronology of his pupils indicates that he had none from 1776 to 1784, a major part of his most active and prosperous period. An exception may be James Sharples (1750–1811). However, he delighted in youthful talent, befriending and encouraging a number of young artists, notably Flaxman, George Morland and Tom Hayley. Among his pupils was the Lakeland-born artist Thomas Robinson (active 1775–1810), who was born near Windermere, close to John Christian Curwen's summer home on Belle Isle. Robinson was introduced to Romney by Curwen as a prospective pupil in 1784 and lived at Cavendish Square during the time when the artist was painting Emma Hart.[55] In Ireland, under the patronage of Bishop Percy of Dromore, Robinson had considerable success, becoming President of the Society of Artists in Dublin. Several of his paintings are still in Ireland, notably his *Battle of Ballynahinch* (Malahide Castle), which evokes Romney's lost *Death of General Wolfe*. His unusual work *A Hermit and a Young Couple before a Tomb* (sold Sotheby's, 31 March 1976), inscribed 'Wynandermere', parallels his master's protoromantic interests. It is to Robinson that we owe some knowledge of Romney's daily routine and studio technique. His son, the Reverend Thomas Romney Robinson DD (1792–1882), named after the artist, became an astronomer, inventor of the cup anemometer and President of the Royal Irish Academy.[56]

Another pupil in the late 1780s was James Rawlinson (1769–1848), an architect's son from Matlock in Derbyshire, of whom Romney wrote 'there is no-one in my house that can be of as much service to me in my profession'.[57] Regrettably, after his father's death Rawlinson returned to Derbyshire against Romney's advice, and for fifty years he was familiar to 'the lovers of the fine arts' in the county. He painted landscapes and portraits, including a copy of Joseph Wright's *Erasmus Darwin*, exhibited once at the RA, and for the rest of his life would express pride in his association with Romney.

James Sharples (1750–1811), a Lancashire man, is also thought to have been a pupil, probably in the late 1770s. He exhibited at the RA from 1779 to 1785 and although he was principally a pastellist, he painted oil portraits of a number of Romney sitters, frequently in profile. In 1793 he went to America with the son of Bishop Law of Carlisle, a major Romney patron. Imprisoned by the French en route, he settled in Philadelphia where four presidents sat to him. After his death in New York, Sharples's third wife Ellen returned to Bristol, where she eventually bequeathed £3,500 for the establishment of the Royal West of England Academy.[58]

Another American portraitist who was influenced by Romney but was not a pupil was Gilbert Stuart (1755–1828). Stuart was in England from 1775 as West's assistant and Priestley and Henderson both sat to him. He was influenced by Romney's neo-classicism, and his own self-portrait borrows the other artist's folded arms design; furthermore, the quality of his brushwork, especially in the treatment of the hair, is very like Romney's. After he returned to America, five presidents sat to him, and his Athenaeum portrait *George Washington* (Boston, Museum of Fine Arts) was engraved for the dollar bill. Urging his artist daughter to purchase Romney heads, Stuart described these as 'exceedingly beautiful and more true to nature than any others I have seen, not excepting those of Sir Joshua'.[59]

Henry Morland (1730–97), who had exhibited candlelight pictures at the Society of Artists in the 1760s, was the father of George Morland (1763–1804). Young George was offered a further training by Romney, also in 1784, and though the offer was declined they maintained a relationship throughout the 1780s, notwithstanding Morland's hard drinking.[60] An apprenticeship was more readily arranged with Willoughby, the youngest son of Sir John Trevelyan, Bart, of Nettlecombe, Somerset (see Pl. XIV). Willoughby Trevelyan (1767–85) was only a pupil for a short time, but Romney painted a fine bust portrait of the boy (England, private collection) which is not recorded in the sitters books. Willoughby died suddenly while at Cavendish Square in August 1785, but his father and brothers continued to sit to the artist, suggesting that they did not blame Romney for this event.[61]

Romney also gave instruction to Mary Barret (*c.*1770–1836), the daughter of George Barret RA who had himself painted in Romney's studio and collaborated in numerous works with Zoffany and Gilpin. Barret had been one of the first artists to be inspired by the landscape sublimity of the Lake District.[62] Mary painted portraits and still lifes, and exhibited several works at the Royal Academy from 1797 to 1799 using Romney's address. Her work includes the miniature *George Romney* (London, National Portrait Gallery) painted on ivory. She later became a member of the Old Water Colour Society and shared the artist's friendship with the Walker family, to whom she was known as 'Little Barret'.[63]

In January 1777 young John Romney came to Cavendish Square for the first time. Thereafter, following four terms at Manchester Grammar School, he was admitted as Duchess of Somerset scholar at St John's College, Cambridge, graduating in 1782. Evidently his time at the 'good Lattin school' had paid off. Next he was to spend six months as usher at Hawkshead Grammar School, where he coincided with the youthful William Wordsworth, but vowed that he could do better for himself back at Cambridge.[64] Soon afterwards he returned to St John's and lived in college as a Fellow until 1806. Although there was little contact between father and son, the artist housed him at Cavendish Square from time to time, in particular when he was recuperating from an illness in 1787. One of these stays coincided with the residence of a Frenchwoman, perhaps the dancer Thelassie. John Romney certainly was upset by this 'unfortunate connection' which eventually 'drove [him] from his [father's] house'.[65] It is also clear that John sometimes 'wounded [his father's] feelings by his harsh and coarse manners and language', and this may not have enhanced his relations with Hayley.[66] Indeed, similar anxieties about Molly's social acceptability may also have hinged upon such details. Nonetheless, surviving letters suggest a gradual improvement in the relationship between father and son following their crucial fifteen years of separation.

It is likely that John Romney's first visit to Cavendish Square was in order to bid farewell to his uncle James Romney, who was leaving for the subcontinent as an officer in the Honourable East India Company. To establish him in this role, in a bond dated 19 February 1777, the artist had lent his handsome younger brother £600. Considering Romney's perilous financial state in Paris in 1775, and the demands made on him by his family following his return, this was an immensely generous act and represented 60 per cent of his annual income in the years immediately before his visit to Italy. He had also just paid off Peter Romney's debts and was meanwhile vigorously chasing payments for pictures.[67] Sitters were often cavalier about paying and obtaining his rightful income was consistently a problem. A few days after accepting his brother's loan, James, then aged thirty-two, sailed south. He was moderately successful in India, becoming a Lieutenant at the strategic seige of Darwar and Commanding Officer of Paulgautcherry in 1796, rising by the time of his retirement to the rank of Lieutenant-Colonel.[68] His financial affairs were always precarious, however, and interwoven with Peter's, and the loan was not finally repaid until after the death not only of the artist but of James himself, who was buried in Bath Abbey in 1807.[69]

Like Peter, and to a lesser extent George, James was unhappy in love; like several of his brothers he also suffered from severe melancholy. His proposal of marriage was refused by the widow of Governor Halsey of Salsette, Bombay, at some time after 1785; another unhappy affair followed. His physical health was poor, following a fall from his horse, and he complained that he had suffered 'almost every severe disorder that is peculiar to this part of India'.[70] An enthusiast with his pen, as well as a tolerable violinist, James also wrote several unpublished plays and verse in profusion.

Apart from paying Peter's debts, Romney had to experience the chagrin of this brother being imprisoned for non-payment of his account with the frame makers Allwood and Murray.[71] Peter did have success with a number of wealthy patrons, including Professor Lambert, Professor of Greek at Cambridge, but he lacked drive, and the 'morbid melancholy' which preyed upon him 'so unhinged his mind . . . that he neglected his profession'. Having escaped the clutches of 'an artful female' who posed as his wife, he also suffered several experiences of unrequited love and on one occasion, following the death of a Miss Brierley in 1770, wandered the Pennines in a distracted state.[72] Such drawbacks and misadventures, coupled with abuse of alcohol, contributed to his death in 1777 aged only thirty-four. Peter displayed a lively intelligence in his letters and was well enough liked by his nephew John, who described him and other malleable youths as 'light skiffs upon the wide and dangerous ocean'.[73] He certainly shared his brother

George's powerful creative impetus, but his material, psychological and social difficulties made the fulfilment of this, for him, a mere dream.

On 3 May 1778 old John Romney, described as 'late of Cocken', died in Kendal and was buried at Dalton.[74] After the death of little Ann Romney in 1763, Molly had generously looked after her father-in-law at High Cocken; but thereafter the threesome evidently moved to Kendal to facilitate young John's schooling. In 1763 Molly was thirty-eight and old John was only sixty, the same age as his own father had been upon marriage. Whether or not the closeness of this ménage increased Romney's reluctance to return north, it was he who inherited his father's modest estate even though they had not seen each other for ten years. By now his brothers William, Lawrence and Peter were dead too, and even the wayward John was only to live for a further four years. His sister Jane still lived at Bardsea near Ulverston, while Molly continued to live in Kendal to be near her sister Esther.[75]

Romney was habitually a generous man, having, like Gainsborough and Lawrence, 'a noble portion of genuine philanthropy'.[76] His consciousness of the extreme generosity of Thomas Greene in the 1760s and 1770s in lending him considerable sums may have catalysed this altruism. Nonetheless, his purse was 'always at the service of his friends', even in the days when he had difficulty supplying his own simple wants. He lent money to Hayley, and to Cumberland on his return from a secret mission to Spain in 1781, and often painted portraits gratis for his friends. Taking every opportunity to 'succour young artists of talent', he would happily lend pictures to amateur artists; his son suggests, however, that he sometimes was imprudent in giving to artful and designing people. John Romney resented these disbursements and estimated that they lost his father an income of 2,000 guineas.[77]

According to Thomas Robinson, the way of life that facilitated Romney's income was hard-working and orderly. During the 1770s and 1780s he would rise between seven and eight o'clock and often walk to Gray's Inn for breakfast with Greene or other associates from the legal profession. Once he had been shaved by his Turkish barber, his servant would dress his hair; he then drew until ten o'clock, when his first sitter was expected.[78] If a sitter failed to arrive, he would resort to his unfinished canvases or his legions of designs. At noon he would take some broth or coffee; he would then dine simply at four. After dinner, always taking a sketchbook, he walked in the country, still accessible to the north of Cavendish Square.[79] On his return he would look through his portfolio and draw until he retired at midnight.[80]

From the outset Romney knew that, despite his creative impulses, he needed to adopt such regular habits in order to achieve success. This may have stemmed originally from observation of his father's brilliantly squandered imagination, as well as from a desire to make up for his own late start as an artist and from his proximity to Steele's chaotic activities. In his Italian journal he comments somewhat unreasonably and at some length on the 'idleness and sloth' of monks and nuns, in words which evince a fervent adherence to the Protestant work ethic.[81] When initially in London, Peter wrote to him, 'For God's sake do not confine yourself too much, I cannot think such very close study as you represent yours to be is most profitable.'[82] Hayley noted his 'cheerful ardour and perseverence', but wondered whether he should have encouraged him in 'the science of retreat'.[83] Despite the timetable described above he would sometimes work at his easel 'from early morning till the sun went down', thus regularly achieving the prodigious daily stint of twelve hours.[84]

Though many men in the eighteenth century worked longer hours, Romney eventually was 'worn out before his time', having exhausted himself by working even on Sundays, a widely deplored habit at that time.[85] Indeed, between 1776 and 1789 he worked on ten out of thirteen Christmas Days. His habit of overworking was noted in a sonnet by Walker, and even the press observed in 1787: 'industry, which we almost fear in our good salutations of Romney's health, is another of his great qualities'.[86]

Rarely indulging in visits for pleasure, Romney did occasionally take exercise on horseback. Apart from his visits abroad he also took a few small holidays. These included excursions to Cambridge, Stonehenge, Wilton House and the Isle of Wight.[87] One reason for his reluctance to indulge in recreation was that he found that if he stopped work it was difficult to regain his professional momentum.[88]

Romney's demon of diligence generated more than two thousand completed portraits. Considering his battle with melancholy and his avoidance of drapery men, this was a phenomenal achievement and it is unsurprising that he paid a high physical price. Although he was criticized for avarice, the truth is that, once established on his professional treadmill, he did not have the strength of will to step off; the consistency in the standard of his work might have been greater if he had.

Throughout his life Romney was sensitive to 'captious criticism, a touch of smart wit, or even a little humorous raillery, [which] damped and disconcerted him and paralysed his hand in whatever he was engaged on'.[89] A potent example of this aspen-like timidity occurred in 1782, when one Captain Thomas Dalton of the 11th Dragoons made 'ludicrous and unchaste' remarks about one of his rare departures from portraiture, *The Initiation of a Rustic Nymph into the Mysteries of Bacchus* (Pl. 41). Considering the blatant sexual resonance of the title, Romney was particularly naive in being surprised by this. He never touched the canvas again and as it was far from complete, it soon perished entirely.[90] Fortunately several drawings remain, revealing a delightful group of bacchantes performing elaborate rites around a splendidly coy neophyte (Cambridge, Fitzwilliam Museum).[91] It might

41 *The Initiation of a Rustic Nymph into the Mysteries of Bacchus*, c.1782–4, 38.9 × 56.7 cm (15.3 × 22.4 in). Here is evidence of Romney's fascination with antique dress and arcane ritual.

have been this incident he had in mind when he expostulated 'What is wit? Wit is a cursed impudent thing and I hate it.'[92] He also held that a painter needed a 'daily portion of cheering applause' to offset such 'phantoms of apprehension'.[93] He was fortunate to have received sufficient praise not to have been immobilized more frequently by such remarks or by unpleasant comment in the press. Hayley was especially supportive and potent in his defence, on one occasion expostulating to Greene:

> How can he be so tender with his confirmed powers and Reputation to tremble at the paltry wet pellets of ill chewed paper shot at him from the Pop Gun of a Blackguard [?] . . . if He will only cease to read and think of Newspapers I would stake my life on him never losing a Grain of his professional Emoluments or of his true Glory by such despicable attacks on his Genius.[94]

Being aware of the need for such support himself made Romney a more sensitive critic of other artists' work: 'he was not fastidious, nor slow to admire where admiration was due and where it was not, he was uniformly silent'.[95]

Romney's arid emotional life exacerbated his depressive tendency. In the

1770s his subject drawings of lovers tragically reunited, or reaching out to each other but unable to connect physically, relate to his own sense of emotional isolation.[96] To a lesser degree this is true of the extraordinary peeping self-portraits, in *Flaxman Modelling Hayley's Bust* (New Haven, Yale Center for British Art; Pl. 16) and *The Four Friends* (Kendal, Abbot Hall Art Gallery), where the artist's head appears tentatively at the edge of both compositions. When the latter was engraved by Caroline Watson for Hayley, the self-effacement was completed by the removal of the artist's head altogether, as the poet considered that his friend had 'slighted himself'.[97] The peeping head motif reminds us of the artist's love of being an observer on social occasions and in public places, as a relief from being centre stage in his studio. It also echoes voyeuristic subjects like his lost *Susannah and the Elders*.

Differences of mood can be seen among the drawings, some of which show a relative state of ease, while others include 'slashing attacks'.[98] Emma Hart's departure for Naples in 1786 is often given as a reason for Romney's increased melancholy during the late 1780s; the deaths of his brother John in 1782, Henderson in 1785, Sheridan in 1788 and Meyer in 1789 doubtless contributed to his dark mood.[99]

His troubled approach to drawing the 'fiends and spectres of the yawning deep' and other protoromantic subjects suited Romney's darker times.[100] Brighter moods may have led to the production of the *Titania* series (see p. 149), though in both his drawings and in his recorded life it is the bleak side that predominates. He also responded to the gloomy aspects of other artists' work, notably the despair registered by the Carracci. Romanticism 'is not in the work of art so much as in the mind of the artist' and Romney was fortunate to live at a time when dark subjects were of significant cultural interest. This may explain Fuseli's remark that 'the times were made for him'.[101] As it is, Romney has been labelled as 'paranoid'; but though his drawings of crowd scenes include some such elements, in his behaviour he exhibited nothing more than normal healthy suspicion.[102] Lacking more detailed evidence, it is a diagnostic distortion to attribute a psychosis to one who was merely neurotic.[103]

There was one mysterious aspect of Romney's personality, of which Flaxman wrote that it was difficult to 'speak the truth without offence'.[104] Whatever this was, it probably deterred Bishop Richard Watson from cultivating an intimacy with him. John Romney blames Hayley, however, for confounding the distinction between vice and virtue, and while admitting that his father 'had his share of infirmities', he was at pains to explain that these were 'exempt from all gross propensities'.[105] Why did he feel this was necessary? He was partly responding to the 'scurrilous' *Memoirs of Lady Hamilton*, which refers to the artist's 'propensities to sensual indulgence (which) were well known to all his acquaintance'.[106] Writing more immediately after Romney's death, Cumberland says: 'he was betrayed into impurities which morality cannot pardon though candour may fairly plead that he kept his weakness out of sight and never offended the Decorum of Society or lost his respect for Virtue though his practice did not strictly conform to it'.[107]

In an age when men openly flaunted their mistresses, disapproval of 'impurities' was unlikely to have its source in mere heterosexual activity. Neither Romney's rejection of his wife, nor his relationship with Emma Hart, nor his propensity for lightly clad sitters, nor his liaison with Thelassie, the French dancer, are sufficient to have given 'offence'.[108] It may be that his considerable ability in painting attractive young men like William Beckford indicates homoerotic leanings, or at least an ambiguous sexual orientation. Why did he need to apologize to George Carter on leaving Italy? In France he reflected upon monks having the choice of 'choking their passion' or gratifying 'a more dangerous one'.[109] John Romney, who certainly bowdlerized other records, alters the wording here to 'clandestine and criminal attachments', which indicates a degree of embarrassment. Some kind of ménage-à-trois is hinted at by Hayley's reference to the dancer Thelassie being keen to 'attend us together'.[110] Despite the tendency of contemporary critics to associate radical politics with libertinage, this in itself cannot explain the mystery of why Romney's son, two of his close friends and a prominent client made oblique references to a secret life.[111]

John Boydell and the closet romantic 1786–90

In 1786 Romney became central to one of the most elaborate schemes of patronage in the history of British art: John Boydell's Shakespeare Gallery. Boydell (1719–1804) was an engraver and print publisher who had become successful by exploiting the rising domestic market for cheap engravings: his catalogue at around this time listed more than four thousand prints.[1] One of his most successful ventures was Woollett's engraving after West's *Death of General Wolfe*. Boydell had dealt in engravings after Romney from as far back as 1770, when he had published Dunkarton's *Two Sisters Contemplating Mortality*.

The idea of a gallery to celebrate Shakespeare's genius was first mooted at a dinner held at Hampstead in November 1786 by Josiah Boydell, the engraver's nephew. Romney is said to have discussed the idea with John Boydell, both in advance of the dinner and the next morning, at the latter's print shop in Cheapside.[2] The other guests besides Romney were Hayley, West, Braithwaite, Hoole, the watercolourist Paul Sandby and George Nichol, the bookseller, who was married to Boydell's niece.[3] The project progressed and in February 1787 one newspaper report declared that 'in this stupendous undertaking of Boydell's, Romney rises to especial note as an enthusiast'.[4] Thurlow, however, although ostensibly a Romney partisan, observed to Carwardine that the artist would make 'a balderdash business of it' and urged him to read Shakespeare's texts in advance, a thing that Romney was always reluctant to do.[5] Carwardine defended his friend, and in due course the Chancellor and the artist were to discuss the potential of Shakespearean subjects over dinner at Thurlow's house.

Until the foundation of Boydell's Shakespeare Gallery there had been no established place in British culture for history painting.[6] By funding such an opportunity for native artists, Boydell was dubbed the 'Commercial Maecenas' by the Prince of Wales and ranked by *The Times* with the Medici.[7]

He thus achieved what the Academy had so far failed to accomplish and singlehandedly 'did more for the advancement of the arts in England than the whole mass of the nobility put together'.[8]

The subjects chosen covered most of the Shakespeare canon and appealed to both polarities of feeling, the fraught and the serene.[9] A major snag arose from Boydell's failure to allocate subjects; Romney's early *Macbeth* designs were pre-empted by Reynolds, who was given a generous advance payment for *Macbeth and the Witches*. Romney next began with *Marjorie Jourdain and Bolingbroke Conjuring up the Fiend*, a subject from *Henry VI, Part II*, but he was beaten to this by the youthful John Opie. In the surviving drawings (Cambridge, Fitzwilliam Museum) the head of Bolingbroke can be related to Le Brun's illustration *Terrour or Fright*.[10] Romney's frustrations, which arose both from an overload of sitters and from his tendency to prevaricate, eventually led him to embark instead upon *The Tempest* (Pl. 42).

The earliest sketches for this project were made in the summer of 1787 in Hayley's wooden riding house, with its distant sea view, where the poet would read to Romney from Vasari's *Lives of the Artists*. Meyer, a fellow guest, generously left Eartham early so as not to disturb Romney's progress. Later that year both men were to visit Windsor Castle to meet Benjamin West and to view the Raphael cartoons. Meanwhile at Eartham, the house was to prove so conducive to progress that Hayley had it converted, with a skylight and fireplace, albeit at the artist's expense.[11]

The Boydell Gallery building, designed by George Dance, opened at 52 Pall Mall in 1789 before some of the paintings, including Romney's, had arrived.[12] The façade was embellished with unusual ammonite capitals, a variant upon the Ionic, and surmounted on the pediment by Thomas Banks's *alto relievo, The Genius of Painting Pointing out Shakespeare to the Dramatic Muse*.[13] Among the pictures on display was a scene by Edward Edwards from *The Two Gentlemen of Verona* and another by Joseph Wright from *The Winter's Tale*.

Romney's design for *The Tempest* (Pl. 42), which originally included Caliban, shows Prospero and Miranda on the shore with Ferdinand jumping from the threatened ship, an action reported by Ariel.[14] The image was modelled by Hayley, whose later reference to his 'marine cell' at Felpham was a deliberate evocation of Prospero's island.[15] Other friends gave encouragement, though the artist felt himself 'sinking under this mighty undertaking'.[16] From September 1788 he refused sitters before noon, devoting the time to *The Tempest*, and on 21 April 1790 there was great rejoicing at the 'birth' of this huge canvas, which measured ten by fifteen feet.[17] A further cause of delay in finishing this painting may have been the premature death at Kew Green in 1789 of Meyer, who was buried at Kew beside Gainsborough

42 *The Tempest* (engraving by Benjamin Smith), 1797, 58.8 × 43.6 cm (23.2 × 17.2 in). Romney's most complex work and the strongest evidence of his passion for history subjects. The figures in the sky are notably Blake-like.

and Joshua Kirby, former President of the Society of Artists.[18] It was an unexpected loss of a friend Romney had known for more than twenty years.

The Tempest was an heroic venture, but not an entirely successful one as an excess of portraits had diminished Romney's skill in composition. The vast majority of his canvases show single figures and of these many were bust portraits, requiring little ingenuity of design. On the other hand, *The Tempest* contains the challenge of more than twenty figures, many in energetic attitudes. Romney was also beginning to show the symptoms of his long decline. He fully appreciated the defects of this, his most ambitious picture, which despite its force suffered from the juxtaposition of land and sea in a conflated narrative design. His influences included the Raphael cartoons at Windsor Castle, notably the billowing cloaks and central grouping in the master's *Sacrifice at Lystra* cartoon.[19] The composition may also owe something to Michelangelo's *Last Judgement* in the Sistine Chapel with its crowded figures in Charon's boat, while the depiction of Ferdinand jumping over the side parallels the figures being tumbled over the ferryman's gunwale. The diversity of these likely sources, conflated with difficulty by Romney, may have contributed to his relative lack of success.

For this complex composition Romney was eventually paid only £600, as opposed to Reynolds's fee of £1,000: negligible compensation for the £2,000 of portrait income lost during its incubation. However, this may have seemed a worthwhile sacrifice in that this was the first historical painting he had completed for many years.[20]

Once *The Tempest* was in place at the gallery, viewers were uncomplimentary about it. The *Gentleman's Magazine* complained that the picture was 'overcharged with figures'.[21] Hayley, despite his usual adulation, admitted that 'it seizes and enchants though it does not absolutely satisfy the mind'. The Reverend James Tate, although referring to the 'very masterly stile', preferred Fuseli's *Tempest* composition.[22] Romney's own mental state was in a sense a benefit here, as he understood that there was 'another tempest raging [in the play, which was] . . . psychological rather than physical'.[23] Recent scholarship suggests that he was 'more faithful to the unique aesthetic of this late romance than any other conventional adaptation', and that his conflation of events effectively captures 'the play's experiment with time' and depicts what is 'beyond the visual capacity of the stage'.[24] He regarded the painting as his greatest work, a staff-breaking and book-drowning performance, worthy of Prospero in preparation if not in achievement and the closest he had come to the fulfilment of his aspirations as a history painter.[25]

Nevertheless, Romney's persistent enthusiasm for the Gallery led him to give gratis to Boydell *The Infant Shakespeare, Nature and the Passions* (Washington, Folger Shakespeare Library; Pl. 43) and the full-length axe-wielding *Cassandra* (sold Christie's, 8 May 1985). Emma had sat for Cassandra in this canvas which, sadly, is now cut down and can only be appreciated through Legat's engraving. Romney also added the figure of Jacques to *Jacques and the Wounded Stag*, a composition from *As You Like It* by the 'kind-hearted and high spirited' William Hodges (1744–97).[26]

The Infant Shakespeare, Nature and the Passions is, like Reynolds's *The Infant Dr Johnson* (Bowood, Marquis of Lansdowne), a secular example of the tradition which heroized the infancy of both pagan and Christian figures, as in Poussin's *The Childhood of Jupiter* (Berlin, Bodesmuseum) and innumerable Nativities.[27] Romney's design shows the baby sitting between Joy and Sorrow, who offer a choice of gifts, either a musical pipe or a phial of poison, while the hooded Nature shines her blessing upon her 'favourite child' and his powers-to-be in dramatizing both comedy and tragedy.[28] On either side of the composition are ranged neo-classical personifications of the passions, derived from his study of Lavater and Le Brun: to the left, Love, Hatred and Jealousy; to the right, Anger, Envy and Fear.[29] Unusually for Romney, both versions of *The Infant Shakespeare, Nature and the Passions* (Pl. 43) were com-

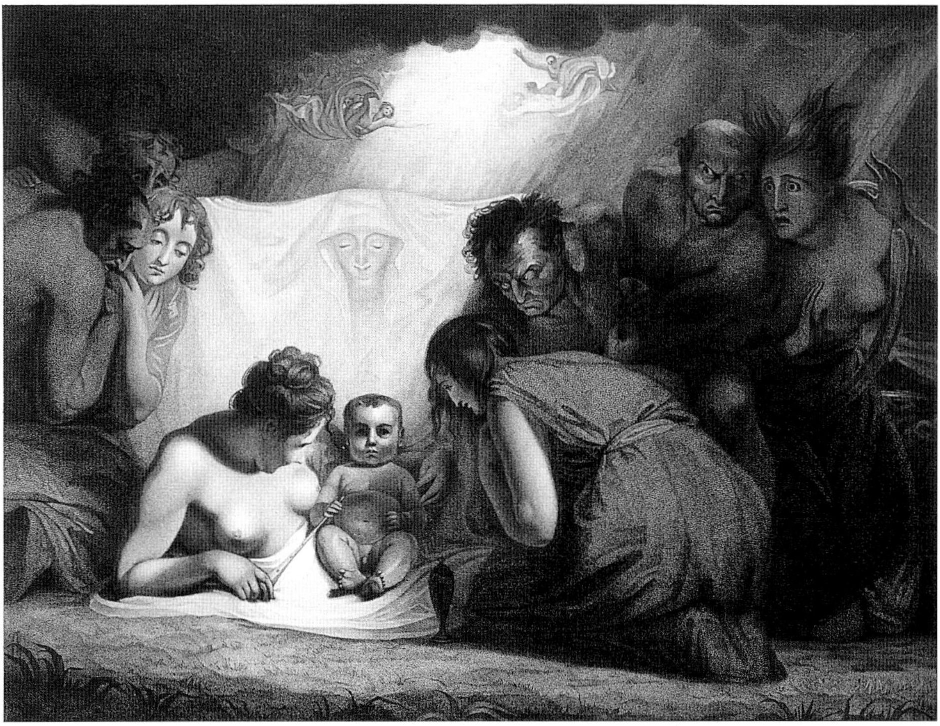

43 *The Infant Shakespeare, Nature and the Passions* (engraving by Benjamin Smith), 1799, 59.5 × 43.6 cm (23.5 × 17.2 in). Nature is flanked by Love, Hatred, Jealousy, Anger, Envy and Fear.

pleted on panel.[30] The composition relates to his simpler transitional design entitled *The Infant Shakespeare with Comedy and Tragedy* (Petworth House, The National Trust), again painted in two versions, where some observers have seen in the face of Comedy a nostalgic resemblance to Emma Hart.[31]

Romney's *Infant Shakespeare* series, an allegory also treated by Fuseli, derives from various legends featuring a life choice, such as the choice Hercules made between vice and virtue which was realized on canvas by West (London, Victoria and Albert Museum).[32] Romney's composition may reflect the painful choices he had made in his own life: between his family and his art, between portraiture and history painting, and also between vice and virtue. Certainly they parallel the duality of darkness and light in his own personality, evoking his *Mirth* and *Melancholy* pictures of 1770; significantly, the child is depicted chosing Comedy's pipe, symbolic of passion or vice, rather than Tragedy's phial, representing the painful path of virtue.[33] His principal literary source was Thomas Gray's *Progress of Poesy*, and an earlier lost version of this design was much admired by the poet

Helen Maria Williams, who wrote verse in its praise.[34] The artist's name appears, in reciprocation, on the subscribers' list of her edition of *Poems* in 1786.

By 1805 there were 167 pictures exhibited at the Boydell Gallery. Many subsequent commissions had proved vastly inferior, however. Both Walpole and Fuseli were critical of the scheme, while Gillray satirized it in his print *Shakespeare Sacrificed*.[35] James Northcote (1746–1831), who had previously praised the concept and in 1791 contributed *The Murder of the Princes in the Tower* (destroyed by enemy action), now denounced the bulk of the collection as nothing more than 'slip-slop imbecility'.[36]

Boydell had intended to bequeath the Gallery to the nation, but sales of the resulting Shakespeare engravings were disappointingly slow and after 1793 his wider markets were damaged by the war with France. He was thus compelled to avert bankruptcy by selling lottery tickets, with the Gallery as the prize.[37] Following the draw, the collection was dismantled and sold off and *The Tempest* (Pl. 42) vanished into oblivion.[38] An additional problem in appreciating this major work is the quality of Benjamin Smith's engraving. The lack of fidelity to Romney's work is significant, and although the composition is clear, the detail has lost much in the engraving process. This confirms another of Boydell's problems: there simply were not enough good engravers to produce high-quality prints. The vibrant energy of Romney's concept can be more clearly seen in the large oil sketch at the Galleria Nazionale d'Arte Moderna in Rome.[39]

Shakespeare subjects, as Boydell and Romney knew, offered a potential route to immortality. But although the bard's ghosts, witches and violent deaths were popular, there was much debate regarding their propriety.[40] Romney was not an avid reader, but throughout his life in his treatments he achieved a 'vital and original visual expression of the poetry' of these protoromantic elements.[41] A couple of lines was sufficient to trigger his vivid imagination and too many words impeded him.[42] Most of his designs were not realized on canvas but it is nonetheless worth examining the variety of plays he illustrated. From the tragedies come many drawings from *Macbeth*, including *Banquo's Ghost* (Pl. 44) and *A Foregathering of Witches* (both Cambridge, Fitzwilliam Museum).

Apart from the large series of such works from *King Lear* such as the drawing *The Death of Cordelia* (Washington DC, Folger Shakespeare Library), there are several references to works inspired by *Hamlet*. Romney completed an oil entitled *Ophelia* (untraced) and began a composition featuring the Prince of Denmark.[43] He responded to the histories by producing several Falstaff drawings (Cambridge, Fitzwilliam Museum), and several of *Joan of Arc upon the Walls of Rouen Holding a Torch* (*Henry VI, Part I*; Cambridge Fitzwilliam Museum).[44] This design relates in concept to drawings of Cas-

44 *Banquo's Ghost (The Banquet Scene: Macbeth)*, c.1791–2, 38.2 × 51.2 cm (15.3 × 20.5 in.). The spirit of the murdered Banquo comes to haunt Macbeth at dinner.

sandra and Circe. The comedies elicited an unfinished canvas, *Falstaff and the Merry Wives of Windsor* (destroyed), and Romney made numerous studies of Titania, Bottom and the Fairies from *A Midsummer Night's Dream*, resulting in the completed *Titania, Puck and the Changeling* (Dublin, National Gallery of Ireland) and *Tom Hayley as Robin Goodfellow* (Brighton Art Gallery; London, Tate Gallery).

Post-war scholarship has greatly raised awareness of the 'convulsive virtuosity' evident in many of Romney's drawings. This private and empowering aspect of his work was consistently closer to his heart than the 'drudgery' of his more public portraiture.[45] Indeed, he had admitted to Adam Walker before coming to London that he found 'more pleasure in . . . contemplative excursions than in bodily enjoyments'.[46] Drawings were Romney's 'delight by day and his study by night and for this his food and rest were often neglected'.[47] Despite this enthusiasm, the confining servitude of portraiture, which was railed against by most artists in this period, certainly hindered him. As late as 1794, in a letter to John Romney he observed, 'I have had all the critics and they are surprised I do not pursue history.'[48] Fuseli believed that expanding his work further beyond 'face painting' was Romney's desideratum for the future, 'when satiety of gain should yield to the pure desire of glory'; in the event, failing health prevented this being realized.[49] Avarice has been given by others as an explanation for his postponing such a future, but the reason cannot be so simple. Today, any comparable drawing which does not result in a completed picture is regarded as 'a typical feature of the Romantic Movement'.[50] Such artistic suggestion can often be more potent than completed designs on canvas, as the viewer must look harder and achieve a closer sense of identification, in order to penetrate the artist's multiple resonances of meaning. In this sense Romney was, with Fuseli, well ahead of his time.

At different points in his career, and even from month to month or week to week, Romney was effectively a different human being, with varying needs, skills and incapacities. The elucidation of these shifting realities of his creativity, exacerbated by his manic-depressive condition, remains almost impossible to attain. Probably he did not have very clearly focussed priorities, and merely soldiered on with little analysis of his situation.

Despite the condition of the market, the years following the 1750s witnessed a distinct shift in sensibility, as artists mined a new seam of inspiration anticipating romanticism. In Italy from 1745, Piranesi populated his Roman ruins with dwarves and hunchbacks and, sometime before 1761, he produced the *Carceri*, his nightmarish prison drawings. In England, Richard Wilson's *Landscape with Banditti: the Murder* (Cardiff, National Museum of Wales), with its elements of horror, its jagged cliffs and blasted oaks, was in 1752 one of the earliest manifestations of protoromanticism, while Burke's *Enquiry into the Sublime and the Beautiful* (1757) identified images of terror as a spring of aesthetic emotion. Romney, to whom Burke sat in 1776, had in the late 1750s produced his own early contribution to the movement in *King Lear in the Storm* (Pl. IV). It was through protoromanticism that English painting was to have its greatest impact upon European art since the middle ages. Hayley's *Epistles to Romney* show a similar influence, demonstrating:

> With pity's tender throbs and horror's icy chill[51]

that it was intrinsic to protoromantic sentiment, not only to observe the impact of terror, but also to empathize with the victim.

In Italy, Romney had been exposed to the sinners and devils of Michelangelo's *Last Judgement*; there too he had copied such subjects as the boy tormented by spirits in Raphael's *Transfiguration*, and drew *The Laocoön* (Pl. 46), the antique sculpture of the disloyal priest of Apollo and his sons being attacked by snakes.[52] As artists such as Romney shifted their sensibility from neo-classicism towards protoromanticism, they could view these early masters in a new light. Romney now had license to exploit his real interests, which lay in the irrational forces of the mind and the horrors of the gothic.

45 Sketch for *Circe* or *Cassandra*, 1782–6, 50.3 × 31.1 cm (19.7 × 12.2 in). An appealing vigorous study with sinuous curves and powerful gesture.

In portraiture, too, he was able occasionally to bridge the gulf between the Apollonian and the Dionysian outlets in his life, by introducing proto-romantic elements into formal works, for example the chasm in *Miss Warren as Hebe* (Pl. 18), or the fraternal lock of hair held in the hand in *John, Lord Somers* (Eastnor Castle, Hervey-Bathurst Collection; Pl. 47).

Few contemporaries were interested, however, in 'the Romney of Burke's terrible sublime', though a study of his drawings, often seen as 'excesses of impetuous and undisciplined imagination', more readily gives an idea of his genius than a familiarity with his portraiture.[53]

More than 5,000 drawings survive: a vast output which indicates the scale of Romney's historical ambitions and demonstrates his prodigious graphic invention.[54] In Hayley's words,

> Thy happy genius springs a virgin mine
> Of copious, pure, original Design . . .[55]

Relatively few are preparatory designs for portraits, as such preparation was generally 'alien to his practice', but survivors include those for *Mrs Banks, The Beaumont Family* (Pl. 27) and *John Flaxman Modelling the Bust of William Hayley* (Pl. 16).[56] Alternatively, it is possible that other portrait drawings were destroyed by the artist or his family, since there are unusually as many as forty extant for *Miss Warren as Hebe* (Pl. 18) alone.[57] Ordinarily Romney produced few drawings for his numerous portraits, and quantities of drawings for his handful of imaginative canvases, a paradox reflecting two totally different goals.

Despite the pressures of portraiture, Ordinarily Romney continued to give thought to subjects from world literature. He acknowledged, however, that in this he needed the assistance of literary friends, and he was fortunate in having several such contacts including Cumberland, Hayley, Reed and Potter. His designs were drawn from hugely varied subject matter, ranging chronologically from Virgil via Boccaccio to Bishop Percy's *Reliques of Ancient English Poetry* (1765), and comprised a minimum of two hundred wholly different titles.[58] The Percy collection awakened widespread interest in traditional lyrics and inspired not only Romney and Flaxman, but in due course the romantic poets. Many other titles for drawings 'floated in the busy mind' of the artist but perished before being fixed on paper.[59] In Italy Romney had jotted down a list of mythological ideas, including stories featuring Venus, Cupid, Jupiter and Niobe, all of which were realized as drawings.[60] When glutted with such stimuli his imagination was apt to fly hither and thither, in Hayley's words 'like a bee, who flies off from a flower, before he has gathered half the honey'.[61] The Hermit's criticism was nothing if not hypocritical, since he himself was frequently the source of distraction.

Despite the loss of numerous ideas, a great deal of thinking nonetheless

46 *The Laocoön*, *c*.1774, 43.8 × 30.5 cm (17.2 × 12 in). Numerous Grand Tourists of Romney's time were struck by this dramatic scuptural group.

47 *John, Lord Somers*, c.1785–6, 253 × 143 cm (100 × 57 in). Several members of the family, neighbours of the artist at Cavendish Square, sat to Romney.

preceded the realization of each series of identifiable drawings. Romney asserts as much in his unpublished 'Discourse on Art': 'when the soul of man receives impressions from its own impulse or from fine poetry or history it [ought to] possess that arrangement or combination in the mind perfect and whole before it is delivered on paper or canvas'.[62] Generally he was faithful to the textual details; an exception is *Alope*, where the marauding lions are his own invention, introduced perhaps to enhance the tension of the woman's isolation.[63]

In addition to the 'Discourse', another unpublished project, planned with Hayley, was an edition of de Fresnoy's *Art of Painting*.[64] Romney was most reluctant, however, to produce drawings as illustrations for publications, as Hayley discovered when he solicited a drawing of *A Maid on a Rock* for Charlotte Smith. The artist's reluctance may have been exacerbated by the apparent plagiarism by Stothard of several of his designs, such as the *Virgin Leucippe in the Cave of Pan* (Cambridge, Fitzwilliam Museum) for Hayley's own *Essay on Old Maids*.[65] The sculptor Joseph Nollekens (1737–1823), who periodically converted the likenesses of Romney's two-dimensional portraits to three-dimensional busts, was likewise 'cordially' hated.[66]

In general Romney 'lacked the conviction to transfer his sketches into large-scale, grand compositions'. He was influenced in this by his awareness of the 'idiosyncrasies of the London art-market', which offered little encouragement to the history painter.[67] Although his confidence in transferring drawings to canvas had been knocked by his difficulties with *The Tempest* (Pl. 42), it may also be that on occasion he was satisfied to produce the drawings alone, seeing them as finished works of art and not done merely for recreation.[68] After his flurry of history canvases in the 1760s, the drawings were an essential foil to the interminable parade of portraits. They can be viewed as a form of strategic withdrawal, the more so as quantities of such design progress justified a planned procrastination and explained the lack of histories on the easel. It was in some respects a blessing not to have to complete such designs, though he may well have sensed the value of their spontaneity in the eyes of posterity.

When grouped by subject the drawings tend to be repetitive, but with minor alterations which subtly shift the emphasis.[69] Like Henri Daumier, Romney was reliant partly upon happy accidents rather than reasoned steps as he sought a compositional solution, so that his sketchbook drawings do not always show logical sequences of design.[70] The stylistic restrictions of his portraiture increased the need for freedom and experimentation in his drawing. This he did mostly 'by the light of the inner eye' without the object before him, a tendency he shared with Fuseli and Blake.[71]

Always having a sketchbook in his pocket, he reserved some for pencil studies and others for ink. He used a wide variety of media: with various

48 *Head of a Fiend*, c.1792–4, 35.4 × 36.7 cm (14 × 14.5 in). A rapid delineation of one of the threatening faces in Milton's *Paradise Lost*.

combinations of pencil, pen, charcoal, chalk and black, brown and grey wash he achieved a 'splendid audacity and poetic feeling', whether loosely delineating the weird *Head of a Fiend* (Eton College; Pl. 48), precisely outlining *Psyche in Charon's Boat* (Cambridge, Fitzwilliam Museum) or using wash over pencil, as in the series of drawings inspired by the work of the reformer John Howard (Pl. 52).[72] Usually, though not always, he began with under-drawing in pencil. Despite the erratic progress of some series, in numerous subjects the genesis of designs and their progress to near-completion can be traced stage by stage, as for example in *Banquo's Ghost* (Pl. 44) and *Samson Overpowered* (Pl. 4).[73]

An intriguing aspect of Romney's creative process is that he periodically reversed the design, as an engraver would do, for example in at least one of *The Gower Children* studies.[74] Periodically he transferred sketchbook drawings to larger sheets of cream-coloured, laid paper; coarse, beige, speckled paper;

or Whatman paper, using pen and wash; none, however, was highly finished as they were never intended for display.

The pen and wash drawings, such as *Antigone and Polynices* (Kendal Town Hall), demonstrate an aesthetic derived ultimately from Poussin, which was common to neo-classical British artists. Winckelmann described this by asserting that 'just as the first pressing of the grapes gives the most exquisite wine, so the . . . sketch on paper of the draughtsman affords us the true spirit of the artist'.[75] Romney himself was able to dash down his ideas 'with the speed and economy of a Rembrandt', the eyes, nose and mouth often indicated simply by three short lines.[76] Some of these drawings, attractive in their form, in fact depict stories of violence: live burial in the series entitled *Canidia and the Youth* (Washington, DC, Folger Shakespeare Library), or death by lightning in *Celadon and Amelia* (Kendal Town Hall). In a lighter mood, others such as the *Pastoral Scene from Longus* (Cambridge, Fitzwilliam Museum), depicting cattle, a flute player and a young girl, convey nostalgia for an idyllic life of Arcady, or perhaps the artist's own rustic childhood. Another, in parallel with Reynolds's *Mrs Lloyd* (England, private collection), shows a woman carving initials on a tree, an idea reminiscent of Orlando in Shakespeare's *As You Like It*. Lively subjects of erotic pursuit were popular at the time, and Romney's *Lover Springing out of a Thicket to Surprise a Young Girl* (Cambridge, Fitzwilliam Museum) has parallels in designs on the *Townley Well Head* (London, British Museum) and later in Keats's *Ode on a Grecian Urn*.[77] It is, however, a positive aspect of romanticism that rarely finds an outlet in his work.

Rather than merely illustrating a scene, in other drawings Romney is able to initiate a response of heightened feeling in the viewer, in keeping with beliefs adopted from Winckelmann. Brandishing sharp weapons or making threatening gestures, the crowds in drawings such as *Scene of a Massacre* (Cambridge, Fitzwilliam Museum) convey an overwhelming violence. There is also a sense of helpless struggle as massed human beings writhe fearfully below figures of dominance.[78] In the *Flood* series, the *Rape of the Sabine Women* series (both Stanford, University Art Gallery) and some of the Milton subjects, the figures become 'metaphors of [Romney's] battle with critics and his own complex personality' and have similarities with the work of Goya.[79]

Goya's iconography embraces horses, shipwreck, witches, prisons, torture and violent death, all elements which appear in Romney's own work. The latter also features nightmares, storms, conjuration of fiends, vivisection of sleeping maidens, infanticide and grotesque states of mind. Romney's delight in 'darkness, threat, mystery, the weird and the supernatural' was not universally shared.[80] Horace Walpole wrote in 1783 'of late, Barry, Romney, Fuseli, Mrs Cosway and others have attempted to paint deities, visions, witchcrafts etc but have only been bombast and extravert, without true dignity'.[81]

It is true that Romney's subjects plumb the gloomy depths of his conscious and unconscious mind, and that the results of these explorations are potent manifestations of the protoromantic movement, for which he had by then a well-established taste. His bleakest drawings present a grim vision of reality in keeping with his mordant spirit, indicating at times a general lack of faith in humanity.

That his subjects include King Lear, Prometheus, and the prison reformer John Howard expresses awareness of the limitations of his personality through his familiarity with mental disorder and with the personal metaphor of imprisonment. Both elements were present in the drawing, now destroyed, entitled *The Madhouse* (formerly in the Edgar Kauffman Collection).

A recurrent theme is that of innocence threatened.[82] The young mother *Alope* (Kendal, Abbot Hall Art Gallery) and her baby are exposed in the wilderness to predatory lions. The protomartyr *St Thecla* (in the former Truro collection) is likewise left to the lions, while tied to a tree. *Eurydice* (cartoon, Liverpool, Walker Art Gallery) flees from Aristaeus and is bitten by a snake. Prospective infanticide is portrayed in *Medea Contemplating the Murder of her Children* (Cambridge, Fitzwilliam Museum). This latter subject, a powerful myth of female aberration, is one of the 'fiercest' undertaken by Romney. Medea is the personification in one of his portraits of Emma Hart (Pasadena, Norton Simon Museum), and became one of her most potent 'Attitudes'. For this role Emma would enlist a visiting child who would suddenly and unexpectedly be grasped by the hair: this, with a brandished dagger, would elicit the requisite emotion on the child's face.[83] Apart from this infanticide series, Romney also drew *Medea on her Chariot* (Cambridge, Fitzwilliam Museum), a subject comparable to the myth of paternal violence expressed in Flaxman's sculpture *The Fury of Athamas* (Ickworth House, The National Trust), and more powerfully explored by Delacroix in the 1830s with his own *Medea* (Lille, Musée de Beaux Arts).

Romney's most extraordinary subject, 'a combination of fascination and horror', appears in the pair of drawings entitled *The Wronged Maid* (Cambridge, Fitzwilliam Museum; Pl. 49). A virtuous maidservant, having resisted her master's advances, was falsely accused by him of theft. After being hanged on the gallows she was found to be warm by a surgeon who, in a time when felons were the only legitimate source of cadavers for dissection, was about to anatomize her 'corpse'. The second drawing shows her waking up and thinking herself in heaven. Such a Hogarthian moral subject, which relates to a scene in Edward Ravenscroft's *The Anatomist* of 1696, held great appeal for the artist as a man of essential humanity.[84]

Throughout Europe in previous centuries several hundred thousand

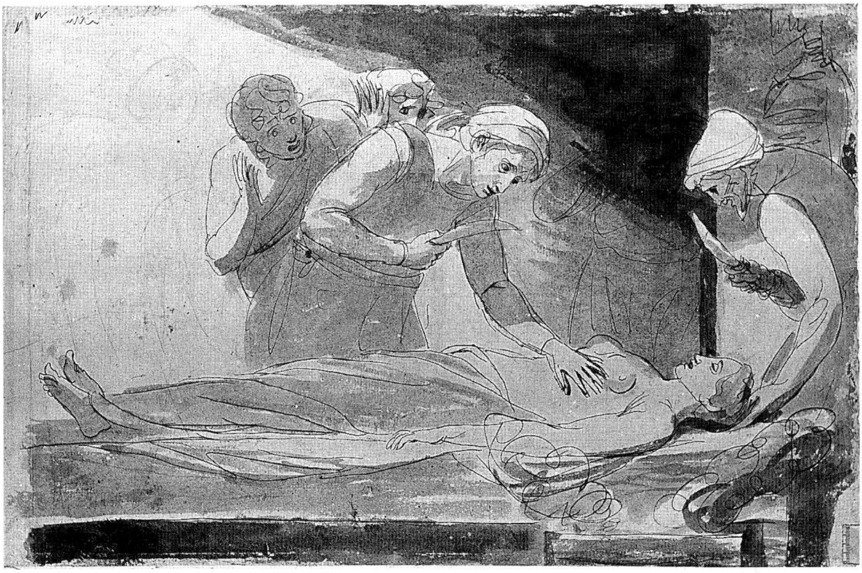

49 *The Wronged Maid*, late 1770s, 31.9 × 50.8 cm (12.5 × 20 in). A narrative scene possibly influenced by Romney's friend William Long, a surgeon and anatomist.

witches had been executed, but by the late eighteenth century the concept of witchcraft survived only in folklore. Whatever the proportion of folk stories as stimuli for his drawings, most nonetheless are found in literature. Other than the Shakespearean witches, the depiction of his most 'sublimely malignant' crone arose from Gray's translation of *The Fatal Sisters* in the form of *The Lapland Witch* (Cambridge, Fitzwilliam Museum; Paris, Musée du Louvre; Pl. 50).[85] Meyer was one who delighted in this design, so different from his own restrained miniatures, and in response to it Hayley wrote

> What lust of mischief marks thy witch's form
> While on the Lapland rock she swells the storm.[86]

These turbulent drawings are greatly satisfying compositions with the curves of the ship echoed by those of the waves. Meanwhile the members of the coven circle in a *danse macabre* and the largest figure watches a vessel in distress, an echo of *Macbeth*.[87] Her ghastly profile has similarities with the Spirit of Despair in Flaxman's drawing of Chatterton's death (London, British Museum) and is the kind of subject enthusiastically described by Payne Knight as eliciting 'pleasing awe and veneration'.[88] Another lost drawing, *Hecate Holding a Snake*, prompted Blake to call the artist 'our Admired Sublime Romney'.[89] As symbols of evil, various other forms of snake arise including those in *Mrs Yates as the Tragic Muse*, *Medea* and *Eurydice*. One

50 *The Lapland Witch*, 1780s, 31.4 × 47.9 cm (12.6 × 19.2 in.). Dramatic light and shade add vigour to the setting of this evil crone.

drawing in the *Canidia and the Youth* (Washington, DC, Folger Shakespeare Library) series shows the group of hags preparing to bury their victim up to his chin in sand, to starve him to death as an ingredient for their leader's love potion.[90] Another drawing of Canidia (Yale Center for British Art), the story taken from Horace's *The Witches' Orgy*, shows the evil crone with Medusan vipers in her hair, a motif whose adoption was in keeping with the spirit of gothic horror.[91]

Various degrees of terror are depicted by Romney in works with a nautical subject such as *The Tempest* (Pl. 42), *The Lapland Witch* (Pl. 50) and *Boys in a Boat Drifting out to Sea* (England, private collection); a less well-known drawing is *The Devil Rowing Himself out to one of two Wrecked Ships* (England, private collection). His most unusual subject of this kind is *The Shipwreck at the Cape of Good Hope*, taken from the travels of Carl Thunberg and depicting Woltemad, a menagerie keeper, rescuing sailors from a wreck on horseback.[92] Both the turbulence of the sea and the muscular strength of horse and rider were emphasised in Romney's oil sketch (untraced) which was subsequently drawn and engraved by Blake (London, British Museum).[93] There is added poignancy in the impending death of the valiant Woltemad, on his seventh journey through the waves, an event anticipated by the female corpse on the shore.[94] The idea, an allegory of Christ saving souls, came from the

Reverend James Stanier Clarke (1765?–1834), whose grandfather had been a friend of the Hayleys in Chichester and who was now rector of Preston in Sussex.[95] Shipwrecks were to be Clarke's lifetime interest; he later wrote *Naufragia or Historical Memoirs of Shipwrecks* and edited Falconer's *Shipwreck*.[96]

Goya, West and Turner were among many artists who developed the tensions of the marine theme, but it is possible, through Flaxman, to establish links between Romney's infernal ferryman in the drawing *Psyche in Charon's Boat* (Cambridge, Fitzwilliam Museum) and Géricault's *Raft of the Medusa*.[97] Indeed, Woltemad's naked muscular back, like those in Michelangelo and that of a sailor in *The Tempest*, anticipates the epic quality of the French artist's work.[98]

Lashing seas and threatened vessels had an enduring appeal for Romney. In 1794 he imagined, but did not draw, a ship striking the rocks on the Isle of Wight: a moment that 'hit [his] taste'.[99] Gentler resonances arise from the painting *Serena in the Boat of Apathy* (sold Christie's, 17 June 1966) and from *Emma Hart as Calypso* (Waddesdon Manor, The National Trust), this being the name of the nymph upon whose island Ulysses was shipwrecked. Indeed, recording in retrospect his own dealings with 'the greatest siren of the age', Romney has here elaborated the metaphor of his own emotional shipwreck.

His achievements notwithstanding, throughout his life Romney remained sensitive to criticism, as well as secretive and anxious about plagiarism.[100] Wounded by a friend's suggestion that he was thus neglecting his portraiture and indulging 'his vanity in doing things that do not turn to account', Romney groaned: 'O, what a damper!'[101] Despite prodigious industry in some areas of his work, he also had a lifelong tendency towards procrastination. Concerning a group that included *Adam and Eve* (Canada, private collection) and *The Flood* (Stanford, Calif.: University Art Gallery) he wrote how he had 'ideas for them all; and I may say sketches; but, alas! I cannot begin anything for a year or two'.[102] His 'alas!' demonstrates the anguish of delays that left many tentative sketches sleeping 'in oblivion'.[103] Considering his lurching resolve and unsettled patterns of mood, it is extraordinary that he achieved so much.

It is difficult to establish a chronology of stylistic development in Romney's drawings, since he was capable of retaining a method over a long period as well as reverting to old methods; but there are identifiable stages.[104] In the 1770s his drawing produced elegant, calligraphic loops and curves, whereas in the 1780s and 1790s his approach was more frequently that of a robust and slashing attack.[105] Some of the later spontaneous drawings appear childish and scribbled; however, their forms are distilled with greater clarity through the use of pen and wash.[106] One unusual characteristic is the 'almost incredible length, combined with seemingly limitless changes of direction, which his speeding lines possess'.[107]

As 'a closet romantic' in his responses to the supernatural, Romney achieved an 'expressionist abstraction, prophetic of Edvard Munch'.[108] His foreshadowing of various modern masters was to elicit a conscious response earlier this century in the writing of Picasso's friend Apollinaire.[109] Largely through subsequent exhibitions, his drawings have continued to attract admiration for the way in which 'the fluency and ease and the insistent energy of his rapid fire manner make the bulk of [them] fascinating and the best of them brilliant'.[110]

9

Prisons and philanthropy 1790–92

Through many of Romney's friendships and, more privately, in his art there runs the theme of a shared awareness of the misfortune of others. Amidst the swelling wealth of the age, a result of colonial expansion and world trade, there was a growing public awareness of social problems: one object of the Society of Artists' exhibitions in the 1760s was 'for the relief of distressed artists, their widows and children'.[1] During his early childhood Romney had lived near the ducking stool at Cuckstool Farm pond, and Dalton Castle was still used as a debtors' prison. At Kendal, the market place had been a scene of public whippings.[2] In 1764 he noted the hardships of fisherwomen near Dunkirk; he sketched destitute people observed anonymously near Cavendish Square, with 'singular sensibility', and frequently gave extensive alms.[3] Travelling from Sussex in 1793 he noted how 'Deep design, disappointed ambition, envy, hatred, melancholy, disease and poverty' were etched on the faces of the urban population, in contrast to the healthy contentment on the ruddy faces of the Eartham country folk.[4] Such awareness in his pre-Eartham days had led to his exhibiting in 1771 *A Beggar* (England, private collection), described as a work that did 'great honour to the artist', and in Rome he drew an indigent dwarf, *Baiocco* (untraced), named after the coins he begged.[5] In subsequent years his sympathy was reflected in private drawings such as *The Beggar Girl* (Cambridge, Fitzwilliam Museum; Pl. 51) rather than in public canvases, perhaps through the realization that most of his sitters did not share his concern. Pliny's *The Grecian Daughter*, now a play by Arthur Murphy that Romney saw with Reed in 1785, inspired his drawing of the young woman Euphrasia suckling her imprisoned father (Cambridge, Fitzwilliam Museum), a blend of philanthropy and eroticism, in a scene which modestly occurs offstage.[6]

Philanthropically inclined friends and sitters included Jeremiah Meyer, who proposed a pension fund for the Royal Academy; Dr Potter, author of

Observations on the Poor Laws; Bishop Barrington, founder of the Society for the Bettering of the Conditions of the Poor; and Robert Raikes, who provided food and clothing for prisoners at Gloucester.[7] Such social contacts fed Romney's radical politics, which further expressed themselves in his enthusiasm for the early stages of the revolution in France. Among other expressions, the sensibilities of the age found an appeal both social and aesthetic in 'the lyricism of the prison cell'.[8] In Romney's case this initially led him to draw the cartoon *Caius Marcus in his Dungeon* (untraced) some time after 1777, the year of Peter Romney's death and three years after his spell in prison. Numerous artists, including his associates Thomas Banks, Edward Edwards and George Carter, responded to prison subjects that not only make a humanitarian appeal, but also evoke the helplessness of the human condition.[9] Two of the period's finest are Reynolds's *Count Ugolino and his Children* (Knole, The National Trust) of 1770, taken from Dante, and Wright's *The Captive* (Vancouver Art Gallery) from Laurence Sterne's *Sentimental Journey* of 1774. The fullest expression of Romney's own fascination with the subject is in his series of drawings depicting prison visits made by John Howard (1726–90).[10] In 1780, the year Newgate prison was burned by the mob, Hayley published his *Ode to Howard*, illustrated by Bartolozzi's engraving after Romney's first drawing in the series, reminiscent of the *Dying Gaul* sculpture in the Museo Capitolino, Rome.[11]

Howard was a wealthy Bedfordshire landowner who, in researching his book *The State of the Prisons* (1777), travelled 42,000 miles and spent £30,000. This epic project provoked the construction of the first cellular prison by the Duke of Richmond at Horsham in 1775, and prompted John Wesley to hail Howard as one of the greatest men in Europe. With Italian precursors such as Cesare Beccaria, who in 1764 had advocated not only judicial and penal reform but also the abolition of the death penalty, Howard's writing gradually changed public attitudes in Britain.[12] The modest philanthropist rejected Hayley's idea of a portrait by Romney, although he was prepared to make suggestions for Romney's pictorial designs.[13] Howard also vetoed John Warner's scheme for a statue; though in 1796 his cousin Samuel Whitbread II commissioned a monument by John Bacon for St Paul's.[14]

Howard's second book, *An Account of the Principal Lazarettos in Europe* (1789), was written again from harrowing personal experience. Following Howard's death in Russia in 1790, the books evoked a passionate response from Romney, as a huge number of drawings of prisons and pest houses erupted onto paper from the artist's imagination.[15] This followed a more 'sentimental' treatment of the subject produced in 1787 by Francis Wheatley (England, private collection). Romney's series has associations with his concern for artistic emancipation, as well as his awareness of social disparities, and held an especially poignant resonance for followers of Howard, as

51 *The Beggar Girl*, 1780s, 38.1 × 31.7 cm (15.2 × 12.5 in). The carriage and contrasted hats convey a sense of social disparity.

the great man had not only travelled in an infected ship but had actually died in a pest hospital. Romney would also have known the engravings after Piranesi's *Carceri*, a remarkable series of imaginative prison fantasies. It was following the same multiple inspiration that Fuseli produced his *Vision of the Lazar House* (engraving, London, Victoria and Albert Museum), but Romney's designs were never realized on canvas.

52 *John Howard Visiting Prisoners*, 1790s, 35.9 × 49.5 cm (14.1 × 19.5 in). Romney identified strongly with energetic philanthropy of Howard.

There are an estimated five hundred drawings in Romney's series, many of which depict a 'jumbled mass of wretched humanity' looking towards their deliverer (Pl. 52). They stress most powerfully the horror of Howard's exposure of the treatment of half-naked, ill and dying prisoners.[16] From its bulk, the series also demonstrates Romney's belief that 'impressions should be heated and fermented long in the mind'.[17] Apart from the muscular power of jailers bearing large symbolic keys, the drawings are 'notable for the use of silhouette, distortions and overcrowding' and the exposure of the joint housing of men and women, 'an economy which Howard deplored'.[18]

This phenomenal output, the most extensive manifestation of Romney's protoromantic tendencies, was also by far the largest group he produced on a single subject. These drawings have been described as the most 'grandiose, original and complex in Romney's oeuvre', expressing the 'cumulative personal and artistic crisis in his life' as he struggled once more to resolve the complex problems of history painting in a monumental and heroic way. Through the expenditure of colossal amounts of time and energy, he formulated a new mode of feeling, one demonstrating an 'epic romantic style which is more difficult to discern in his other works'.[19] The drawings' characteristic jailer figure is 'surely representing the inherent cruelty of despotism'.

Howard himself, in a virtually Christ-like role, represents 'not only mercy and courage but the power of reason to liberate humanity from suffering'.[20] Unsurprisingly, alongside such aspirations Romney complained of being 'shackled' to portraiture, a metaphor resonating in the gloomy cell of his own mind and one which he shared with William Blake, whose *Urizen* (London, Tate Gallery) is depicted fettered.[21] The notion of being restrained by ropes finds expression in the surviving cartoon on a theme of imprisonment, *Prometheus* (Liverpool, Walker Art Gallery).

Along with a growing movement towards philanthropy, the eighteenth century witnessed a number of challenges to the establishment which derived in part from progressive thinking. In seeking to increase parliamentary power and curb that of the monarchy, the Whig party had an appeal for Romney. This was an element of his relationship with the Duke of Richmond, but he could not afford to alienate patrons of other political persuasions. In general his circle of associates rejoiced with many others at the fall of the Bastille, 'that dreadful building', an event which moved Wedgwood to design commemorative medallions and Blake to write verse.[22] More overt pointers to the politics of Romney's circle are Cumberland's writing of the play *Wat Tyler*, a drama about the leader of the rebellion of 1381, and Hayley's membership of the Revolution Society, for whom he composed verse.[23] Thomas Banks was considered 'a violent democrat'; so too the Rev. John Warner, who, despite having a private chapel in Long Acre and being dubbed 'His Holiness of Barnard's Inn', was particularly 'imbued with revolutionary ideas'.[24] Romney's own work at this period was 'fundamentally conditioned by the French Revolution', although his early biographers were to underplay this aspect of his life, to safeguard his reputation, from the Napoleonic period onwards.[25]

In 1790 from his post as chaplain to Lord Gower, the British Ambassador in Paris, Romney's friend John Warner urged Romney to visit the city and experience directly one of the most cataclysmic political events in the history of modern Europe. Others of Romney's acquaintance had recently observed Paris at first hand. They included Helen Maria Williams (1762–1827), a friend of the great radical writer Thomas Paine (1737–1810); Mary Wollstonecraft (1759–97), who had lived in the French capital from 1788 and whose letters (not to Romney) record events in the city from 1790 to 1795; Adam Walker, who had gone there in 1789; and in the early 1790s, Charles Este's son, who was in Paris to study medicine.[26] On 31 July 1790 Romney, Carwardine and Hayley hired a post coach to Brighton, where they took ship for Dieppe.[27] At this early bloodless period of the revolution they shared the widespread optimism concerning its outcome, being hopeful for the liberty of the French people from tyranny.[28]

Putting up at the Hôtel de Modène, they dined with Lord Gower twice at the embassy in the Hôtel de Monaco. His lordship was the elder son of Romney's major patron, now the Marquis of Stafford, and the half-brother of the smaller dancing children immortalized in *The Gower Children* of 1777 (Pl. IX) – he himself had sat to the artist in 1778. Later, as the Duke of Sutherland, Gower became notorious for his involvement in the Highland clearances, but at this point he too appears to have sympathized with the French revolutionaries. With Gower, Romney and his friends went to view the 'houses of foreign artists', seeking out Greuze who dined with them.[29] Twenty-six years after their first meeting, Greuze was not as celebrated as he had been. Aside from his sentimental portraits of girls, he shared a tendency with Romney in that his genre scenes, for example *The Death of the Paralytic* (St Petersburg, The Hermitage Museum) were infused with explicit moral feeling, in a way reminiscent of Romney's John Howard series.

The other prominent artist Romney encountered was Jacques-Louis David (1748–1825), whose more austere neo-classical style was now in the ascendant. As France's leading history painter, who also painted portraits and had an interest in the theatre, David was already moving in revolutionary circles. He too had been influenced by Winckelmann, and by Mengs and Fuseli in Rome in 1775. The three British visitors dined together with David and toured the Luxembourg gallery. Next Romney visited David's studio in the Louvre, and the public display of several of his paintings including *The Oath of the Horatii* and *The Death of Socrates*, which threw into relief the disparate possibilities for history painters in France and in Britain.[30]

During their visit to Paris, Romney and his travelling companions also met Madame Stéphanie-Félicité de Genlis (1746–1830), writer of *Tales of the Castle* and various volumes on education. Though officially governess to the children of the Duke of Orléans, the cousin of Louis XVI, she was probably also his mistress. Her ability to speak English was a boon for Romney, who still could not speak French. He was also much taken with Madame de Genlis's attractive adopted daughter Pamela. The governess took them to the Duke's seat at Rancy, where Romney toured the Orléans collection for a second time, his guide on this occasion being the Duke's sixteen-year-old son, the Duke of Chartres, who became Louis-Philippe, the last king of France, in 1830. Back in Paris, Romney noted that 'The people are still gay and good humoured but not so fantastic as they were.'[31] The Terror, in which the French revolution destroyed so many of its own begetters, was still three years off.

Crossing the Channel again on 21 August, Romney caught cold; he recuperated at Eartham, deferring sittings for *The Beckford Sisters* (San Marino, Huntington Art Collections).[32] He wrote to Humphry on 18 October that he hoped 'in a little time to be able to resume the functions of my art', which he was to, although the sketchy quality of this delayed picture may relate, like others, to both his psychological and physical health.[33]

The following year, 1791, saw Romney's liaison with a Parisian dancing girl called Thelassie, whose native city he had recently praised as 'a pleasant place to live when a man wishes to dissipate . . . (indeed) one of the most licentious and splendid places in Europe'.[34] In May she wrote requesting money: 'I am glad that you are still in the sentiment of coming to meet me for I think of leaving for Paris the 9th day of June . . . O dear, my life, your Thelassie wishes very much to see you . . . you may be assured of my heart and therefore of my conduct.'[35] Hayley wrote that he would 'promote their passion' if Romney was 'completely in love with this fair rustic Parisian'.[36] He then offered her a domestic situation at Eartham of a rather ambiguous nature.[37] Exactly how long the liaison lasted is not clear, but it coincided with the painting of *John Flaxman Modelling the Bust of William Hayley* (New Haven, Yale Center for British Art; Pl. 16), which indicates that the 'Great Picture' was painted in 1791–2, earlier than the date at present assigned to it.[38] Considering Hayley's apparent role as Pandarus in this liaison and his own unabashed sexually predatory behaviour in his search for a wealthy second wife, it is ironic that his plays such as *Lord Russel* 'sought to persuade theatregoers to a high standard of morality'.[39] It might appear to be inappropriate to blame Hayley entirely, as according to the poet himself Romney had 'as many secretaries as well as [as] many sultanas as an Asiatic Prince'.[40] Thelassie, it appears, was the Frenchwoman much disapproved of by John Romney as he believed her 'meretricious arts entirely supplanted the chaste and coy muse of painting' in his father's life and contributed to the early decline of his creativity.[41]

Also in 1791, the Duke of Orléans displeased the court with his support of the revolutionaries and was exiled to England. He brought Madame de Genlis and Pamela with him and was to become intimate with the Prince of Wales, likewise at that time an associate of Whigs and radicals. In January 1792 Romney belatedly repaid the hospitality he had received in France from Madame de Genlis by beginning portraits of both her and Pamela and attending them to the theatre. Later that year Pamela married Lord Edward Fitzgerald, brother of the Duke of Leinster and friend of Thomas Paine. On 8 November her new husband dramatically renounced his title at a republican dinner near the Petit Palais, in a gesture aimed at the abolition of feudal distinctions.[42] Fitzgerald's belief that insurrection was the only future for his country led to his participation in the Irish rebellion of 1798 and his untimely death in Newgate prison.[43]

A further radical acquaintance of Romney was Charlotte Smith (1749–1806), Hayley's neighbour in Sussex, who struggled to support her children with her pen and whose work has been praised in the twentieth century as 'brisk, ironic and confident'.[44] Smith's *Elegiac Sonnets* (1784) ran to five editions and her novel *Desmond* (1792) was tinged with revolutionary interests and radical attitudes to conventional morality.[45] Her verse refers to melancholy, lunacy and imprisonment and in 1785 she also translated Prévost's *Manon Lescaut*.[46] She met Romney a number of times after 1787, when Hayley promised her on his friend's behalf a drawing of 'a pensive pathetic muse on a rock' as an illustration for her verse. Having unreasonably made such a promise, Hayley used all his bullying charm to extract the sketch: 'I know you would almost as soon be sent into Hell as set about such a task but Coraggio Signor!'[47] The drawing was eventually provided and was engraved by Stothard, who does not acknowledge its origin;[48] it was followed in 1792 by a hasty pastel portrait (untraced). At a dinner for the Friends of the Rights of Man in 1792, both Charlotte Smith and Helen Maria Williams were toasted as 'The Lady Defenders of the Revolution'.[49]

Many of Romney's associates had links with Thomas Paine, who came to sit in June 1792 at the behest of one of his admirers, Thomas Cooper of Manchester.[50] Paine's *Common Sense* had been central to the literature of revolution in America at the time of the colonies' Declaration of Independence. Subsequently he took up the cause of the French revolution, publishing *The Rights of Man*, perceived as a textbook for radicals, in 1791–2. Following four sittings Romney completed *Thomas Paine* (untraced), an unusual smiling portrait which, with its long nose and determined chin, reveals the strength of Paine's character. William Sharp's excellent engraving after the original was described as 'devilish like' (Pl. 53) and Millière's copy is in the National Portrait Gallery. This powerful man, painted by Romney beside manuscripts of his major works *Common Sense* and *The Rights of Man*, is now increasingly accepted as one of the makers of the modern world. He himself famously wrote that 'a share in two revolutions is living to some purpose'.[51]

Thomas Cooper himself (1759–1840) was a versatile radical and a co-founder of the Manchester Constitutional Society with his friend Thomas Walker (1749–1817), a cotton manufacturer. On a visit to France in 1792 he had given a paper in the Hall of the Jacobins, had been awarded the title 'Citizen of France' and had fled from Paris following his involvement in a plot to assassinate Robespierre. Denounced by Burke in Parliament, he published a powerful riposte and in 1794 settled in America, where he became first a judge and then a Professor of Mineralogy.[52] Thomas Walker, another leading Manchester Whig, also sat to Romney for a portrait – later engraved by William Sharp – in 1793, the year before he was acquitted of a charge of treasonable conspiracy.[53] Sharp, who was a member of the Society for Constitutional Information in London, was in turn arrested and narrowly

53 *Thomas Paine* (engraving by William Sharp), 1793, 23 × 19.3 cm (9.1 × 7.6 in). This radical is depicted with manuscripts of two of his major works beside him.

escaped indictment for high treason, for producing for this organization a print entitled *The Declaration of Rights*.[54]

Paine himself was said to be safe only in four houses in London: William Sharp's, Lord Edward Fitzgerald's, Mary Wollstonecraft's and Romney's.[55] As the bookseller Richard Phillips (1767–1840) was jailed in 1793 merely for selling copies of *The Rights of Man*, Romney was here treading a political tightrope, the more so since by 1794 Pitt had established a spy network to suppress radical activity. In communicating effectively with both aristocrats and revolutionaries during this period, it may be that Romney's natural tendency to secrecy helped him to avoid accusations of constitutional disloyalty. Had he been marked as a 'dangerous radical', his sitters would have declined rapidly in numbers. As it was, he had been in fashion now for a remarkable eighteen years, during which time he achieved the bulk of his best work.[56]

Benjamin West, like Romney, experienced divided allegiances as an American who had entertained Paine but who had strong links with the royal family.[57] In walking his own tightrope, Romney took sitters from both sides of the American conflict: Lord George Germain, uncle of the Duke of Dorset, who was Secretary of State for the Colonies from 1779 to 1782, and David Hartley, the radical pamphleteer who in 1783 was selected to negotiate the terms of American independence with his friend Benjamin Franklin.[58] Enduring the rigours of these complex political polarities, in addition to his immense workload, contributed fatally to Romney's premature decline.

In August 1792 there occurred the massacre of Louis XVI's Swiss guard at the Tuileries, a terrible demonstration of the power of the French people following the repudiation of both parliament and king. This event led Romney to identify himself further with the 'Government of Blackguards', writing, 'I hope to God they will prevail.'[59] In October he wrote to his son of the 'Sublimity' of this 'epock in liberty' which 'has interested and agitated me much'.[60] When in late 1792 the bloodshed increased, Romney became disillusioned, and by the time Louis XVI and the Duke of Orléans were guillotined in 1793 he had lost faith in the 'liberalising effect of the Revolution'.[61] Among his own acquaintances Helen Maria Williams was imprisoned as a Girondist, narrowly escaping execution. Madame de Genlis was also to survive, and became Inspector of Schools under Napoleon; her memoirs contain numerous anecdotes of her long life of privilege and intrigue.[62]

During this period many anticipated a 'French tragedy upon the stage of England' if reform were not achieved, but demands for change subsided with the bloodletting.[63] As became a moderate republican and a humanitarian, there was a 'strong Girondin flavour about Romney's (own) ardent temperament'.[64] Both he and Greene abhorred the use of the guillotine; the lawyer was to become involved in assisting aristocrats to flee the Terror.

His descendants still possess a silver loving cup designed by Flaxman and engraved with thanks for his heroism.[65] By 1797, when he was depressed, ill and doubly disillusioned, Romney was recorded by Joseph Farington as believing that 'Monarchy is best after all', though this is certainly a simplification of his views. More accurately he has been described as 'perhaps the British artist most influenced by revolutionary ideas'.[66]

Among the radicals of various shades included in Romney's acquaintance, another potent voice of humanitarianism in a largely uncaring age was that of William Cowper (1731–1800). It was at Eartham, on his annual holiday in August 1792, that Romney met Cowper, the archetypal poet of sensibility, whose poem *The Castaway* is a powerful evocation of the melancholy he, like Romney, both endured for much of his life:

> But I beneath a rougher sea
> And whelm'd in deeper gulphs than he.[67]

Hayley had invited Cowper to Sussex as they were both working on Milton: Hayley on a biography and Cowper on an edition of the verse. The 'Hermit' hoped to 'drive off that depressive spirit of Melancholy' from this new friend. Enticed to travel with his old companion Mrs Unwin, Cowper made his first major journey for twenty-six years to enjoy Hayley's company, the garden, 'silence and retirement in perfection', and to have his likeness taken in pastels by Romney.[68] *William Cowper* (London, National Portrait Gallery; Pl. 54) is a rare work by Romney in this medium, described by the sitter as 'my exact counterpart'. After a delay attributed to 'costive' brains, Cowper responded further with a complimentary sonnet, acknowledging the insight Romney had into their mutual affliction:[69]

> To George Romney Esq.,
> Romney – expert infallibly to trace
> On chart or canvas, not the form alone
> And semblance, but, however faintly shown,
> The mind's impression too on ev'ry face –
> With strokes that Time ought never to erase
> Thou hast so pencill'd mine, that though I own
> The Subject worthless, I have never known
> The Artist shining with superior grace.
> But this I mark – that symptoms none of woe
> In thy incomparable work appear.
> Well – I am satisified it should be so
> Since on maturer thought, the cause is clear;
> For in my looks what sorrow could'st thou see?
> When I was Hayley's guest and sat to thee?[70]

The portrait is indeed a superb late head and one of Romney's finest works; though usually modest with regard to his own performance, the artist

54 *William Cowper*, 1792, 57.5 × 47.5 cm (23 × 19 in). The poet and hymn writer is shown without a wig, his shaven head kept warm by a cap.

himself considered it one of his best.[71] Hayley retained the pastel and instead sent Cowper his own portrait by Romney, an exchange typical of the period.

Cowper's eventual breakdown provided a harrowing version of what Romney feared was in store for himself. In October 1794 the poet's deterioration elicited from him a powerful sympathetic response:

> If there is a blessing in nature above all others, it is when a man recovers his lost reason. And if there is a situation more deplorable than any other in nature it is the horrible decline of reason and the derangement of the power we have been blessed with. How hard it is for a man with a feeling mind to preserve that balance in his understanding that carries him well through life! Bless all those who dedicate their time to the weakness of the human mind.[72]

Painfully conscious of his own frailties, which were compounded by the ramifications of his social, professional and political life, Romney was grateful to those who dedicated their time to his support. His anxious words, ostensibly about Cowper, were a form of self-reassurance or even an implicit prayer. He needed a bulwark of friends and family to protect him from his depression and these words express the anxiety which hovered in and out of his conscious mind. Before he arrived at Eartham in 1792 he wrote that if ever he were 'to worship an allegorical divinity' it would be kindness.[73] Despite the kindness of his friends, like Cowper, he found it increasingly impossible, in his own words above, 'to preserve that balance in his understanding'.

The fall of a rebel angel: years of decline 1793–6

Following the deaths of Gainsborough in 1788 and of Reynolds in 1792, Romney was at the head of his profession. According to Nathaniel Marchant, a friend of Romney's had asked George III in 1792 to appoint him as Portrait Painter to His Majesty; the King had unsurprisingly replied that the vacancy had been filled. Farington maintained that, although Reynolds himself had disdainfully described the post as 'of near dignity to His Majesty's Rat Catcher', Romney, had he been so appointed, would finally have been prepared to exhibit at the Royal Academy.[1]

Despite his more general attainment of fame, there are several reasons why Romney, unlike a number of lesser artists, did not receive many royal commissions. He was not a member of the Academy and had not exhibited there; furthermore he had radical tendencies and did not venture regularly into grand society. In 1773 he had also obtained from the King's brother, the Duke of Gloucester, an introduction to the Pope. This ostensibly useful royal contact was effectively worthless, since by his injudicious marriage Gloucester had become *persona non grata* at court. In 1790, the Duke's son, Prince William of Gloucester (Pl. 34), sat to Romney, followed by his elder sister Princess Sophia in 1791. Other minor members of the royal family did sit to him, however, the first of whom was the Duchess of Cumberland (Los Angeles, J. Paul Getty Museum) in 1788. A subsequent consort of royalty, painted by Romney in 1782, was Lady Augusta Murray, who secretly married the Duke of Sussex in 1793. The Prince of Wales promised to sit, visiting Cavendish Square in 1790 and again with Charles James Fox in 1796.[2] In the event he never did so, either on received advice that Romney's powers were waning, or because of the intervention of John Hoppner, or because of the Prince's own financial problems. At any rate the Prince did buy two Emma Hart pictures, the *Calypso* (Waddesdon Manor, The National Trust) and a *Magdalen* (New York, private collection), paying £300 in debentures for them in May 1796. This sum also covered the fee for *Mrs Fitzherbert* (untraced), a portrait of his mistress, for which payment had been overdue since 1789.

Reynolds's death also significantly increased the number of patrons sitting to Romney, who in April 1793 wrote to his brother James, 'I have no time to go in quest of pleasure to prevent a decline in health. My hands are full and I shall be forced to refuse new faces... There is a delight in the novelty, greater than the profit gained by sending them home finished, but it must be done.'[3]

Apart from his consciousness of being more burdened by portraiture than usual, there was a growing awareness of the success of the new generation of rivals: William Beechey (1753–1839), John Hoppner (1758–1810) and Thomas Lawrence (1769–1830). Beechey had exhibited since 1776, was elected ARA in 1793 and was to be elected RA and knighted in 1798, the year of his ambitious *A Review of the Horse Guard with King George III and the Prince of Wales*. Hoppner had received royal favour from 1785 and in 1789 was appointed Portrait Painter to the Prince of Wales. Having success with the members of the Prince's set, he was elected ARA in 1792 and RA in 1795. Of the three, it was the youngest, Thomas Lawrence, who was to be the most significant both in Romney's lifetime and afterwards, following his major success with *Queen Charlotte* (London, National Gallery) in 1790. In his process of self-instruction he may have visited Romney's studio and was deeply influenced by the older artist.[4] Lawrence's strong sense of colour, loose handling, racing skies and brilliant drapery all have their antecedents in Romney's work. He was young to be elected ARA in 1791, but this reflects his precocious yet powerful talent, which reached its greatest expression in the Waterloo Chamber portraits (Windsor, Royal Collection).

It was also in the early 1790s that Romney's life began to show the opposing pull of nearly unmatched success on the one hand, and on the other the approach of decline and retirement. He had schemes in mind for helping young artists. He also cherished desires as a collector. By now he possessed a small collection of casts after the antique, including the work of John Flaxman Senior. In the early 1790s he planned the expansion of this collection, to form 'one of the finest museums in London for antique sculpture'.[5] For years Romney had hankered after owning a significant group of casts, partly from the wish to make such a collection available to others. This project was the more worthwhile in public terms, since in 1791 fire had destroyed the Duke of Richmond's collection and the Royal Academy still did not hold many good-quality casts. Despite Romney's present affluence, he decided he could not afford genuine antiquities to match collections such as those of Paul Methuen, Sir Roger Newdigate, Lord Lansdowne and Charles Townley, but settled for new casts to be ordered from Italy.[6] John Flaxman Junior was currently visiting Rome, and, having confidence in his judgement, Romney sent him £100 with which to obtain some representative examples.

Accordingly, on 12 September 1792, Flaxman despatched in ten large cases from Leghorn 'the cream of the finest things in Rome', including casts of the Apollo Belvedere, the Laocoön, a colossal bust of Minerva, Cupid and Psyche, Apollo as the python-killer and a bas relief of Niobe's children.[7] His choice included several of the most famous works in Italy, and furthermore expressed the tension between neo-classical and protoromantic fashion. Romney acknowledged how valuable these figures would be to him, as even now he found himself 'very deficient in the knowledge of that kind of muscular character which is . . . of so much use in historical pictures'.[8]

A rare burst of 'huzzas' broke from him when, on 4 November 1794, he heard of Flaxman's own imminent arrival from Italy.[9] On returning, as a token of esteem, the sculptor presented his friend with a Campagna-shaped vase carved with the Three Graces.[10] Romney was further delighted when the sculptor moved into a house in Fitzroy Square, not far from his own. Soon thereafter, gaining access to Flaxman's outline drawings of subjects from Homer and Aeschylus, he wrote that he had 'caught a portion of his soul' from them, a light which dissipated some of his 'thick gloom'.[11] In addition to the glories of Flaxman's sculpture evident in his *Aphrodite* and *St Michael Slaying Satan* (Petworth House, The National Trust), these designs were to have a great impact upon Ingres and Delacroix.[12]

The arrival of the casts overtaxed his already cluttered accommodation, so that it was not possible for them all to be displayed effectively.[13] He nonetheless gained immense satisfaction from setting them up in his gallery, as a step towards establishing a 'domestic academy'. Their arrival prompted his aspiration for a larger gallery to be built to his own specifications.[14]

Using candelabra, lamps and reflectors, Romney experimented meanwhile by shedding light on the casts from different directions, blurring the distinction between flesh and plaster and seeking illusions of perfection.[15] Dramatic candlelight effects had long appealed to him, and at night he would sit silently, alone or with friends, rapturously admiring his favourite casts. This recreation was effectively recorded, albeit with different protagonists, in Wright's *Academy by Candlelight* (New Haven, Yale Center for British Art).

Early in 1792 Romney had also expressed a need for a larger painting room, where he planned to make available to young artists the study facilities he had lacked in his youth. By November he was in treaty for a piece of ground two to three miles from London. Supervising such studies and sharing his expertise would have given him something interesting to do when he was no longer able to paint himself; once again, the pressure of existing work ensured that the scheme was not realized.[16] In April 1793 he wrote to his brother James that he sought air and exercise, and later in the year he complained that the city had 'an unpleasant effect upon his senses'.[17] It was now further to walk to the fields and he compensated by taking trips out to the Assembly Room at Kilburn Wells, three miles from Cavendish Square, to drink tea.

On a visit to Kilburn in June 1793 Romney discovered Pine Apple Place, a new villa on the Kilburn Wells Road, where he arranged with the nurseryman tenant to take breakfast for seven and sixpence a week as a break from the bustle and smog of the city. The name of the exotic fruit was set high on the building around which bloomed 'flowers in perfection'.[18] Here, with eight fine children to wait on him and 'soften the steps down declining life', he made numerous domestic sketches.[19] On one visit the children were in tears as their father was in debt for £200. Much to their relief and delight, with customary generosity, Romney paid the sum directly.[20]

In 1794 Romney was seeking further retirement and in July revived his 'contemplation of a little academy next winter in the room under my gallery . . . when each can set his figures, as suits him, and with the quiet of only three persons'.[21] By November he was expressing his excitement that his academy would soon be available for Tom Hayley and 'another promising young artist'.[22] The notion of this project persisted until 1797, but he was never able to attain his goal on the scale for which he had hoped.[23]

In his latter years Romney gradually withdrew from portraiture and became increasingly preoccupied with a late series of commemorative paintings, a series of drawings related to the writings of John Milton, and a group of drawings entitled *The Seven Ages of Man*. Of these late works, those that reached the canvas tend to display more sombre colours, broader, coarser handling and signs of a failing control of the brush.[24]

The eighteenth century in Britain saw a special value placed on commemorating moral exemplars and exalted talents. In part this was inspired by the customs and values of ancient Rome, and led to a widespread fashion for series of related portraits and busts. Outstanding series include the literary heroes depicted in the Rotunda at Vauxhall Gardens and the sequence of busts in the Library at Trinity College, Dublin. Hayley's own library contained one such collection of literary busts and Thomas Sheridan's sitting room at Quilca, north-west of Dublin, was decorated with literary medallions.[25] Romney himself planned to paint large canvases depicting scenes from the lives of John Milton, Sir Isaac Newton, Sir Francis Bacon and Sir Christopher Wren. It was to be a late gesture towards some of the great cultural heroes of the past, occupied as he had largely been with the living.[26]

The first canvas in this series was *John Milton Dictating to his Daughters* (England, private collection; Pl. XVI) which shows the poet in the later stages of his blindness. Romney himself by now wore bifocal spectacles, an invention of Benjamin Franklin, and suffered growing anxiety for his own sight;

indeed, the scoring on later sheets of drawings may indicate his inability to spot graphite worn down to the wood.[27] In this composition Milton is shown seated, with his daughters at a table beside him. Historically this is inaccurate, as they were both illiterate and the poet used a different amanuensis.[28] Strongly evoking the power of inspiration, the illuminated pallor of Milton's face contrasts greatly with the background shadow, a chiaroscuro effect also evident in a drawing relating to this canvas (Cambridge, Fitzwilliam Museum) which shows the poet with a leg thrown over the arm of the chair, as he was described in Dr Johnson's biography.[29] The painting was completed by the autumn of 1793 and bought, upon the advice of Charles James Fox, by the brewer Samuel Whitbread II, who had just come into his inheritance.[30] Whitbread's father had, in the late 1780s, commissioned Romney to paint portraits of his employees Mr Delafield and Mr Yellowby. His son, who sat to Romney while he was at Eton, was, with Lord Egremont, one of the first patrons to profess the aim of collecting only British art. It was precisely such patronage of which Hogarth had dreamed; in Romney's circle it had been urged by Richard Cumberland for many years.[31] Whitbread, a cousin of John Howard, was to strike up friendships with a number of other reformers including William Wilberforce. As commemorative prints were very marketable, in 1797 George Nicol paid the artist £50 from the Boydells to have an engraving taken from the Milton painting.

In 1792, Romney was also making a series of 'secret' designs from Milton's *Paradise Lost*. His anxiety that his strength and talent were deserting him stands in contrast to the physical and psychological strength of Satan, 'the arch-apostate', who was already associated by the press with Romney's portrait of Thomas Paine.[32] Both Hayley, as a biographer of Milton, and Cumberland had suggested the subject of Satan, whom Romney eventually conceived as a 'powerful but beatific guardian angel', nowhere nearing 'the bestial fiend of conventional theology'. This paradox turns on the name 'Lucifer', a source of light, given to him in medieval drama.[33] Regrettably, Romney's numerous designs were never realized in oil. His *Satan Summoning his Host* and *Expulsion from Paradise* (both Cambridge, Fitzwilliam Museum) did, however, have several close parallels in the work of Fuseli, whose Milton Gallery opened in 1799, as 'an implicitly social and political project under the aegis of the great blind republican himself'.[34]

Elsewhere in the series, *The Fall of the Rebel Angels* (Cambridge, Fitzwilliam Museum; Pl. 55) echoes the artist's fascination with revolution, suggests his largely hidden defiance against unjust authority and evokes elements of Michelangelo's *Last Judgement*. It seethes with figures centred on the shield-bearing figure of Satan about to be 'Hurl'd headlong, flaming from the ethereal sky'.[35] Satanic themes of this kind, together with the allegory of Prometheus and the subject of imprisonment, as used in the *Howard* series, served as a common ground on which Romney's neo-classical idealism could merge with his political radicalism.[36] In this, during the closing years of the century, he was not alone. Thomas Banks, a fellow radical, under suspicion at the time of the trial for treason of Horne Tooke, produced in 1794 his own artistic parallel in his *Falling Titan* (London, Royal Academy). Satan appears in several of Blake's works, while his *Last Judgement* (Petworth House, The National Trust), has a crowded design which is directly reminiscent of Romney's *The Fall of the Rebel Angels* (Pl. 55). Devils also freely inhabit Blake's texts as metaphors of oppression, in the same way that Romney would be beset on his melancholy days by a 'legion of blue devils', a notion which gave rise to Tom Hayley dubbing him 'the Admiral of the Blues'.[37] Despite the energy of these drawings, his portrait practice was in terminal decline, which created an intense polarization of his interests.

Descriptions of the acquaintance between Romney and Blake, fellow artistic spirits, are many if oblique. Soon after Romney's death, Blake reported Braithwaite's description of the medallion portrait of Romney by Tom Hayley (Chichester, Record Office; Pl. 56), a fine strong profile, as 'the most exact resemblance'.[38] Blake's own drawing of Romney (untraced), although almost certainly not taken from life, was also said by Mrs Flaxman to be a good likeness.[39] Blake hoped to make the engraving after this drawing 'a Supernaculum', but although proofs intended for Hayley's 1809 biography were sent to the author, it was never used.[40] Romney and Blake each had a high regard for the other's art, despite Blake's general dismissal of portraitists.[41] In 1784, when Blake was only twenty-seven, Flaxman wrote that 'Mr Romney thinks Blake's historical drawings rank with those of Michelangelo.'[42] Blake reciprocated with the remark that 'Romney's drawings should be "engraved by the hands of angels".'[43] He was not prompted by mere sycophancy: Romney in several ways anticipated Blake's style and iconography, and both artists held motifs with Fuseli and Flaxman as a 'common property'.[44] Romney comes 'close to the spirit of Blake' in the musculature of his naked torsos and in such inspiration as the bearded figure in *Providence Brooding over Chaos* (Cambridge, Fitzwilliam Museum), and his aerial forms above the ship in *The Tempest* (Pl. 42).[45]

Romney's friends in general were described by Blake as 'amiable like himself'. In particular they had common bonds in the acquaintance of Paine and, through Adam Walker, with Priestley. From 1800 to 1803 Blake also enjoyed Hayley's patronage in Sussex. Eventually, though, he became frustrated with the Hermit's tendency to meddle, and wrote, 'As a poet he is frightened at me and as a painter his views and mine are opposite; he thinks he'll turn me into a portrait painter like poor Romney, but this he nor all the devils in hell will never do.'[46] He did however, co-operate further with Hayley in his biography of Romney by tracking down paintings, including

55 *The Fall of the Rebel Angels*, early 1790s, 54 × 39 cm (21.2 × 15.2 in). A great sense of scale is achieved in this vigorous, uneven study.

56 Thomas Hayley, *Portrait of George Romney*, c.1796, 13.9 cm diameter (5.5 in). This profile shows the artist's prominent nose, receding chin and downturned mouth.

those owned by Walker and Braithwaite.[47] He also drew and engraved Romney's lost drawing of *The Shipwreck at the Cape of Good Hope* (London, British Museum), which appears in the same volume and which he called 'the noblest of his studies'.[48] Notwithstanding a tendency to hyperbole, he was not exaggerating his admiration when, proud of this work, he declared that Romney's 'spiritual aid has not a little conduced to my restoration to the light of art'.[49]

Miltonic infernal metaphor had come to pervade Romney's mood, however. Following one physical illness, he described the experience as if 'some fiend presided' and complained that 'the tyranny of the disease was terrible for four days'.[50] He was increasingly worried about his health, complaining of 'lassitude' and, writing in April 1793, he observed 'my hand is weak and trembles'.[51] Possibly this arose from his first small paralytic stroke; poor circulation may indeed have afflicted him for years as he tended to require his studio to be 'immoderately hot'.[52]

During a visit to Eartham in summer 1793 he was chiefly intent upon consolidating his health by dint of 'air and exercise' and drawing took a second place.[53] However, although his summer drawings tended to languish forgotten once he had returned to London, in 1793 he did produce his canvas *Boys on a Seashore* (United States of America, private collection) which may have originated from an outdoor sketch made in Sussex. Though ostensibly this is a nostalgic portrayal of the joys of childhood, one of the boys is dramatically lit against a forbidding black breaker, a metaphor of the abyss, in a work described as 'one of the most remarkable paintings produced in Britain in the 1790s'.[54]

From 1793, he also persisted with a series entitled *The Seven Ages of Man*, related not to Shakespeare so much as to the busts of Romney (old age), Flaxman (middle age) and Tom Hayley (youth) at Eartham.[55] Prominent in the group is old age, as discussed by the angel in *Paradise Lost*:

> I perceive
> Thy mortal sight to fail; objects divine
> Must needs impair and weary human sense . . .
> [And] ye may live, which will be many days,
> Both in one faith unanimous, though sad,
> With cause for evils past; yet much more cheer'd
> With meditation on the happy end.[56]

For the artist these lines held irony, spoken as they were to Adam and Eve as a couple. Apart from the onset of old age, Romney's own meditations upon death held the additional frustrations of his being effectively single and isolated. Conscious of his own frailty, by 1794 Romney was writing of Tom Hayley becoming a great sculptor 'when I am looking down from the stars'.[57] In the same year he wrote that he was 'now without a friend here that I dare speak to', an exaggeration that demonstrates the irrationality visitors now had to deal with.[58] Some friends were loyal until his departure north and afterwards, but it was nonetheless loyalty maintained at a distance.

This may explain the relative intensity of the 'last considerable picture' he painted at Eartham in August 1794. *The Four Friends* (Kendal, Abbot Hall Art Gallery) is a group portrait of Hayley, Tom Hayley, William Meyer and Romney himself.[59] Hayley deemed this symbolic and romantic work 'sacred to friendship', as indeed is indicated by the copy of Cicero's *On Friendship* which lies on the table before them. The group relates closely to *Flaxman*

Modelling Hayley's Bust (New Haven, Yale Center for British Art; Pl. 16) where Hayley's costume recalls 'the prototype of the classical orator'.[60] The dramatic lighting and the exaggerated size of the sitter and his bust in the latter painting, not only provide 'an analogue to Romney's mental frenzy', but successfully merge romantic feeling and classical form.[61] A poignant resonance in *The Four Friends* was that both William's father and his brother, Charles Meyer, were dead, the latter having shot himself in Calcutta in 1793. The two older men had, since 1787, been surrogate fathers to William, who was now an undergraduate at Trinity. Tom Hayley was in fact absent when this painting was done, being in London, and his likeness was obtained via a drawing by the portraitist Henry Howard (1769–1847).[62]

Later in 1794 Romney was still under pressure from sitters, though his response was largely directed at completing pictures rather than beginning anew. His new appointments were tailing off and by September his only sitters were his friend Francis Newbery and Mr Abraham Newland, chief cashier of the Bank of England. His popularity remained intact but now for the first time he was turning down new sitters, being too chronically depressed to deal with the necessary pleasantries of the studio. Meanwhile, existing appointments had to be cancelled, and his sitters book bears references to sending for sitters 'when Master is well'. Romney's decline was not a steady one: in May 1794 he reported that he had reached four and a half out of five stages of recovery.[63] However, in August, John Romney was summoned from Cambridge by his friend Dr Henry Ainslie, who had been very concerned to find the artist 'in a disturbed state'.[64]

He had accumulated an immense unsaleable stock of unfinished paintings, which were propped in every corner of the studio at Cavendish Square and even obstructed the passages.[65] Young Tom Hayley noted in 1795 how inundated Romney was with incomplete portraits, reporting to his father that 'portrait painting knocks him up'.[66] The resultant financial losses were not entirely his fault as gentlemen were generally reluctant to pay for portraits of divorced wives or rejected mistresses, and many lady sitters were dead, divorced or dismissed 'before he would bestow half-an-hour's pains on their petticoats' to complete them.[67] Several only lacked a few brushstrokes, but the size of the backlog oppressed him into a state of inaction. Eventually, in Hayley's words, he fell 'like a Titan overwhelmed by the mountainous fragments that he had piled upon himself'.[68] Many portraits thus languished for years in the studio. *Viscount Wellesley*, an Eton leaving portrait, was begun in 1781 and not sent to Eton until 1791.[69] *Mr and Mrs Wogan Browne* (sold Sotheby's, 21 October 1987) was commenced in 1787, but as he had never been pressed to finish it, the portrait was not collected until 1805, three years after Romney's death. By the time *Jeremiah Milles* (San Marino, Huntington Art Collections) arrived at the sitter's home, Milles himself was on his deathbed. His widow confined the crate in an attic for forty-nine years.[70] Several history paintings, including *Cupid and Psyche* and *Joan of Arc*, both now lost, were likewise unfinished.[71] Mislaid props or the difficulties of obtaining animal models, such as the wolves for *Emma Hart as Circe*, also conspired to thwart completion. Even child models generated problems, as one died and another was dismissed for misbehaviour.[72] Although Romney usually avoided using drapery men, and refused to let his pupils touch a canvas, several works were eventually finished by other artists, including John Hoppner, Michael Keeling, Martin Archer Shee and Thomas Stewardson.[73] A few survive in an incomplete state; *The Misses Hill* (private collection), which was in the studio sale, is notable for the exquisite head of one of its girl subjects.

Despite the erratic patterns of Romney's health, a painting to celebrate Isaac Newton's achievement was the next goal. He was acquainted with 'the principles of mathematical science', and had an interest in the related disciplines.[74] It was still possible in his lifetime for a well-educated individual to be conversant with developments in most areas of knowedge. Romney himself had already written of 'the great light that is thrown on all the sciences, the extraordinary industry of the men in that line and our superiority to all nations'.[75] In 1789, he and Carwardine had heard their friend Walker lecture publicly at Covent Garden; Walker had been encouraged to do so by Joseph Priestley, for whom he had designed at least one demonstration model.[76] For himself, Walker built an orrery to demonstrate Newton's theory of the universe. Such lectures are paralleled by Joseph Wright's depiction of a natural philosopher lecturing on the orrery (Derby, Museum and Art Gallery).[77] Walker's expertise was wide: he had designed rotatory lights for St Anne's lighthouse on the Scilly Isles, and had sold one version of his own celestina, a modification for the harpsichord, to Thomas Jefferson, the American statesman, who described it as 'a divine thing'.[78] He had also experimented with steam power and thermo-ventilation and had written an early study of air pollution. In 1791 he was with Priestley, known as a radical dissenter, on the day the great chemist's house was destroyed by a 'church and king' mob.[79] Like Romney, his old Troutbeck friend sometimes trod a precarious political path, but was nonetheless sufficiently highly regarded to be hailed as 'the celebrated Adam Walker'.[80]

As a great colourist, Romney would have been fascinated by the understanding of colour established through Newton's spectrum analysis, a parallel of the magic of an artist's palette. In *Newton Displaying the Prismatic Colours* (England, private collection), Romney set out not only to demonstrate the science of colour but also to indicate the close relationship perceived in the eighteenth century between the natural sciences and the visual arts.[81] In his composition, the rainbow colours of the spectrum are projected onto a wall, 'in many a hue divine', to the astonishment of one of the scientist's attendants.[82] With his concern for likeness, Romney defied the late Sir Joshua's strictures and used Newton's death mask for his principal subject's face.[83] Though harshly described as 'a late and deplorable work', this painting is important as a unique manifestation of the artist's broader interests.[84] Scientific curiosity was widely associated, not without reason, with moral and political dissent; some indeed saw current circles of its enthusiasts as 'breeding grounds for radical politics'.[85] The painting was probably started in 1795, but it was as late as 1799 that Romney repainted one of the girls' faces and spoiled his work, a defect later made good by another hand. Newton was depicted at this time by numerous artists, including Blake, whose painting of the scientist in profile, holding compasses (London, Tate Gallery), was likewise executed in 1795. Blake also produced *Milton Composing with Newton Looking On*, a juxtaposition of the two great men already painted by Romney, which suggests another link between them.

Sir Francis Bacon and Sir Christopher Wren, Romney's other two projected subjects, were probably not even sketched. Bacon, the great polymath, whose example inspired the foundation of the Royal Society, was to be represented engaged in his fatal refrigeration experiment, stuffing a fresh chicken with snow. Wren was to be seated, contemplating his major achievement under the dome of St Paul's cathedral. The last great portrait he actually completed was *Warren Hastings* (London, India Office Library).[86] A former Governor General of India, Hastings sat in 1795, the year of his acquittal following charges of corruption. The portrait can be seen as one in which Romney's own chronic unhappiness enhanced his insight into mature character, for Hastings, like Romney, had stoically endured both triumph and disaster.

In spring 1796, following another winter bout of illness and depression, Romney wrote that he felt 'like one escaped from an enchantment', a slightly paranoid description that has led some readers to doubt his sanity.[87] But the impact of Romney's metaphorical dark fiend may be best likened to the 'black dog' of Sir Winston Churchill's melancholia, an evil presence which only temporarily affected his ability to function.[88] Indeed, the seasonal component in his melancholy suggests a proximity to Scandinavian 'cabin fever', now known as seasonal affective disorder.

Having fondly followed the progress of the precocious Tom Hayley through the young man's apprenticeship to Flaxman, Romney was to describe his sculpture as 'of a pure gusto'.[89] The Eartham visits had spanned Tom's childhood, so that Romney came in time to write that Tom 'had grown into my mind as a relative'.[90] In London, busy though Tom was in studying and running errands for his father, Romney remained to him 'the really great man whom it delights me to visit'.[91] Tom's medallion portrait of the artist (Pl. 56) is evidence of the boy's considerable ability, which was hampered by a painful disease of the spine.[92] His sweet disposition brought comfort to his worried father, who described the disabilities of both his son and the ailing Romney with considerable sensitivity.[93]

In late December 1796, Sawrey Gilpin reported that his fellow artist was 'past the time of new and great exertions', and the work on Romney's easel was his 'last' painting, *The Walker Family* (London, National Portrait Gallery).[94] In this group, his old friend Adam, his wife Eleanor and their adult children are depicted with tokens of his life in science: a mathematical drawing, a telescope, and his published volume on astronomy. The unfinished portrait group was much appreciated by the gentle, white-haired patriarch, who later praised it as 'the great lion of my parlour'.[95]

In fact Romney's last painting was probably the climactic retelling of *The Temptation of Christ*, an ambitious work taken from the fourth book of Milton's *Paradise Regained*, for which several drawings survive (Cambridge, Fitzwilliam Museum; New Haven, Yale Center for British Art; Washington, DC, Folger Shakespeare Library). Like *The Fall of the Rebel Angels*, the subject involves numerous supernatural figures, including Satan, in this case attempting to distract Christ with wealth, glory and political triumph. Begun in oil on a large canvas in 1796, it showed the defenceless Christ alone and assailed by boisterous and noisy fiends:

> Infernal ghosts, and hellish furies round
> Environed thee; some howled, some yelled, some shrieked
> Some bent at thee their fiery darts, while thou
> Sat'st unappalled in calm and sinless peace.[96]

This painting, which may be viewed as a parallel of Romney's own social isolation and moral struggle, soon became another victim of his physical deterioration.[97] Only the head of Christ was salvaged for posterity, having been engraved by A. Raimbach for Hayley's biography; the canvas was last seen by Blake, in 1803, rolled up in the workshop of Saunders, Romney's frame maker.[98]

These late religious subjects were not the only sacred paintings he produced. Despite his tendency not to attend church, according to Hayley he would often look heavenwards and 'read in the skies, with a contemplative and devout spirit, both the power and beneficence of God'.[99] In his earlier years he had painted a *Holy Family, Tobias and Tobit* and *Susannah and the Elders* (all untraced). However, numerous designs remain including *Head of King Saul* (Cambridge, Fitzwilliam Museum; Pl. 57), *Samson Overpowered* (New Haven, Yale Center for British Art; Pl. 4), *Adam and Eve* (Canada, private collection), *The Descent from the Cross* (Montreal, Museum of Fine Arts) and *Christ in Glory* (Cambridge, Fitzwilliam Museum).[100] One notable drawing is *The Holy Spirit Moving on the Face of the Waters* (Cambridge,

Fitzwilliam Museum), which relates to the painting *Providence Brooding over Chaos* (untraced), executed in Rome.[101] However, after the débâcle of the King's College altarpiece project, Romney tended to be more enthusiastic about Milton than the Bible as a source of religious inspiration.[102]

By 1796, Romney had lost many members of his family and numerous friends, and once again thought of death, writing 'my prospect of future life grows dreary'.[103] He also planned drawings to show an alchemist in quest of the philosopher's stone. His own quest for perfection and the alchemy of his own career had conjured many unparalleled images into being. As an allegory of thwarted hopes, this concept nonetheless parallels his largely frustrated desire to be a history painter and echoes the disastrous explosion of the crucible of his Dalton mentor, John Williamson. Romney also conceived the Faust-like motif of yet another fiend or devil.[104] An equally pejorative metaphor is found in *The Flood* (Cambridge, Fitzwilliam Sketchbook), in the form of Noah's ark (New Haven, Yale Center for British Art). As Dr Johnson had observed, being in a ship was like being in jail with the chance of being drowned. In this recapitulation of two of Romney's favourite subjects, the prison and the shipwreck, the ark, as both a haven and a prison, intimates the material and psychological duality of his portraiture.[105]

Though Romney had expressed a desire to 'wrap himself in retirement', his feelings were ambivalent; though only sixty years old and certainly wealthy enough to retire, he somehow could not bring himself to make such a decision. It was at this time that he began to produce designs for *The Seven Ages of Man* series, one of which he called 'the grandest that has been thought of', but adding 'if my name was mentioned I should hear nothing but abuse and that I cannot bear. Fear has always been my enemy. My nerves are too weak for supporting anything in public.'[106]

Though his portrait practice had almost ceased, his working life had regained some impetus through the patronage of the connoisseur Earl of Egremont, a friend and benefactor praised for his 'liberal hand and feeling heart' by, among others, Charlotte Smith.[107] As well as providing J.M.W. Turner in his later years with a studio at Petworth, the Earl was to maintain a lifelong respect for Romney's ability, and as late as 1834 he made a point of buying *Mirth and Melancholy* (Petworth, The National Trust) from the Reverend John Romney's sale.[108] In the spring of 1795, Lord Egremont called at Cavendish Square to propose that Romney should paint a picture of his mistress, Miss Elizabeth Iliffe, known as 'Mrs Wyndham', with their four children.[109] As Hayley was godfather to one of the Egremont boys, Romney knew the family well and dined regularly as the guest of the Earl and Miss Iliffe.[110] At Eartham that summer, Romney made a daily walk of ten miles over the downs to execute the portrait at Lord Egremont's great house at

57 *A Head of King Saul*, 1776–7, 43.8 × 31.1 cm (17.2 × 12.2 in). A noble study for a composition of David playing his harp to Saul.

Petworth, whose treasures included a van Dyck collection described by one near contemporary as 'the finest in the world'.[111]

In *The Egremont Family* (Petworth House, The National Trust), the sitters are placed in the open air at dusk. The elder boys are aiming their arrows at a bat, a slightly sinister protoromantic element echoing Romney's preoccupation with *A Midsummer Night's Dream*. Archery was furthermore one of the leisure pursuits of the Hayleys and Romney at Eartham, while Thomas Greene was a 'Prince of Archers'.[112] A further odd feature is the awkward angle of Miss Iliffe's head as she reclines in apprehension of the flying devils. Other bats appear in one of his *A Midsummer Night's Dream* series of paintings, *Titania's Attendants Chasing Bats* (Florida, private collection) as the fairy queen is falling asleep to the fairies' unusual lullaby 'You spotted snakes', from Act II. Related metaphors recur in his language as he described the Egremont children as 'my elves and fairies' and referred to the 'innocent little sprites' at Pine Apple Place. *The Egremont Family* was not a success, but it has 'beautiful passages of colour' and its execution evidently gave the artist some pleasure.[113]

'An owl in the desert' 1796–1802

Apprehensive of retirement and the likely loss of motivation, Romney was all too aware of his flagging energies. In June 1795 he wrote: 'I am going to decline business . . . and then build me a house which I hope will inspire me with new vigour . . . I have still the same passion for art.'[1] At the end of the same month he continued, 'I am still unsettled where and when I shall fix my first stone, and make my gravel walks and plant my cedars; but to build my house and to plant my cedars I am determined.'[2]

Though Adam Walker believed that Romney had 'laid aside all schemes of pastoral felicity' by moving to London, his friend continued to hanker for fresh air and in 1788 had experimented with sleeping in lodgings at Hampstead, three miles north of Cavendish Square.[3] Other artists such as West had long ago established themselves in a 'country box', the better to avoid the harassment of life in the city, the noise of which, for Romney, had long had 'an unpleasant effect upon (his) senses'.[4]

Aware of his friend's restlessness, in 1788–90 Hayley had urged Romney in vain to build a 'picturesque cottage' in Sussex near the sea.[5] This suggestion was not taken up, but the idea of a new home continued to develop in his imagination. Indeed, Romney's aspirations survive in tangible form as numerous drawings of fantastic buildings for a variety of other sites (England, private collection). These are a late echo of the metaphorical 'castles in the air' he conceived in his youth at High Cocken.[6] He even referred to building a theatre, evidence enough to justify John Romney's anxiety that his father was becoming irrational and liable to dissipate his patrimony.[7] Another crazy scheme was to build a house on the Edgware Road, not far from where Emma Hart had lived with Greville, which would have reverted to the ground landlord on the artist's death. With necessary tact, in October 1796 John extricated his father from this 'ruinous project'. He persuaded him instead to buy some land and an old property called The Mount, on Holly Bush Hill at Hampstead, for £700.[8]

The village of Hampstead, set on a hillside amid commons, oak woods and parkland, had become a popular place of recreation by the late eighteenth century. Visitors took the chalybeate waters of its wells and enjoyed opportunities for dancing, music and gambling. The Bull and Bush at North End was a popular meeting place for artists, and Romney dined regularly at the Hampstead Long Room, which was decorated with pictures of the nine muses.[9] Several of his associates and sitters had houses there, including Josiah Boydell and William Beckford.

Financially, The Mount seemed a safe option, though eventually Romney did spend more than his son had anticipated. Initially, he leased the house itself to Mr Thomas Rundell, a member of the firm of silversmiths Rundell, Bridges and Rundell, who realized in silver several of Flaxman's designs. He then had the stable demolished and on its site he erected 'a whimsical structure' consisting of a large studio, a curious series of smaller rooms and a few domestic conveniences, together with a vast eighteen-foot-high picture and cast gallery.[10] A virtually hidden marble staircase enabled visitors to arrive or depart incognito: an architectural parallel of his secretiveness. He was the first artist to live in the village, and this unusual dwelling reflects in its design his quirky character. On completion it was known as Prospect House, so named because it had a 'magnificent view of the metropolis' from windows and balconies, which also looked over Hampstead Heath.[11] This was the finest panorama Romney had lived with since he left his parental home more than forty years earlier. As a valetudinarian, this was tellingly a pleasure that he could enjoy 'without moving from his pillow'.[12]

Today, as Romney's House, it still retains much of the artist's original conception.[13] As with other nearby properties at this time, although the interior structure was of brick and in places even marble, the exterior is clad with white-painted weatherboarding, which caused it to be described in Farington's diary as 'a quaint wooden house'.[14] Maintaining his concern for exercise, Romney had part of the garden covered in to provide a riding house.[15]

The gallery was undoubtedly the *raison d'être* of the project and was built in keeping with current fashion, with pilasters bearing Ionic capitals. It reflected several comparable structures Romney had known: in London at Richmond House, in Rome at the Villa Albani, and more recently at Udney House, in the fashionable riverside village of Teddington. Here in 1796 Romney had visited the Adam-designed gallery built by the West India merchant Robert Udney, brother of his old acquaintance John, the consul.[16] At Prospect House the elegant pilasters of the new gallery effectively comprised a series of frames in which large sculptures might be displayed. A similar arrangement existed in the Cortile del Belvedere in the Vatican, where Romney had gone to see the Laocoön.[17] It enclosed a volume of space approaching that of Walpole's extensive gallery at Strawberry Hill, and one large enough to include an interior balcony offering a different perspective of his cast collection.[18]

The architect for Prospect House was a pupil of James Wyatt named Samuel Bunce, whom Flaxman had met in Rome. He began work for Romney in August 1796, probably on the Edgware Road scheme. At the same time he was helping to realize Hayley's conception and design of a modest marine villa at Felpham, to which he would remove from Eartham, a change necessitated by a lifetime of incorrigible extravagance.[19] Having also been appointed architect to the Admiralty in this year, Bunce was clearly over-committed, and although Hayley described him as 'little Palladio', by the summer of 1797 Romney was sufficiently dissatisfied to have sacked him.[20] Henceforth the artist supervised the workmen himself. Having formerly assisted his father as a builder, and being acquainted with the principles of architecture, his experience enabled him 'to construct every part of the building'.[21]

As depression ruled him for much of the time, many of Romney's friends found his mental as well as physical state a considerable disincentive to visit. Hayley remained loyal, however, and responded by taking him in October 1796 to see the sculptures at Wilton House, collected by the 8th Earl of Pembroke, which included Roman sarcophagi; they also saw the vaster masonry of Stonehenge nearby on Salisbury Plain.[22] Such visits were a tonic, as Romney had also found in 1796 when he visited Cambridge with Carwardine.[23] He continued to be oppressed by a tremor in one hand and in 1797–8 his hypochondria increased.[24] In May 1797 Cumberland made his last recorded visit to Cavendish Square, 'by appointment', to eat a mutton chop.[25]

In June 1797, concerned for Tom Hayley's health, he accompanied the boy to Sussex and its 'fine balsamic air'. He travelled again to Eartham in August, when he explored the east of the county and went sea-bathing with Tom. During this visit, they were surprised by the arrival from Goodwood of the recently widowed Duke of Richmond, the Duchess of Devonshire and Lord Thurlow. After their departure Romney remarked: 'we have been honoured by a curious trio of visitors today; grandeur! beauty! and genius! but all so much in their decline, that they excite rather more pity, than admiration'.[26] Very much in decline himself, he was all the more aware of the condition of others. Flaxman was pleased that Hayley was giving their friend support, but described it as 'hard duty', which indicates that such time was now recognized as arduous rather than pleasurable. He added: 'We all love his virtues, reverence his talents, and therefore cannot be indifferent to his welfare.'[27]

Among his friends, death, as well as decrepitude, extended its presence. Early in 1797 came the 'calamitous' expiry of William Hodges. Disillusioned with art as a livelihood, Hodges had taken up banking in the provinces, but following the unexpected collapse of his bank he had committed suicide, leaving a wife and small children. Romney visited his widow in March and expressed how moved he was by the encounter:

> I shall never forget what I saw one morning when I found her at breakfast with her little children; her voice, her face, more enchanting and beautiful than I had ever thought them before . . . For the gratification of the same look and voice, I think I could travel one hundred miles. I must content myself with the vision; the reality I shall never see again.[28]

Amidst the loneliness of separation from his remaining family, he nonetheless was aware of his own lack of the psychological resources necessary to maintain regular contact. Meanwhile Anne Hodges, 'her fair and gentle frame dissolv'd by grief', did not survive her husband long.

Regardless of his own decline, and maintaining an interest in his notion of an academy, Romney continued to take pupils. One of the last and most successful of these was James Lonsdale (1777–1839), the son of Richard Lonsdale, a portrait painter of Lancaster. It was not an ideal time to request expert teaching from Romney, but the Duke of Hamilton, a cousin of Greville, had made the introduction and could not be gainsaid.[29] As well as suffering mood swings, the artist was now absorbed in his Hampstead project. In order to supervise the builders he regularly walked up the hill to Hampstead, a round trip of seven miles. Lonsdale, who was living at Cavendish Square, complained at having to accompany him when walking or riding rather than being able to study.[30] One appeal for Lonsdale, however, was being able to draw from Romney's casts after the antique, which required less supervision than oil painting. In the long term the young man's development does not seem to have been harmed, as he achieved an extensive practice and became one of the founders of the Society of British Artists. His self-portrait with his brothers, *The Chess Players* (Nottingham, Castle Museum) and his *Sir William Congreve* (London, Royal Collection) are prominent among his productions. He was also to design a large Magna Carta window for Arundel Castle.[31]

Another 'highly promising domestic disciple', Isaac Pocock (1782–1835), became Romney's penultimate student in September 1797. He was the son of Nicholas Pocock (1741?–1821), a marine painter, who became a founder of the Old Water Colour Society.[32] Pocock often used to read aloud to the artist and copied the Newton and Milton compositions, in the great men series, in watercolours. In 1798 Isaac sat as Edgar in Romney's final Shakespearean composition, *King Lear in the Storm*, which like so many others remained

58 *A Head of Edgar (King Lear)*, 1773–5, 35 × 53.3 cm (14 × 21.3 in.). This line of the nose was a feature recommended by Winckelmann.

unfinished.[33] This and earlier drawings such as *The Death of Cordelia* (Cambridge, Fitzwilliam Museum; Washington, DC, Folger Shakespeare Library) and *A Head of Edgar* (Pl. 58), indicate how *King Lear* was a text consistently central in his imagination for forty years. Pocock was to win £100 at the British Institution in 1807 for *The Murder of Becket* (untraced) and eventually exhibited seventy-three oils at the RA.[34] Later he became a successful musical dramatist, adapting Scott's *Old Mortality* and influencing the development of melodrama with *The Miller and his Men*. Pocock was probably also the originator of the lyric 'Home Sweet Home', which was set to music by the first musician ever to be knighted, his collaborator Sir Henry Bishop.[35]

Throughout 1797, Romney's manual dexterity was increasingly impaired, and his depression became deeper. Aware of his decline but not wishing to be resented for interfering, his family had encouraged his old bachelor friend William Cockin to travel south to support him. Cockin had retired from his Nottingham school in 1792. By now his achievements included published verses on *The Death of Dr Johnson*, and volumes on oratory, arithmetic and the siphon; and he had also had a meteorological paper read to the Royal Society entitled 'An Extraordinary Appearance in a Mist'.[36] Perhaps the advent of Cockin contributed to the brighter mood during which Romney wrote that he planned to see the Hayleys 'next winter upon the hill at

Hampstead where I hope to have my new mansion thoroughly dried, fit for your reception and my gratification'.[37] However, the old schoolmaster's benevolent compliance was insufficient to cope with Romney's black despair, which, by July 1797, had thrown the building project 'almost to the ground'.[38]

At the year's end Hayley found him 'much dejected' in his new house. He was, however, impatient actually to move in, which he managed to do by Christmas, before the plaster was dry.[39] The removal of his remaining belongings was a protracted business which lasted some months. Horses, pulling cartloads of fragile paintings and casts, struggled up the hill with the help of several carriers, young Pocock and a carpenter employed by Poole, the artists' supplier.[40] Having wound down his business, Romney no longer needed the same range of servants on a daily basis, but for this major task he had had to bolster his staff with the help of Poole. The increase in stress led meanwhile to another slight stroke, which affected his eye, gave him 'a swimming in the head' and left a numbness in one hand.[41] His symptoms suggest cerebral arteriosclerosis atheroma, which is often associated with severe depression.[42] The move was achieved with so little publicity that his old patron and friend the Duke of Richmond only wrote to him in May 1800 to wish him well in his new home.[43]

Another blow fell in 1798 with the news of the painful death in Newgate prison of Edward Fitzgerald, Pamela's young husband, following the failure of the Irish rebellion. Word from home brought little comfort: that year a report from Mr Burnthwaite, Romney's agent in Furness, stated that High Cocken and the two farms he had bought at Ormsgill in 1786 had fallen into disrepair and the tenants were neglecting the land.[44]

Under pressure from his family to recuperate, in 1798 Romney briefly returned north. In persuading him to visit, his son's ulterior motive was the purchase of an estate. Accordingly, they toured properties in Furness, up the coast at Bootle and Whitehaven, and in Lancaster. They settled on Whitestock Hall, in the Rusland valley to the west of Kendal, a house which had been recently destroyed by fire.[45] As the estate lies between the Lake valleys of Windermere and Coniston, it had great appeal for both of them. Not far away was Force Forge, a monastic bloomery to which Romney and Adam Walker had ridden in their youth. Romney, now allegedly worth £50,000, was prepared to finance the lease of this, his son's project, but, being reluctant to make a full commitment at this stage, he released funds for neither the purchase nor the rebuilding of the house. He did not actually purchase the property until 1801.[46]

Now sixty-four years old, Romney retained some physical vigour but his cerebral decay was accelerating. Prospect House, and especially the gallery, with the Laocoön, the Apollo Belvedere and other casts now spaciously laid out, initially raised his spirits. He still had sufficient motivation to attack the backlog of portraits in a desultory fashion, stacked as they now were in his new studio in reproachful heaps. Since he had failed to design enough interior storage space, some paintings, including the unfinished *Orpheus and Eurydice*, found themselves left out in the weather in an arcade.[47] Ten years after Romney's first experiment with living in Hampstead, it was too late for him to enjoy fully the fruits of a life of almost constant labour. He still retained a temporary foothold in his familiar past life since, having advertised the remaining nineteen years of the lease of Cavendish Square, he was initially 'so struck with his own description of it' that he temporarily resolved to continue there.[48]

However, in December 1798 an aspiring young Irish artist, Martin Archer Shee (1769–1850), having just been elected ARA, astutely purchased the lease. Like Romney before him he was delighted with the 'extra suite of spacious and well-lighted rooms built expressly for the reception and display of pictures'.[49] He was the third significant British portraitist to reside there and he was elected President of the Academy after the death of Lawrence.[50]

Part of the transfer price of the lease of Cavendish Square was that Romney would sit to Shee, an effective recommendation to other sitters.[51] Romney, the doyen of London portraitists, appears in this portrait (sold Christie's, 20 May 1927) as a bulky figure, his increased weight being an inevitable contribution to his vascular disorders. An examination of Bond's engraving after Shee (Carlisle Library, Jackson Collection; Pl. 59) reveals the inclusion of the gunwale of a ship and several shadowy figures, which can be identified as visual quotations from Romney's *The Tempest* (Pl. 42). Romney, like Prospero, was now becoming reconciled to death and the portrait is a form of farewell to the easel, rather as Shakespeare's play has been viewed as a farewell to the stage.[52]

On 7 February 1799, with Pocock, Romney made what was to be his last visit to Sussex. A premonition of never returning tempted him to stay for as long as a month, and he was able to sketch a little. On 20 February, Romney still being active in philanthropy, Hayley wrote to Greene on his behalf requesting that 'the Person in Leicester Fields', doubtless one of his many unknown dependents, should be given the sum of £20.[53] By 28 April he had declined further, when Hayley saw him for the last time at Hampstead.[54] Most of his remaining friends were ageing and probably found the extra three or four miles a disincentive to visit. He had hoped to share the premises with a quantity of pupils, whose youthful energy would have invigorated him once he himself was unable to paint. The lone presence of Pocock was insufficient, and it was becoming clear that the vast gallery and studio provided more space than he now needed.

In early July, both Flaxmans, father and son, now friends of thirty years' standing, dined at Holly Bush Hill 'by particular invitation, and were

59 Martin Archer Shee, *George Romney* (engraving by W. Bond), 1810, 19 × 15.5 cm (7.5 x 6.1 in). Heavily dressed and with tousled hair, Romney is here the epitome of romanticism.

received in the most cordial manner', words which speak of infrequent entertaining and dissuasion of casual visitors. By now John Flaxman Junior was a prominent artist in his own right. He noted: 'Alas! I was grieved to see so noble a collection in a state so confused, so mangled, and prepared, I fear, for worse and not better.'[55]

After years of being obliged to present a formal professional welcome, Romney had lost interest in maintaining appearances. The studio was littered not only with unfinished portraits, but with numerous portfolios bulging with sketches. He never summoned the energy to be able to sort the salvage from the rubbish, an omission which was to have repercussions upon his future reputation. Despite his avoidance of the Academy for so long, he was reported by Shee early in 1799 as saying that he wished he had been an Academician and that he ought to have sought the society of the men of his own profession more than he had done. He also recommended that Shee should pursue a different course. This understandable change of heart is doubly poignant, as Shee added that Romney was also anxious to know what the Academicians thought of him.[56]

Romney's family had again prevailed upon him to travel north in late 1799. He set off intending to return, leaving only a couple of his staff to supervise the house, but he was never again fit enough to attempt the long journey back to Hampstead. Before October 1800, he arranged from Kendal to reduce still further both his domestic staff and his team of riding and carriage horses, leaving one rather dilatory servant in charge of Prospect House.[57] The family delayed selling the property as he stubbornly refused to accept that his Hampstead project was now a shattered dream. This contributed to the delapidation of the fabric and the opportunistic pillaging of the contents by villagers, who came with carts and barrows.[58]

Prospect House remained forlorn for eighteen months, until 18 May 1801, when some of the surviving contents were sold. The Royal Academy had a shortage of good-quality casts after the antique and Flaxman, since he knew Romney's collection well, was authorized to bid.[59] Thus fourteen of Romney's casts were acquired for the benefit of the next generation of Academy students. At the same sale, Sir John Soane purchased *Crouching Venus*, a cast which is still in the Soane Collection and whose dark golden patina may indicate Romney's own particular taste.[60] Benjamin West, now President of the Academy, attended a later Romney sale and was so shocked at the state of the collection that he went home resolving to tidy up his own portfolios.[61] To this resolve Farington added that, in his view, a man should be 'his own executor'.[62]

Although Prospect House had cost Romney £2,700, it realized less than £1,000 for his family.[63] It was to be briefly inhabited by Mrs Maria Rundell, probably the widow of the tenant of The Mount and author of *A New System of Domestic Cookery* (1808).[64] The village of Hampstead was meanwhile in need of accommodation for balls, dinners and public events, and in 1806 fifty-six local residents, including Josiah Boydell, bought £50 shares to cover the purchase and conversion of Romney's former home.

The studio became known as the card room and the gallery was converted to a ballroom, where, in the mid-nineteenth century, both Charles Dickens and Marie Lloyd were to give performances.[65] The stable buildings were leased to Thomas Lovelock, a victualler of Kilburn Wells, in 1807, and were soon converted to become the Holly Bush Inn. Although parts of the surviving house postdate Romney's occupation, and the building has been restored several times, many of the artist's unique features have been retained.

Despite Romney's neglect of his wife, Molly accepted him back into her home. He had supported her financially for thirty-seven years, and the welcome she gave to her absentee husband was probably more rooted in duty than affection.[66] It was unfortunate that the impression her fidelity later made on the poet Edward Fitzgerald led to the 'unpardonable impertinence' of his friend Tennyson's poem *Romney's Remorse* of 1889, which suggests, against all the evidence, that by the end of his life the artist regretted ever leaving Kendal.[67]

The sense of separation experienced by his wife had been exacerbated by her illiteracy, as this had prevented their direct communication. This fundamental lack of education, the common experience of women in this period, is clear from her use of Peter Romney as a scribe for her early letters. On the other hand, to live apart for reasons of work was less usual in the eighteenth century than it is now.[68] The fact that Molly had been content to housekeep for 'Honest' John Romney at High Cocken until his death in 1778 suggests that she was not wholly at odds with her husband, though her motivation may have been economic.

On whatever terms, Romney settled into the modest limestone house in Kendal, one of the southernmost in the town, which had been leased by his son for some years past.[69] It stands beside the River Kent, downstream of the Nether Bridge and not far from the parish church in which he and Molly had been married. The house had an orchard and a steep, east-facing garden, with what was then a fine view across the river to Kendal Castle, and it was here that Molly became his 'attentive affectionate nurse' during his final decline.[70] Adam Walker wrote that if he returned to Kendal himself, he would have no contacts left, 'like an owl in the desert and a stranger in my first home'.[71] Romney himself knew very few people there now. To begin with, he continued to correspond with Hayley, Greene and others, thus knowing of the final stages of poor Tom Hayley's stoical suffering. When increasing debility prevented Romney from writing altogether, William

Cockin was invited to live at Nether Bridge and to become his amanuensis.[72] Thus it was Cockin, on Romney's behalf, who conveyed his condolences to Felpham following Tom's death and interment, below a small Flaxman memorial in Eartham church, in 1800.

On 13 December 1800, in one of his last letters to Hayley, Romney regretted that he would not see London again, writing 'I feel every day greater need of care and attention, and here I experience them in the highest degree.'[73] Once it was clear that he would never more attend the meetings of the Unincreaseables, Greene wrote that the club had elected Haworth, an apothecary of Chancery Lane, in his stead.[74] That they had not done this sooner shows much concern for his feelings. To the dismay of all the family, on 30 May 1801, Cockin predeceased the artist and was buried at Burton-in-Kendal. His friend was succeeded as amanuensis by William Kennel, the son-in-law of the artist's sister Jane Barrow.[75]

As the old man's condition gradually worsened, in March 1801 Dr David Pitcairn of Craig's Court off Whitehall, physician to St Bartholomew's hospital, corresponded with William Long about his treatment. Pitcairn, after whose brother the eponymous island had been named, recommended that the artist should be bled and purged, that his liquid intake should be controlled, that he should be given doses of bruised white mustardseed moistened with white wine, that he should avoid fruit and vegetables and that Cheltenham water, 'if drunk with caution . . . would be beneficial'.[76]

During this final phase, wrangles over the ownership of several paintings led relations between John Romney and Hayley to deteriorate further. Following his son's death, Hayley somewhat transparently used Tom's mother Mrs Cockerell to write and request that *John Flaxman Modelling the Bust of William Hayley* (Pl. 16), should be sent to Sussex, as one of the few surviving images of her late son.[77] The 'Great Picture', as this was known, consequently hung at Felpham until the poet's death, after which it reverted to Greene. The decision to accede to this request may have been Romney's own, even at this late date, as his son would not have countenanced further portraits being accumulated by Hayley. His inability to hold a pen may also have clouded a precise determination of the point at which he became senile in earlier accounts.

The patient suffered a series of strokes, becoming increasingly frail and vague, and when in late 1801 James Romney returned from India, he 'did not recollect the brother, whom he had so anxiously wished to see; on being asked if he did not know him, he looked eagerly in his face, burst into an agony of tears, that spoke his tender remembrance, and then immediately lost all recollection of his person and character'.[78] This tearful recognition was virtually the last significant recorded moment of his life.

In February 1802 John wrote to Greene that his father had signed his will and would probably 'linger some time yet'. The artist was described as being 'good humoured' and did not 'appear sensible of pain', but he was 'quite incapable of doing anything for himself'.[79] Romney's last visitor at Nether Bridge, towards the end of 1802, was the faithful Greene, but by then the artist had lapsed into total oblivion. Having hovered between life and death for several months, he died on 15 November 1802, just a month short of his sixty-eighth birthday. The *Cumberland Pacquet* inaccurately recorded the event: 'Yesterday se'ennight at his house in Kendal where he had resided some time in a poor state of health, George Romney Esq., well known for his eminent abilities as a painter . . . in the metropolis.'[80] His body was taken to St Mary's churchyard in Dalton, where he was interred on 19 November near the graves of his parents and paternal grandparents, in a grassy hollow to the south of the choir.

Cumberland wrote to Greene, 'We were prepared for the loss of Mr Romney, in fact he was lost to us before his death. He will however live in our Remembrance by his virtues and in the World's remembrance by his works.' Greene wrote to John Romney, 'We ought to be thankful considering the melancholy situation he has been in for some time without a prospect of being better.' Carwardine had intended, too late, to 'whip into the mail' to make a final visit. He wrote to Greene, 'Having experienced his friendship for somewhat more than thirty years, I have found in him many excellent virtues blended with some human frailties, yet with all his eccentricities, his heart was ever good.'[81]

News travelled slowly to other friends. Estranged from John Romney, Hayley read of the death in his newspaper. Characteristically, he resolved to write an epitaph, which John Romney did not deign to use. An elegiac verse, later published in Hayley's biography, was written by the ten-year-old Thomas Romney Robinson; in a portrait of the boy, his father Thomas Robinson painted him standing by an urn engraved with the name of his old master (sold Sotheby's, 31 March 1976).[82]

Romney's tombstone, which was restored in 1895 by the artist's great-grandson John Orde Romney, bears the inscription:

Georgius Romney Armiger
Pictor Celeberrimus
obiit November 15th 1802
Requiescat in Pace.[83]

John Romney also commissioned a fine black marble cenotaph for the interior of St Mary's but was refused permission by the lord of the manor to erect it. Outraged, the cleric put it up inside Kendal parish church, adjacent to the west door, where its inscription reads:

To the memory of
GEORGE ROMNEY ESQUIRE,
The Celebrated Painter
who died in Kendal, the 15. Nov. 1802,
in the 68. year of his age, and was interred
at Dalton the place of his birth,
So long as Genius and Talent shall be
respected, his fame will live.

In his will, dated 14 February 1802, Romney left an annuity to Molly and the bulk of his estate to his son, including 100 unfinished oils, the large cartoons and many drawings. However, he also waived the old loan to his brother James and left considerable sums to members of his sister Jane's family, including her granddaughters Hannah and Jane Kennel. To Hayley he left £300 and the poet commissioned six specially designed coffee cups in his memory.[84] He remembered his other friends, leaving a gold ring each to Greene, Long, Hayley, Braithwaite, Carwardine, Walker, Flaxman, Stanier Clarke and George Tennant of Gray's Inn, one of his executors.[85]

John Romney had lived most of his adult life in Cambridge, but after his father's death he chose to return to his native territory, there to establish himself as a landed gentleman. Having inherited the Whitestock estate he found his social position was more secure, and he designed and built a fashionable country house flanked at either side by a small pavilion. It stands as a powerful statement of the artist's success and contrasts significantly with the modesty of old John Romney's construction at High Cocken. In 1803, nonetheless, John Romney told Flaxman that his father died worth only £700 a year, perhaps attempting to play down his own new affluence.[86]

Four years after his father's death, on 21 November 1806, John married his cousin, Jane Kennel, at Colton church. He was almost fifty years old. Twenty-nine years his junior, his wife eventually presented him with two sons and three daughters.[87] Molly Romney moved in nearby at Whitestock Cottage, now called the Dower House, the surviving part of the former building. The old lady outlived her husband by twenty years, dying on 20 April 1823 at the age of ninety-seven, and was buried in Rusland churchyard.[88]

Determined to enhance his father's posthumous reputation, John Romney eventually gave a selected group of 164 drawings to the newly founded Fitzwilliam Museum in Cambridge in 1818, and a group of large cartoons to the Liverpool Institution in 1823.[89] He was profoundly dissatisfied with Hayley's biography of his father, published in 1809, and belatedly published his own *Memoirs* in 1830, only two years before he died. Probably upon the majority of his elder son George, in 1832, his widow Jane moved to Tent Lodge, beside Coniston Water, where she lived with her unmarried daughter

Elizabeth until her own death in 1861. Elizabeth, a neighbour of John Ruskin from his arrival in 1871 at nearby Brantwood, spent her latter years back at Whitestock, where the family continued to live until the beginning of the twentieth century.[90] The Romney family is still represented in England and America. In England there are several direct descendants including Commander Kenneth Cadogan-Rawlinson RN (Retired), and in America there are numerous descendants of the artist's uncle, Thomas Rumney of Dalton, including the late Governor George Romney of Michigan and the Romney scholar Dr Yvonne Romney Dixon.[91]

Although Romney owned a copy of a Rembrandt self-portrait, he did not chart his own physical decline as relentlessly as the great master; but his own self-portraits are as revelatory.[92] There are several known, but the best of them, which represents him as he appeared 'in the most active season of his existence', is the *c.*1780–82 *Self-portrait* (London, National Portrait Gallery; Pl. 60).[93] Here, his superbly painted, sensitive face reveals a complex blend of peevishness and humour, whilst the contradiction of the irresolute mouth with the firm chin is underlined by defensively folded arms.[94] It may be that the pose Romney adopted for this self-portrait relates to the stance of the centurion in Michelangelo's *Crucifixion of St Peter* in the Pauline chapel at Rome.[95] This would have been a deliberate riposte to Reynolds's reference to Rembrandt in one of his own self-portraits. Commenced at Eartham at a busy time of his life, it is characteristic that it is unfinished. As a radical, Romney here wears his own hair rather than a wig, and his clothing appears comparably drab and plain. Described as 'the portrait of a dreamer which hints at the torture of his soul', this very modern work appears to have been painted with scarcely any preliminary drawing, 'the hallmark of supreme confidence'.[96] As he devoted most of his life to preserving the likenesses of his fellow human beings, it is fitting that he left such an individual representation of his own physiognomy.

Although his great rival Reynolds was interred with pomp in St Paul's cathedral, the simplicity of Romney's own grave at Dalton, comparable to Gainsborough's plain tomb at Kew, was more in keeping with his personality and preferences. Not only was he back home, but he was close to open fields beneath an outdoor monument quite free from ostentation. Almost two centuries later, the major galleries of five continents, whose names in themselves are a roll of honour, house his portraits and drawings in their hundreds. It is these, together with a legion of smaller private collections, that are the true memorial to his achievement.

60 *Self-portrait*, c.1780–82, 125 × 101.2 cm (50 × 40 in). This unfinished self-portrait is characteristic in its use of trailing brush strokes.

George Romney's family tree

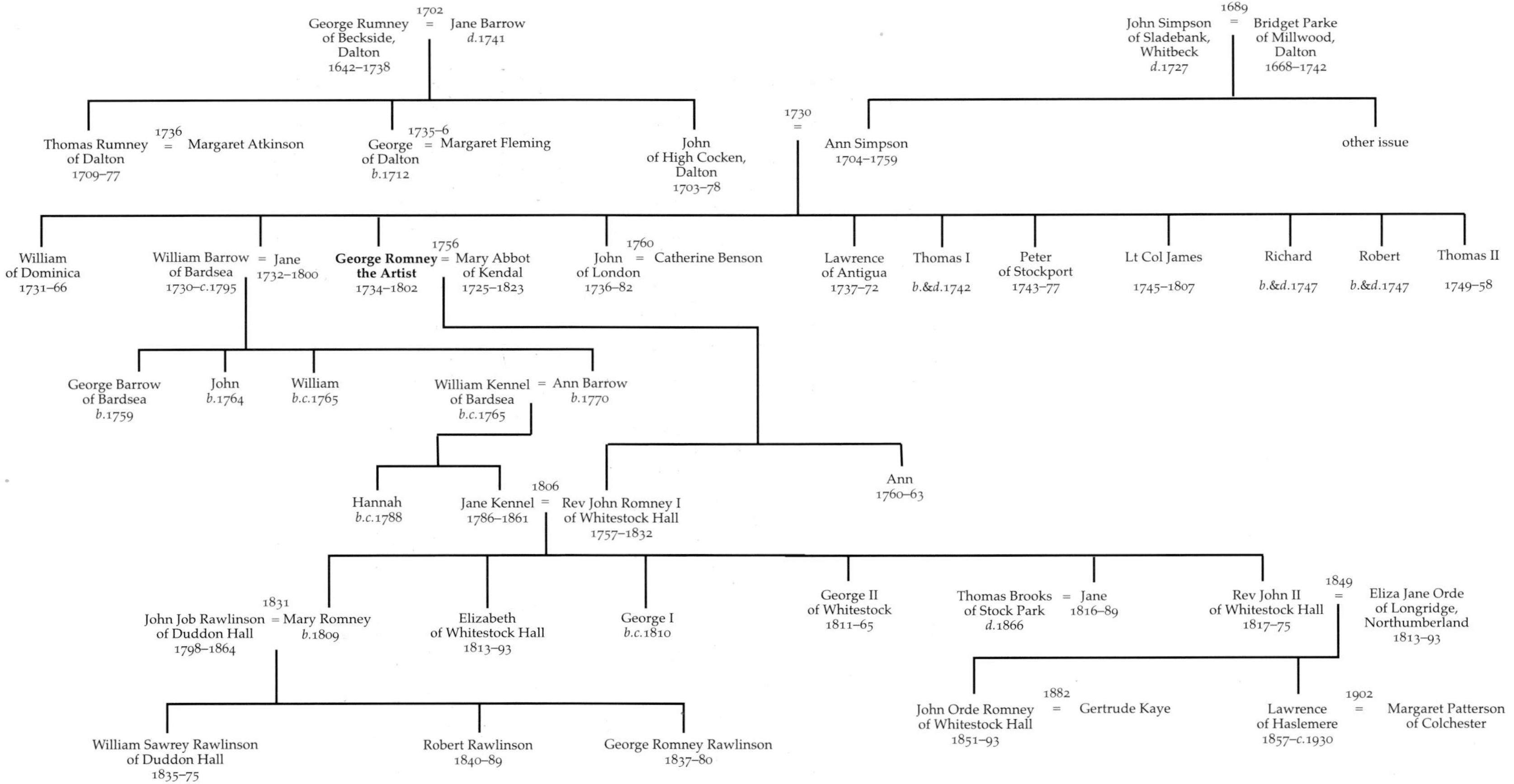

Drawn with assistance
from Tim Cockerill and
the late C. Roy Hudleston FSA

Notes

1. From woodcarver to portraitist

1. Until 1974, the northern part of Lancashire; known as Lancashire over the sands.

2. The parish clerk omitted to record his baptism in St Mary's parish register, although his siblings' names may be found there. He may otherwise have been baptised in an adjacent parish, as yet unlocated.

   In the present volume the family name is spelled Romney, although the artist's father always used Rumney and his grandfather Rumley. It was not, however, until 1764 that the artist changed the spelling to Romney, perhaps having encountered Lord Romney, the then president of the Society for the Encouragement of Arts, Manufactures and Commerce. This was for him a conscious gesture of gentrification, not without precedent in the eighteenth century when Lakeland Hogarths became London Hogarths. The original spelling of Rumney survives in Hayward's List of 1773 and in the Fashionable Court Guide of 1792 (Ford, Brinsley), and as late as 1799 his wife was still recorded as Mrs Rumney in Kendal (Land Tax certificate, Romney House, Kendal, Collection Mr Leach). His servants used both spellings but his cousins in Dalton changed their spelling to Romney in due course. Though the art world pronounces his name 'Rumney', in Furness he is always pronounced 'Romney'. The present writer suspects that the artist called himself 'Roomney', with the same vowel sound as 'room' in received pronunciation.

3. Appleby was then in Westmorland. There is a Joseph Rumney in Appleby listed in the directories of 1885–97. Thanks to Barry McKay; Hudleston, pp. 145–6 and 159.

4. Millwood then housed several families and traces of the earlier buildings survive adjacent to the present Victorian house. Three generations and both sides of the artist's family had links here. As both Bridget Simpson, his maternal grandmother, and John Romney, his father, had links with Millwood, it appears that in marrying Ann Simpson the artist's father had responded to propinquity.

5. There was a farm here called Cuckstool Farm, perhaps too rustic a name for earlier biographers to use. Chamberlain was almost certainly mistaken when he described the farm as being near the railway station. This would have been too far from the beck or stream from which the area takes its name. Several other buildings are claimed as the site of the birthplace and further research into the deeds of this much divided property is needed.

6. Romney, p. 5; Hayley, p. 11.

7. Marshall, J.D. (1958), *Furness and the Industrial Revolution*, Barrow-in-Furness Library Committee, p. 151n; Ann Romney's mother, Bridget Simpson, is recorded as having shipped iron ore from Lowsey Point on the Duddon estuary, and John Romney's neighbour was the jovial ironmaster Tom Kendal.

8. Romney, pp. 4–5.

9. Cumberland (1803), p. 417.

10. Romney, p. 4; Hayley, p. 38.

11. Until 1974 this was in Cumberland.
12. Hudleston, p. 146.
13. Preston County Records Office DDGr misc. bundle 1. There is no indication to which parish this refers.
14. Romney, pp. 306 and 237; Chamberlain, p. 382; Jamison, p. 16.
15. Hayley, p. 232.
16. George painted and played the violin; Peter painted and 'had a turn for poetry and music' (Romney, pp. 7 and 304); James wrote verse and plays and played the violin (*Quarto*, T. McCabe/ Abbot Hall Art Gallery 18/2, July 1980).
17. The present writer has borrowed these very apt words from Roy Porter's review of the play *Crumb*, *Guardian* Arts Review, 1997; thanks to Paul Cross for his newspaper cuttings service.
18. Hayley, p. 10; Romney, p. 177.
19. Aristotle (1936), *Problems*, trans. Holt, W.S., 2/28, Harvard, pp. 155–7; cited Jamison, 51; Jamison, 56; John Romney wrote of the 'superior organisation of the nerves' in men of genius which renders them more liable to injury. Such men have a 'certain elevation of soul which makes the possessor despise those low and mean practices by which vulgar minds prosper' (Romney, pp. 6–7). Patricia Jaffé called for a psychological analysis of Romney's life and work. (Jaffé (1977), p. 67). The present writer, whose first degree was in psychology at Durham, has endeavoured to commence this study here but is aware that further work is needed. Thanks to Professor James Averill of the University of Massachusetts at Amherst and Dr Esther Ross of Morecambe, Lancashire, for their advice.
20. Romney, p. 41.
21. Hayley, p. 123.
22. Hayley, p. 305.
23. Hayley, pp. 214 and 300. This metaphor from archery relates to the interest he shared with Greene. Preston CRO DDGr contains numerous references in the Hayley–Greene correspondence.
24. Romney, p. 273.
25. Hayley, pp. 217, 213, 210, 301.
26. Anna Seward, letter cited by Chamberlain, p. 245; Hayley, p. 317.
27. Hayley, p. 8.
28. Hayley, pp. 117 and 302.
29. Cumberland (1803), p. 423. In Romney's time men were not discouraged from such outbursts of tears. See Farington, 5 July 1810; Pointon (1970), p. 99; Honour (1968), p. 141.
30. Cumberland (1803), p. 423; Honour (1968), p. 141.
31. Hayley, p. 131, Preston CRO DDGr; letter, Hayley to Greene, 14 September 1787.
32. Hayley, p. 271.
33. Jamison, p. 58.
34. Thanks to Dr Esther Ross for this observation; Hayley, p. 270.
35. Jamison, p. 6.
36. Jamison, pp. 5–6.
37. Jamison, pp. 87 and 270.
38. Storr, A., *Dynamics of Creation*, Jamison, p. 121; Kiernan, J.G. (1892), 'Is Genius a Neurosis?' *Alienist and Neurologist* **13**, pp. 119–50; Kiernan, J.G. (1892), 'Art and the Insane', *Alienist and Neurologist* **13**, pp. 684–97, cited by Macgregor, J.M. (1989), *The Discovery of the Art of the Insane*, Princeton, New Jersey, and Oxford. The present writer acknowledges the irony of these titles amidst his endeavour to establish Romney's neurosis rather than psychosis.
39. Iain Gale's review of the James Gunn Exhibition at the Fine Art Society, New Bond Street, March–April 1995, *Guardian* Arts Review.
40. Jamison, p. 153; Chamberlain, p. 5.
41. Kendal County Records Office WD/MM/169, cited in Hudleston.

42. Dalton, St Mary's Parish Registers. 'Cocken' may be a version of Cockayne, the land of luxury and idleness, and perhaps a relic of monastic humour. Today High Cocken is called Romney Cottage. In the early twentieth century visitors came by carriage from Furness Abbey railway station.

43. Hayley, pp. 307–8, citing John Flaxman; Romney, p. 249.

44. Williamson (1921), Chapter 1.

45. Hayley, pp. 306–7, citing Flaxman.

46. Beard, G., and Gilbert, C. (1986), *A Dictionary of English Furniture Makers (1660–1840)*, Leeds, p. 1004. One of Wright's fine mahogany kneehole desks is now in the collection of the Victoria and Albert Museum.

47. Hayley, p. 18.

48. Walton, p. 91; Romney, p. 7.

49. Hayley, pp. 15–16; Walton, p. 91; Romney, p. 9; Sir William Hamilton, the uncle of Romney's friend Charles Greville and himself a Romney sitter, learned the violin from Giardini.

50. Romney, p. 5. A violin with a carved back, said to be by Romney, is in a private collection in London. Also see n. 52.

51. Suggested by the present writer in correspondence with the Yale Center; Brenneman, D.A. (1996), 'The Romney Paintings in the Center for British Art,' *Transactions of the Romney Society* **I**, p. 18.

52. Cumberland (1803), pp. 417–18; Romney, pp. 32–3; Romney's own violin (perhaps not the instrument referred to above in note 50) was bought at Miss Romney's sale, 24 May 1894, lot 146, by Mr Hill, whose family owned it until after 1934 when it was given to 'a London Museum'. Letter, Desmond Hill, 28 October 1991; *Henley's Universal Dictionary of Violin and Bow Makers*, p. 985.

53. Romney, p. 9.

54. Cumberland (1803), p. 419.

55. Hayley, p. 13; Romney, p. 21, says a beautiful woman.

56. Mr Boow, a Duddon farmer, reported this to Fenwick Pattison of Coniston in the 1950s. Thanks to Joan David.

57. *Art's Masterpiece, or A companion for the ingenious of either sex* by C.K. (1697), London: printed for G. Conyers and J. and B. Sprint. Romney, p. 11. Jaffé (1977), p. 3; Romney's copy is in the Fitzwilliam Museum, Cambridge.

58. Romney, p. 11.

59. Romney, p. 11.

60. The present writer suggests that there were two Mrs Gardners, one in Dendron and one in Kendal, who have been conflated into one. They may have been sisters-in-law. One is recorded as having a husband who was an upholsterer; the other's husband was a baker. More research is needed here. This realization may have occurred to Gamlin, p. 7.

61. Hayley, p. 18. William Lewthwaite lived at Kirkby Hall to supervise his mining interests in Furness. His son was apprenticed to Romney's early sitter T.H. Rawlinson, and his descendant became the first Lewthwaite baronet. Timothy Cockerill and C. Roy Hudleston, Lewthwaite of Broadgate, in 'Millom Families' Part I, *Transactions of the Cumberland and Westmorland Antiquarian and Archaeological Society*, **92**, 1992, pp. 93–5.

62. Cumberland (1803), p. 418.

63. Williamson (1921), p. 14.

64. Her son Daniel became Romney's early pupil in Kendal.

65. Cranke's son Malachi was baptised in Ulverston in 1752. See Gaythorpe. Vertue wrote of Cranke that he 'painted strongly . . . at least as well as anyone living'.

66. Romney, p. 15; Sahut, M-C (ed.) (1977), *Carle Vanloo, Premier Peintre du Roi*, exh. cat., Nice (Museum Cheret). Steele's brother Dr Peter Steele recorded that he spoke fluent French. V&A ms. letter 1803, cited Burkett (1987), p. 202; Carle van Loo had been honoured by Pope Benedict XII and was director of the Ecole des elèves Protégés, the school for young artists who aspired to travel to Rome. His *Grand Turk Giving a Concert to his Mistress* is in the Wallace Collection. At Kirkby Hall, home of Romney's Lewthwaite cousins, there is an extraordinary wall painting in the disused chapel. This was probably one of the first large-scale paintings Romney saw. (See the article

by M.E. Burkett in *Transactions of the Cumberland and Westmorland Antiquarian and Archaeological Society*.) Furness was not devoid of important paintings: at Conishead Priory, the Braddylls owned two Titians, four Lelys and four van Dycks. As John Romney worked for the Duke of Buccleuch at Dalton Castle, he could also have worked at Conishead. Thanks to Richard Dean and Mary Burkett for these suggestions. Cumberland's jocular remark that the inn sign at the Red Lion in Dalton was the earliest work of art Romney saw, actually appears earlier (Greene, *c.*1802), but may well originate in the artist's own self-deprecation.

67. This portrait is illustrated in Burkett.

68. The studio was demolished *c.*1960. Photographs at Kendal Reference Library and Abbot Hall Art Gallery.

69. Hayley, pp. 199 and 300.

70. Romney, p. 14; the witnesses were Thomas Ashburner, newspaper proprietor and paper manufacturer, and James Dowker, Coroner of Kendal.

71. Cumberland (1803), p. 419.

72. Hayley, p. 20.

73. Romney, p. 15.

74. Burkett, p. 199.

75. Jaffé, P. (1989), exh. cat., Ljubljana (Narodna Galerija), p. 19.

76. Romney, p. 16.

77. Parish Register, Crosthwaite-cum-Lyth.

78. Romney, p. 16.

79. Romney, pp. 16–17.

80. Parish Register, Kendal; Preston CRO AR11; thanks to Tim Cockerill.

81. Hayley, pp. 25 and 27.

82. Egerton (1984), no. 167.

83. Romney, p. 29.

84. Sterne, L. (1759), *Tristram Shandy*, Book VI, Chapter 10.

85. Paulson, p. 76.

86. Romney, pp. 29–30.

87. Romney, p. 23; Hayley, p. 27.

88. Romney p. 17; as Molly was illiterate, the letters were probably written by a Kendal friend.

89. Hayley, p. 27; Cumberland (1803), p. 419.

90. Romney, p. 17.

91. Romney, p. 18; Hayley, pp. 230–1.

92. Letter from Miss Wallace, Post Office Archivist, 16 September 1992, *re.* St Martin's Le Grand Book, 1924, p. 245.

93. Romney, p. 19.

94. Curwen, p. 190; Romney, pp. 60–61; Hayley, pp. 278–98.

95. Hayley, pp. 199 and 300; Romney, pp. 32 and 272.

96. Cited in Chamberlain, p. 254.

97. Alex Kidson believes that the portraits usually said to be of Charles and Cecilia Strickland are in fact of Walter and his wife.

98. This building is now Abbot Hall Art Gallery.

99. Jacob Morland is sometimes wrongly called James.

100. Pavière, Sidney H. (1950), *The Devis Family of Painters*, Leigh on Sea, Lewis, p. 23; Sartin, Stephen V. (1983), *Anthony Devis: His Life and Art*, exhibition catalogue, Harris Art Gallery, Preston, pp. 30 and 33; Devis exhibited in London at the Society of Artists from 1762 but could have known Romney in the north, Preston being near Lancaster.

101. See illustration in Egerton, Judy (1990), *Wright of Derby*, Tate Gallery exhibition catalogue, London, p. 274.

102. Sartin, pp. 23–4 and 31; Devis's own lay figure was much smaller than life size. In 1770 Romney was asked by the Society of Artists to repair a wooden lay figure; Romney did use a lay figure but preferred to have male or female live models such as Nancy Kemble of Leg Alley, Drury Lane (Yale Center for British Art, Rare Book Room, Romney ms. 32279); Romney was charged by Saunders for a lay figure and gallows from which to suspend it (V&A ms. 86 AA 5, cited Jacob Simon, Romney Society lecture October 1998); Simon, Jacob (1999), 'Romney and the Art of the Picture Frame', *Romney Society Transactions*. Sitters' clothing was often left in the studio to be worn by these models, for example Lady Newdigate's dress and Sir John Pole's suit.

103. R.R.M. See Romney, 'Peter' (1919), *The Connoisseur*, 53, p. 63.

104. Williamson (1921), pp. 14–15.

105. Romney, p. 33.

106. Romney, pp. 23–5.

107. Romney, pp. 24–5. Although Romney may not have kept up with Greene in these intervening years, Greene was actually in London from *c.*1760 visiting the sights, including the early exhibitions of the Society of Artists. Greene ms. *Diary*, *c.*1760–62, Preston CRO DDGr.

108. Bicknell, pp. 23, 27 and 31.

109. Allen, B., 'Watteau and his Imitators in Mid-Eighteenth Century England', in Maureau, F., and Grasselle, M.M., eds. (1987), *Antoine Watteau (1684–1721), le peintre, son temps et sa légende*, Paris, p. 266.

110. As Romney had not visited Shropshire, this last was probably painted after engravings by Vivares, based in turn upon 1758 drawings by Thomas Smith of Derby; Egerton (1990), p. 21.

111. Smith, S. (1979), *A View from Iron Bridge*, Ironbridge Gorge Trust, cited in a letter from John Powell, Ironbridge Museum, 19 June 1992. The idea may have stemmed from Colonel Wilson of Abbot Hall, whose iron chimneypiece had just been made at Coalbrookdale.

112. Burkett, M.E. (1977), 'A Boy with a Candle', *Burlington Magazine* **119**, p. 857.

113. Apprenticeship indenture (Kendal Town Hall); Eddershaw, M. (1989), *Grand Fashionable Nights (1575–1985)*, Centre for North West Studies, Lancaster University.

114. Egerton (1990), pp. 10 and 50, citing Nicholson (1968), p. 18.

115. Egerton (1990) p. 133; Pressly, p. 126, cites Rosenblum, R. (1957), 'The Origin of Painting', *Art Bulletin*, December 1957, pp. 279–90. Both Hayley in his *Essay on Painting* and Cumberland in his verse to Romney refer to this subject.

116. Bignamini (1988), p. 24.

117. Williamson (1921), pp. 14–15.

118. Bradford was apprenticed to T. and W. Dilworth of Lancaster in 1752 and was still operating as a merchant in 1789 (*Tunnicliffe's Directory*). Thanks to Dr White, Lancaster Museum. William Lewthwaite, their cousin, also had interests in the West Indies. Huddleston and Cockerill (1992), p. 94.

119. Chamberlain, pp. 41 and 381–3.

120. V&A mss. 86 aa 25a 4; Chamberlain, pp. 381–5.

121. Chamberlain, p. 382.

122. Chamberlain, pp. 381–5, refers to mss. letters in the collection of the artist's great-grandson Lawrence Romney *c.*1910 (untraced).

123. V&A mss. 86 cc 32a 1/1, Walker to Romney, 12 December 1762; Romney, pp. 42–4.

124. Burkett (1987), p. 202.

125. Romney, p. 35; Hayley, p. 25.

126. V&A mss. 86 aa 25 a4.

127. Chamberlain, p. 257.

128. Keane, p. 77; Chamberlain, p. 3.

2. In London: architect of his own fortune

1. The most likely of numerous Castle Inns listed in Bryant Lillywhite (1972), *London Signs*, London, pp. 93–7. Thanks to the staff at the Museum of London.
2. Romney, p. 39.
3. Romney, pp. 318–19.
4. Johnson, E. M. (1976), Francis Cotes, Oxford.
5. Dr Johnson (1759), *The Idler*, **45**, cited in Northcote, J. (1818), *Life of Joshua Reynolds*, London: vol. 1, p. 239.
6. Letter to a friend in England, April 1773; Romney, p. 75.
7. Romney, p. 40.
8. Elfrida was later the subject of works by Angelica Kauffmann and Rigaud. Strong (1978), p. 116.
9. Molly's inability to sign even her name is clear from the X she wrote in the marriage register on her wedding day. Thanks to Richard Hall.
10. Cumberland (1803), p. 420; Chamberlain, pp. 42 and 351.
11. Romney, p. 40; Rowland's uncle Edward Stephenson had a house in London and died there in 1768. Thanks to George Bott, Keswick.
12. Romney's Dove Court landlord was a Mr Pantry. See Chamberlain, p. 42; Hayley, p. 38.
13. Establishment Book, Post Office Archives. Thanks to Miss Wallace; Royal Society Certificate of Election 14 March 1782; *Gentleman's Magazine*, **87**, 1817, p. 632; *DNB*.
14. For example: the biblical subject, *The Holy Family*; the literary subject, *Macbeth and the Witches*; the mythological subject, *Medea and her Children*; the allegorical subject, *The Infant Shakespeare, Nature and the Passions*.
15. Waterhouse, p. 17; Pointon (1993), p. 38.
16. These are discussed in Chapter 8.
17. Hayley, p. 123.
18. Pointon (1993), p. 49; Northcote was Reynolds's biographer, see note 5 above.
19. Thanks to Brian Allen for this observation.
20. Hutchison, pp. 28–9; Chamberlain, pp. 36–7.
21. Daphne Foskett refers to Humphry in several publications. See Bibliography.
22. Reese, M. (1987), *Goodwood's Oak: the Life and Times of the 3rd Duke of Richmond, Lennox and Aubigny*, London, pp. 58–9, cites Edward Edwards (1808); Gunnis, R. (1951), *Dictionary of British Sculptors*, London; few of the Duke's papers survive, letter to author from Patricia Gill, Chichester County Records Office, 3 August 1992.
23. Waterhouse, p. 20.
24. Chamberlain, p. 59; Watson (1985), pp. 21–6, gives excellent details of Romney's exhibits.
25. Many authorities appear to confuse the Society of Artists and the Free Society of Artists with the Society for the Encouragement of Arts, Manufactures and Commerce (now the Royal Society of Arts). See Bignamini (1988).
26. Illustrated by Solkin, p. 253.
27. Denvir, p. 22; Strong (1978), p.23.
28. Warner, p. 192.
29. Hayley, p. 368.
30. Simon, p. 104.
31. Defoe, D. (1722), *A Journal of the Plague Year*, cited in Stapleton, A. (1930), *London Lanes*, London, p. 105.
32. J.H. Mortimer, cited in Whitley, p. 191; Bearbinder Lane led from the south-east corner of the Mansion House. See Laxton, P., and Wisdom, J. (1985), *The A–Z of Regency London*, London

Topographical Society publication no. 131, p. 15. Thanks to Jan Parkin and Dr Jonathan Harris of University College, London.

33. *Gentleman's Magazine* (1763), cited in Watson (1985), p. 34; Burke, pp. 170 and 246; Allen (1987), pp. 66–7.

34. Cumberland (1803), pp. 417–23.

35. John Halliday, biographer of Lord Mansfield, cited in Romney, pp. 46–7. Gatty, H. (1938–9), 'Notes by Horace Walpole on the Exhibitions of the Society of Artists and the Free Society of Artists, 1760–1791', *The Walpole Society*, **27**, pp. 76–7; Honour (1968), pp. 146–59.

36. Alberts, p. 78.

37. Romney, p. 45.

38. It is worth noting that after 1763 Reynolds appears for the first time in the street directory as 'history and portrait painter'. Postle, M. (1995), *The Subject Pictures of Sir Joshua Reynolds*, Cambridge, pp. 8–9.

39. Edwards, pp. 276–7.

40. Hayley, p. 212.

41. Alberts, p. 413; *Notes and Queries*, cited in Ward and Roberts vol. 2, pp. 199–200; letter Anthony Mould to present writer July 1991; Webster, J.C. (1927),'The Pictures of the Death of General Wolfe', *Journal of the Society of Army History Research*, **6**, pp. 30–37; several oil sketches exist but scholars are divided about their authenticity.

42. Ward and Roberts, **2**, pp. 199–200; Mitchell, p. 31; Alberts, R. C. (1978), *Benjamin West: A Biography*, Houghton Mifflin, New York, p. 105; Edward Penny's *Death of General Wolfe* was exhibited in 1764.

43. Later friendliness between West and Romney suggests no grudges were borne. More recently Romney has been described as having 'set a precedent for future military pictures'; see Harrington, P. (1993), *British Artists and War 1700–1914*, London and Providence, Rhode Island, pp. 31–2. This volume reproduces one of the putative oil sketches for Romney's *The Death of Wolfe*.

44. At the Mews Gate, demolished to make space for Trafalgar Square, his landlady was Mrs Caigow, a tobacconist. Address on V&A mss. 86 aa 25a 4/1.

45. Philips, p. 96. Chamberlain, p. 48; Mortimer had links with Reynolds but his wash drawings were rather like Romney's.

46. King Edmund (921–46) was probably depicted being stabbed by a robber; Gower, p. 17; Romney, p. 52; Ward and Roberts, vol. 2, p. 200.

47. Pointon (1970), p. xxvii.

48. Greene (*c*.1802).

49. Greene (*c*.1802).

50. Greene (1986), 30 August 1764.

51. Letter, Romney to Peter Romney, 16 September 1764, published in Romney, p. 51.

52. Greene (1986), Sunday 2 September 1764.

53. Romney, p. 51.

54. Greene (1986), 10 September 1764.

55. Greene (1986), 2 September 1764.

56. Hayley, p. 43; Romney, p. 51; Greene (1986), 26–7 September 1764.

57. This was said of Vernet by Diderot in 1767; Vernet also painted shipwrecks, such as *Storm with a Shipwreck* (London, Wallace Collection).

58. Crow, T.E. (1985), *Painters and Private Life in Eighteenth Century Paris*, New Haven, p. 141.

59. Mowl, p. 202.

60. Greene (1986), 22 September 1764.

61. Greene (1986), 4 October 1764.

62. Hayley, p. 43.

63. Hayley, p. 103.

64. Romney, pp. 166–7.
65. Jaffé (1977), p. 25.
66. *Dictionary of National Biography*, 'John Henderson', xxv, pp. 398–401.
67. Romney, pp. 235 and 274.
68. Romney, pp. 22–3.
69. Watson (1985), p. 36.
70. Lecture, Dr Andrew White, Curator, Lancaster Museum, The Romney Society, 1996.
71. Chamberlain, pp. 383–5; Romney, pp. 275, 295, 298, 300 and 308.
72. Watson (1985), p. 17.

3. Great Newport Street

1. Chamberlain, p. 240, cites a letter by William Blake of 28 May 1804.
2. Wilton and Bignamini, p. 214.
3. Watson (1985), no. 6.
4. Foskett (1972), p. 345.
5. Egerton (1984).
6. Behrman, pp. 120–23. Thanks to Jean Smith. Walker, D. (1938), 'The Romney Picture Case' in *The Life of Lord Darling*, London, Cassell, pp. 186–94. Thanks to Les Shore.
7. Foskett (1972), p. 131; Hayley, pp. 69 and 373; Walker, pp. 127–35.
8. Ward and Roberts, **2**, p. 103.
9. Hayley, p. 97.
10. Irwin, p. 4; Romney, p. 203.
11. Gower, Lord R.S. (1882), *Lawrence and Romney*, London, p. 24.
12. Piper (1957), p. 144.
13. Leech and Craik, p. 190.
14. Roetgen, S. (1993), *Anton Raphael Mengs 1728–1779 and his British Patrons*, London, p. 153; Cumberland also translated de Azara's edition of Mengs's writings, wrote a catalogue of the Spanish royal collection of paintings and a volume of *Anecdotes of Eminent Painters in Spain*. Roetgen, cat. 61.
15. He must not be confused with his relative George Cumberland, the friend of Blake.
16. Burke, J. (1960), 'Romney's *Leigh Family* (1768): 'Link between the Conversation Piece and the Neo-classical Portrait Group', *Annual Bulletin, National Gallery of Victoria*, **2**, pp. 5–14.
17. Chamberlain, p. 53; Romney, p. 56.
18. Romney, p. 66.
19. Romney, p. 63; Chamberlain, p. 9.
20. Romney, p. 66.
21. *DNB*, 'Richard Cumberland', vol. xiii, pp. 290-93.
22. Cumberland (1805), vol. 2, p. 214.
23. Romney, p. 49, citing James Northcote.
24. This portrait, *Lady Greville*, hangs at the Courtauld Institute Galleries, Somerset House, London; Burke, 'Romney's *Leigh Family*'.
25. Allen (1984), p. 2; Burke.
26. Whitley, pp. 90 and 236–7.
27. Waterhouse, E. (1965), *Three Decades of British Art (1740–1770)*, Philadelphia: American Philosophical Society, cited in Hayes (1991) p. 14.
28. Hutchison, p. 46.

29. Waterhouse, p. 317.

30. The original Society of Artists continued until 1791 to be a 'rallying ground for dissenters' such as Wright and Stubbs whilst the Free Society lingered only until 1783; Burke, p. 273; Pressly, p. 78; Strong (1978), p. 17; Romney's non-membership of the Academy did not prevent him taking an interest in the pseudonymous Peter Pindar's satires on the Academy and he was sent at least one edition of the 'Lyric Ode to the Academicians' by the author, John Wolcot (1738–1819). Romney's copy was sold at Miss Romney's sale in 1894 (lot 7).

31. Solkin, p. 264; 'Fresnoy' was probably the Reverend James Wills; Brewer, p. 250.

32. Society of Artists mss. cited by Helen Valentine, Royal Academy Library, in a letter to me of 16 October 1991; Watson (1985), p. 17.

33. Parker, C.A. (1971), *Mr Stubbs the Horse Painter*, London, pp. 46–7 ; Brewer, p. 238.

34. Chamberlain, p. 40.

35. Whitley, cited by Watson (1985), p. 22.

36. *DNB*, 'James Paine', vol. XLIII, pp. 67–9.

37. Wilton and Bignamini, cat. 14 and 18; Piper, 2nd edn, 162; remarkably enough, Sir George Warren (b. 1735) did not visit Rome himself until 1783–4, a decade after Romney. Ingamells, p. 980.

38. This composition would have been available to Romney via an engraving or a student copy.

39. Tomalin, p. 46.

40. Watson (1992), p. 149; some authorities give Thalia as the Comic Muse.

41. Romney, p. 62. The Barrow sketchbooks contain sketches for *Mirth* and *Melancholy*.

42. Jaffé (1977), p. 50; Ward and Roberts, vol. 2, p. 165, see Miss Wallis entry; Watson (1992), p. 150; RA Council Minutes cited in letter from Helen Valentine, RA Library, 16 October 1991; Lord Duveen associated Romney with sentiments of sadness and melancholy; Robyn Asleson (San Marino, Huntington Art Collections) suggests that his composition of a woman leaning against a plinth is derived from classical funerary images; letter to the author, 5 January 1995.

43. Thanks to Jean Wallis; 1771 was also the year that Thomas Barrow (1737–1822) of Great Eccleston, Lancashire, exhibited at the Society of Artists, using Romney's Great Newport Street address as his own. Sometimes described as a pupil, he sat to Romney and engraved the resulting portrait (Corporation of London, Guildhall Art Gallery).

44. E. Waterhouse, cited by Postle, M. (1995), p. 39.

45. Sheldon, p. 291.

46. Watson (1985), p. 25. Thanks to Alex Kidson for identifying this fragment.

47. Mannings (1991), p. 140; Watson (1985), p. 25.

48. Major Thomas Peirson must not be confused with Major Francis Peirson (sometimes spelled Pierson) whose death, also in 1781, was recorded in J.S. Copley's *The Death of Major Peirson* (London, Tate Gallery).

49. John Martin Robinson's notion is expressed in Hayes, p. 104.

50. Romney, pp. 71–2.

51. Romney, p. 73; Humphry, mss. in RA Library 1/126; see also Jenkins and Sloan.

52. Ms. letter Adam Walker to Romney 2 September 1775, V & A ms. 86 cc 32a 52/1.

53. Hayley, p. 58; Romney, pp. 73.

54. Romney ms. letter from Rome, 20 June 1773, Fairfax Murry Collection, cited in Ward and Roberts, vol. 1, p. 32.

4. 'Egad, George, we're bit!' Italy and neo-classicism

1. A notion supported by Alex Kidson in conversation with the author, October 1996.
2. Wilton and Bignamini, pp. 33 and 93.
3. Ms. versions of this journal are at the Yale Center for British Art and the Fitzwilliam Museum, Cambridge; see also Chapter 5, n. 17.

4. Romney's Italian journal (Fitzwilliam Museum, Cambridge), cover.
5. Romney Journal, pp. 74–5.
6. Romney, pp. 76–8.
7. Romney, p. 80.
8. Romney, pp. 79–83.
9. Mowl, p. 56.
10. Romney, p. 93; Hayley, p. 54.
11. Hayley, p. 54.
12. Sketchbook, sold Christie's 17 May 1966, inscribed 'we arrived Rome' and dated 18 June 1773. Note in Ford, Brinsley.
13. Bell, p. 17.
14. Piranesi designs illustrated in Wilton and Bignamini, cat. 73–4.
15. ibid. p. 112.
16. Letter to Peter Romney, 20 June 1774, V&A mss. cc32a/18, cited Watson (1985), p. 12 n9.
17. Ford, Brinsley, Romney, p. 95.
18. Jones, B., and Dixon, M.V. (eds) (1985), *The Macmillan Dictionary*, London: Macmillan, p. 723.
19. ibid.
20. Hayley, pp. 370–71.
21. Romney, p. 107 n.
22. Romney, p. 111.
23. Romney, p. 107.
24. Romney, p. 110.
25. Letter to George Carter, V&A ms. 86 aa 25a; Pressly, p. 125; Romney, pp. 95 and 107.
26. *DNB*, 'George Romney', vol. XLIV, pp. 191–200.
27. Farington, 28 August 1803.
28. Letters to Lord Arundel, 1 January 1774 and 25 January 1775, in Ford, Brinsley.
29. Wilton and Bignamini, p. 25; Romney, p. 96.
30. Romney, p. 110; Jenkins and Sloan, p. 123; Greene, once again, put up the funds.
31. Jenkins and Sloan, p. 211.
32. Romney, p. 318.
33. Seidmann, pp. 7–9.
34. Seidmann, pp. 11–12 and 29.
35. Seidmann, pp. 15 and 50; Miss Romney's sale, 1894, lot 143; Barrow CRO Z250; Jenkins and Sloan, cat. 113; Marchant's engraved gems are in major collections throughout the world, for example his brown sard intaglio *Cleopatra* (London, Royal Collection) and his chalcedony medallion *Isis* (St Petersburg, Hermitage). This latter gem was copied from the antique reclining statue in the Museo Clementino, Rome, and relates to numerous recumbent female figures in Romney's oeuvre.
36. Wilton and Bignamini, cat. 178 and 212.
37. Romney, who later sent Wright recommendations concerning a visit to Venice, is acknowledged as an influence upon him after 1776; Bemrose, p. 36.
38. Egerton (1990), p. 249; Wright and Romney were both melancholics succoured by Hayley. Romney enquired after Wright's mental health; Hayley, p. 198.
39. Romney, p. 138 and pp. 321–32.
40. Romney, p. 324.
41. Summerson, pp. 413 and 466–8; Rudolf, M. A. (1988), 'The Life and Work of Thomas Harrison of Chester', PhD thesis London: Courtauld Institute, pp. 57 and 74; Hemingway, H. (1831), *History of Chester*, p. 362; Harrison and Romney were both influenced by neo-classicism: Harrison through

French architecture as typified by the Petit Trianon at Versailles (1764), and Romney through the work of Anton Raffael Mengs.

42. Wilson, p. 7; Ford, Boris, p. 301; Chamberlain, p. 173; Jaffé (1977), p. 57; Hayley, p. 166.
43. Wilton and Bignamini, p. 212.
44. Pressly, pp. v and ix.
45. Pressly, pp. xi and i.
46. Symmons, p. 649; illustrated in Tate Gallery (1975), *Henry Fuseli (1741–1825)*, exh. cat., London (Tate Gallery), p. 11.
47. Pilkington, M. (1810), *Dictionary of Painters*, cited in Watson (1985), p. 14.
48. Romney, p. 96.
49. V&A ms. 86 aa 25a.
50. Pressly, p. 125.
51. Wilton and Bignamini, p. 34; Chamberlain, p. 272.
52. Romney, p. 106; Wilton and Bignamini, cat. 26 and 96.
53. Wilton and Bignamini, p. 33.
54. His consciousness of this weakness is recorded in July 1792: British Museum sketchbook folios 63–44, cited in Chan, pp. 141–2.
55. Romney, pp. 79 and 97.
56. Twelve drawings at the Fitzwilliam Museum; Jaffé (1977), pp. 6–7.
57. Bignamini and Postle (1991), p. 75, e cat. 59.
58. Rump, figs. 181 and 182, compares the Romney drawings with Vesalius. Original in Barrow CRO z250.
59. The Mason Chamberlin portrait is illustrated in Bignamini and Postle, cat. 77.
60. Spang's bronze is illustrated in Bignamini and Postle, cat. 90; *Art Instruction* is illustrated in Allen (1984), cat. 4.
61. Romney, p. 20.
62. Wilton and Bignamini, p. 133.
63. Romney sale catalogue, 1801.
64. Jaffé (1977), p. 8.
65. Mowl, p. 125.
66. Watson (1974), p. 34.
67. Hayley, p. 311.
68. Shawe-Taylor, p. 153.
69. Eitner (1970), p. 11.
70. Ward and Roberts, vol. 2, p. 201; Romney, p. 237.
71. Edwards, R. (1930), 'Edward Edwards', *Country Life*, **67**, pp. 840–50; *DNB*, 'Edward Edwards', vol. XVIII, pp. 114–15.
72. Hazlitt (1894), cited in Dorment, p. 309 n. 2.
73. Williamson (1918), p. 50.
74. Pressly, p. x; Dixon, p. 80.
75. Romney, p. 99.
76. Romney, pp. 98–9; Crookshank (1957), p. 44.
77. Italian journal, Fitzwilliam Museum, Cambridge.
78. Romney, p. 120.
79. Romney, p. 113.
80. Humphry file in Ford, Brinsley.

81. Romney, p. 102.
82. Romney, p. 90; Greville also owned a Correggio.
83. Chamberlain, p. 74 and pp. 290–91; Hayley, p. 206; Flaxman, in Hayley, p. 309.
84. Italian journal, front cover, cited in Ward and Roberts, vol 1, pp. 35–6.
85. Greene, 5 and 12 September 1764.
86. Buttery, p. 108; Piper, 2nd edn, p. 75.
87. The apparent van Dyck dress of *John Sayer* (London, Harrow School) is that of the Harrow Archery Club. Thanks to Alex Kidson.
88. The present writer persists in using the outdated term 'protoromantic', as it emphasizes the artist's early involvement with this movement.
89. Usherwood, p. 379; Rump (exh. cat.), p. 4; Waterhouse, p. 317; Pointon (1970), p. xxv.
90. *The Gower Children* is generally known as *The Gower Family,* although it was called *The Stafford Family* by Chamberlain in 1910. The word 'Family' used here has led some authorities to assume that Lady Anne, the tallest figure, is the mother of the other children when she is actually their half-sister (Ward and Roberts, vol. 2, pp. 62–3). For this reason, the present publication uses the less ambiguous title *The Gower Children,* which also has the advantage of consistency within Romney's oeuvre. All other group paintings entitled 'Children' depict a group of siblings; those entitled 'Family' depict at least one parent or, as in the case of *The Beaumont Family,* a brother-in-law. Thanks to Christian Barnes for an interesting discussion on this subject.
91. Dixon, p. 154.
92. Brion, M. (1960), *Romantic Art*, London, p. 40.
93. Mowl, p. 224; Bindman (1979), pp. 37 and 41; Webster, Mary, 'A Poet and his Protégé Sculptor: William Hayley and John Flaxman', *Country Life,* September 1980, pp. 774–7.
94. Burke, p. vi.
95. Romney, pp. 11 and 61.
96. Romney, pp. 102 and 114.
97. Lister, p. 8, illustrated Pointon (1970), p. 119; Levitine, p. 33; Eitner (1970), p. 86.
98. Lavater's book was not published until 1789; Dixon, pp. 64n and 75; Pressly, pp. x and 42; Pointon (1970), p. 136; Bentley, 1743–4.
99. Chamberlain, p. 69. Baiocco was so called after the small coins he begged.
100. Marques, M. B., in Royal Academy (1994), *Goya,* exh. cat. London (Royal Academy), p. 24.
101. Letter from Father Thorpe to Lord Arundel, 4 January 1775, Ford, Brinsley. Romney file contains a transcript from the cover of a sketchbook sold Christie's, 17 May 1966.
102. Letter to Carter, V&A ms. 86 aa 25a.
103. Carter's professional ability in these areas is evident in his *Siege of Gibraltar* (London, National Portrait Gallery) and his *Apotheosis of Garrick* (Stratford-upon-Avon, Royal Shakespeare Company).
104. Williamson (1918), p. 54.
105. Romney, p. 108.
106. Romney, p. 110.
107. Romney, p. 114.
108. Wilton and Bignamini, cat. 91.
109. With Udney's assistance, his brother Robert Udney (1727–1800) was accumulating a fine collection of European art back in Teddington, and had funded Edward Edwards' visit to Italy. *DNB,* 'Edward Edwards', vol. XVII, pp. 324–5.
110. Turner, J. (ed.) (1996), op. cit., vol. 31, pp. 324–5, anonymous contribution on Udney.
111. Romney, pp. 114 and 118.
112. Romney, p. 112.
113. Thanks to John Ingamells, who checked the Brinsley Ford list of Bologna Academy members.
114. Humphry file, Ford, Brinsley; draft letter to Greville, cited in Chamberlain, p. 74.

115. Romney, pp. 120–21.

116. Dixon, p. 101.

117. Dixon, p. 101.

118. Buttery, p. 105 and fig. 3.

119. Ward and Roberts, vol. 1, p. 41; *DNB*, 'Edward Wortley Montagu', vol. XXXVIII, pp. 237–40.

120. Romney, pp. 110–12.

121. Hayley, p. 60.

122. Romney, pp. 130–32.

123. Romney, pp. 116 and 132.

124. Wilton and Bignamini, p. 15.

125. Chamberlain, p. 346; Crookshank (1957), p. 47; Pressly, p. vi.

5. Growing reputation and 'The Hermit of Eartham'

1. Jackson-Stops, p. 18.

2. An impressive residence was recommended by Rouquet, A. (1755), *The Present State of the Arts in England*, London, cited in Denvir, p. 121.

3. Phillips, p. 302; Chancellor, B. (1907), *History of the Squares of London*, London, pp. 56n, 57 and 59. Marylebone Library has a drawing of the house *c.*1904 before its demolition; Johnson, E.M. (1976), *Francis Cotes*, Oxford; a plan of the house by Cotes was in Miss Romney's sale of 1894, lot 27. The benefits of moving to an established studio were also enjoyed by Meyer, who moved to Zincke's studio in 1767, and Lonsdale, who moved to Opie's. Shee was to follow Romney at Cavendish Square.

4. Information from Marylebone Reference Library; Pointon (1993), p. 44.

5. Summerson, pp. 108, 110–11 and 143; Ratebooks 1775–96, Marylebone Library.

6. Preston CRO, DDGr Box 55.

7. Pointon (1993), p. 40.

8. Chamberlain, p. 82; Pointon (1993), p. 43.

9. Hayley, p. 34; Denvir, p. 122; Pointon (1993), p. 43.

10. Some of these would have been by his own hand; others he would have collected. Yet others in the John Romney sale (the source of this list) may have been collected by his son; Chamberlain, p. 233.

11. Whitley, vol. 2, p. 94, cited in Watson (1985), p. 60; sitters book, 24 November 1787; Wenham, pp. 57–8. Thanks to Frank and Brigid Heron. Tate visited Fuseli's studio and was not admitted as the artist was not at home. Mrs Flaxman's visit is recorded in Hayley's *Memoirs*, **2**, p. 149.

12. Shawe-Taylor, p. 17; Pointon (1993), p. 41; Romney's speed of working resulted in numerous *pentimenti*, for example in *Lady Grantham* (Philadelphia Museum of Art).

13. Romney, p. 55.

14. Bindman (1979), p. 25; Pointon (1993), p. 36; Hayley, p. 8.

15. Letter, Walker to Romney, V&A ms. 86 cc 32a 52/1; see also Brewer's *Dictionary of Phrase and Fable*, 'Mundungus'. Walker's request may explain why there are several versions of the travel journal. Thanks to Elizabeth Allen.

16. Romney, pp. 132–4.

17. Pointon (1993), p. 44.

18. Watson (1985), p. 47; Buttery, pp. 104–7.

19. Romney, pp. 136 and 313–19; Cumberland (1805), vol. 2, p. 384.

20. Thomas West's words in the first edition of his *Guide to the Lake District* (1778), cited by the present writer in his lecture to the Lancaster University Lake District Studies Diploma Course, 1995–6; West's *Guide* much influenced Wordsworth; Romney, p. 316. Gray's journal of his Lakes

tour is published in: Mann W. (ed.) (1775), *The Poems of Mr Gray. To which are prefixed memoirs of his life and writings*, London: Dodsley.

21. The Duke also sat in 1788 and visited the artist at Eartham in 1797. The importance of the Duke's patronage has previously been exaggerated. The Duke of Dorset had been a patron before Italy.
22. Ward and Roberts, vol. 1, p. 81.
23. Humphry ms. in RA Library Hu 2/47, dated 10 December 1776.
24. Humphry ms. RA (undated, late 1770s), a letter from Greene (not Thomas). Richter was his landlord at Great Newport Street while Coates (Cotes) was his predecessor at Cavendish Square.
25. Greene 'Life of George Romney'.
26. *DNB*, 'Richard Jebb; vol. XXIX, pp. 262–3; Romney, pp. 137–8; *Dr Richard Jebb* (London, Royal College of Physicians), though attributed to Zoffany, was probably a gift from Romney.
27. Hayley, pp. 68–9; Meyer appears in Zoffany's *Academicians of the Royal Academy* (London, Royal Collection); several Meyer miniatures are illustrated in Foskett (1987).
28. Hayley, p. 69; Romney, p. 138; Bishop, pp. 36–7.
29. Hayley, pp. 73–4.
30. ibid, p. 75.
31. Bishop, pp. 51, 162 and 165. The house, remodelled by Lutyens, is now Great Ballard School. Thanks to Janet Sugden for her guided tour.
32. Hayley, pp. 248–9; Cowper, letter to Rose, 29 August 1792; to Lady Hesketh, 26 August 1792. Thanks to Elizabeth Knight, The Cowper Museum, Olney.
33. Preston CRO DDGr, undated letter Hayley to Greene, 7 September, probably 1797.
34. Hayley, p. 342.
35. Hayley, p. 361; written in 1777, the *Epistles* were first published by Dodsley in 1778; the date in Hayley, p. 339, is probably a misprint.
36. Romney, p. 139; Bindman (1979), p. 27.
37. *DNB*, 'William Hayley', vol. XXV, pp. 295–6.
38. Chamberlain, p. 85; also pp. 77, 98, 115 and 130.
39. Bishop, p. 119.
40. Bishop, pp. 20 and 120.
41. King (1991), p. 140; Lewis, W.S. (ed.) (1955), Walpole letters, vol. 25, New Haven, pp. 225–7.
42. Jaffé (1977), p. 16; Wilson, p. 146.
43. Dixon, p. 12.
44. Egerton (1990), pp. 132–4; Bindman (1979), p. 27.
45. V&A mss. 86 cc 32a, 54/2, letter, Adam Walker to Romney, 14 September 1783.
46. Hayley, p. 7.
47. Hayley, pp. 90–91; Romney, p. 193; Chamberlain, p. 130; Barrow CRO Z251/2, letter, Hayley to Romney, 7 March 1787, also Z251/1.
48. Seward, A. (1782), *Verses on Leaving Eartham*, cited in Romney, pp. 191–2.
49. Chamberlain, pp. 121 and 152.
50. *DNB*, 'Anna Seward', vol. LI, pp. 280–82; Oman, C. (1973), *Wizard of the North*, London, p. 137.
51. Bishop, pp. 132–5.
52. Bindman (1979), pp. 27, 36, 46 and 100; Gower, p. 45.
53. Barrow CRO, ms. Z251/1, letter, Hayley to Romney, 21 January 1787; Hayley, p. 134.
54. Hayley, p. 184.
55. Chamberlain, pp. 129, 131–2 and 148.
56. Hayley, p. 61; Cumberland (1803), pp. 417–23.
57. Hayley, p. 22.

58. Ward and Roberts, **2**, p. 35.
59. Egerton (1984), p. 19.
60. Mowl, p. 234.
61. Romney, p. 125.
62. ibid., pp. 126–7.
63. George Romney, quoted in the obituary of his pupil, James Rawlinson, Derby *Mercury*, 30 May 1849.
64. *Morning Chronicle*, 8 May 1786, cited in Ward and Roberts, vol. 2, p. 143; Chamberlain, p. 248; Edwards, pp. 274–76; Cunningham, p. 77.
65. Mowl, pp. 126–8 and 133–43.
66. Watson (1985), p. 18.
67. Romney, p. 140.
68. Chamberlain, p. 193.
69. Postle (1995), p. 331, cites the Society of Artists' Minutes.
70. Paulson, p. 243n.
71. Romney, p. 136.
72. Pressly, p. 121; the cartoons were presented to Liverpool Royal Institution by the Reverend John Romney.
73. Morris and Stevens, p. 44.
74. ibid. These works are a tangible recapitulation of his desire that John should 'retain the butys and knowledge of the lattin authors', letter from Rome, 20 June 1773, cited Ward and Roberts, vol. 1, p. 32.
75. One from this group was to be wrongly entitled *Ophelia* by a writer who failed to spot the lurking water snake; Gower, illustrations unpaginated.
76. Drabble, M. (ed.) (1985), *Oxford Companion to Literature*, pp. 412–13.
77. Hayley, p. 309; Romney, p. 160; Bindman (1979), Pl. 109.
78. The cartoons from *The Persians* were praised as 'worthy to have been applauded by Aeschylus himself' by the poet laureate Thomas Warton (1728–90), himself a literary protoromantic. In this century they have been hailed as having 'a compositional austerity that is only found a little later in David' (Hayley, pp. 224–5; Rump (1974), p. 3). Although Romney and David did not meet until 1790, at this earlier period they were working on similar themes. Romney's cartoon *The Dream of Atossa* depicts Xerxes falling from his chariot (Morris and Stevens, pp. 46–7); David drew Hector falling from his in *c.* 1778. Both may owe something to Rubens's *Death of Hippolytus* (London, Courtauld Institute Galleries).
79. Honour (1968), p. 14.
80. Chamberlain, p. 354.
81. Sometimes wrongly called Richard Potter.
82. Norwich City Library, C821 LOC 11317.
83. Crookshank (1957), p. 43; Potter's second edition, p. 349, cited Morris and Stevens, p. 48.
84. National Museum of Wales, Potter's letter to Romney, mss. 12433, Wigfair 33D, letter 1; Maxwell, pp. 82–3; Romney, pp. 159–61 and 220–22. By dedicating the translations to Chancellor Thurlow, Potter earned a prebendal stall at Norwich in 1788.
85. Jaffé (1977), p. 22.
86. Bell, cited Denvir, p. 104.

6. 'The man in Cavendish Square'

1. *The Idler*, **45**, cited in Friedman, pp. 9 and 45.
2. Shawe-Taylor, p. 7.

3. Denvir, p. 183.
4. Hayley, p. 342.
5. Waterhouse, p. 306.
6. Pointon (1993), p. 52.
7. Chamberlain, p. 268.
8. Cumberland (1803), p. 423; Frith, W.P., *Recollections*, cited in *London Argus*, **139.6**, 30 December 1899, p. 1.
9. Ward and Roberts published most of these but a very late studio day-book remains unpublished at the Yale Center for British Art; most mss. sitters books are at the British Library: Add. mss. 38081–87; see Watson (1985), p. 97.
10. Whitley, cited in Piper (1957), p. 206; Gombrich, p. 80.
11. Hayley, p. 83; Ward and Roberts, **2**, p. 114, refers to *Mrs Oliver*; Burkett (1987), p. 202, cites a letter from Dr Peter Steele, his brother.
12. Romney, p. 21.
13. Wesley's *Journal*, 5 January 1789, cited in Ward and Roberts, vol. 2, p. 169; letter Stewardson to John Romney, Barrow CRO Z244/1.
14. Newdigate mss., cited in Gower, p. 91.
15. Italian journal (1773). Note on cover relates to shadow effects.
16. Hazlitt, cited in Shawe-Taylor, p. 20.
17. Jackson-Stops, p. 530; Piper, first edn, p. 196.
18. Hayley, p. 104.
19. Shawe-Taylor, p. 125.
20. Ward and Roberts, vol. 2, p. 159.
21. Chamberlain, p. 345.
22. Ward and Roberts, **2**, p. 164.
23. Simon, p. 19.
24. Postle, M. (1995), p. 168.
25. Northcote, cited in Romney, pp. 172–3; Shawe-Taylor, p. 125; Alex Kidson lecture, Romney Society, 10 October 1996. Postle in Strong (1991), p. 39, cites James Barry in Fryer (1809), *Works of James Barry*, vol. 1, London, p. 217.
26. Simon, p. 226.
27. An Italian sketchbook contains a reference to Reynolds's *Discourses*. Photograph in Witt Library, Courtauld Institute, London, Romney Files box 2154.
28. Quoted by Flaxman, in Hayley, p. 313.
29. Romney, p. 108.
30. Redgrave, Samuel and Richard (1866), *A Century of British Painters*, London; new edn London, 1947, p. 61.
31. Greene (*c*.1802); this invitation was probably issued in the early days of their rivalry.
32. Chamberlain, p. 348.
33. Letter to Lord Hardwick (original MS untraced), 15 September 1779. xerox copy of ms. Thanks to Clifford Ellisone.
34. Gower cites Newdigate mss, cited by Gower, p. 91.
35. Sitters Book National Portrait Gallery, cited Pointon (1993), p. 41; letter, John Romney to Hayley, 17 June 1805, Fitzwilliam Museum, Cambridge.
36. National Portrait Gallery ledger October 1791; ms. in possession of private owner; Hayley, pp. 124 and 141; Romney, pp. 44, 142 and 159.
37. Egerton (1990), p. 269.

38. This was the opinon of the late Sir Ellis Waterhouse, which is contentious with regard to Gainsborough.
39. Thomas Robinson, cited in Hayley, p. 323.
40. ibid.
41. Romney, p. 193.
42. Jamison, p. 127.
43. Quoted in Ward and Roberts, vol. 2, p. 169.
44. Allen, E. (1996), pp. 117–20.
45. Dorment, p. 332.
46. Paulson, p. 215.
47. Ward and Roberts, vol. 2, p. 25; Shawe-Taylor, p. 17.
48. King (1991), pp. 161–2.
49. Pointon (1993), p. 192; Buttery, p. 108; Waterhouse, p. 212.
50. Noted by Watson, Jennifer C., 'Romney's Theatrical Portraiture', *Apollo* (September 1992), pp. 147–51.
51. Shawe-Taylor, p. 166.
52. Romney, p. 327.
53. Romney, p. 83; Hammond, N.G.L., and Sculland, H.H. (1970), *Oxford Classical Dictionary*, p. 1074; Hobey-Hamsher, C. (1996), in Turner, J. (ed.), op.cit., vol. 30, p. 893.
54. Simon, p. 16; Allen (1987), p. 219.
55. Simon, p. 97; Chamberlain, p. 345.
56. Yale Sitters Book, New Haven, Yale Center for British Art, Rare Book Room, no. 32279; Watson (1985), p. 14.
57. Romney, p. 25; Pointon (1993), p. 58.
58. Horne, H.P. (1891), *Engravings after George Romney published between 1770 and 1830*, London; copy in British Museum Department of Prints and Drawings.
59. Romney, p. 194.
60. Romney, p. 75; Barrow CRO Z ms., 21 May 1801.
61. Romney, p. 328; Newdigate ms. cited in Gower, p. 91.
62. Gardiner, H. (ed.) (1972), *New Oxford Book of English Verse*, Oxford, p. 450.
63. Eitner (1970), p. 7; Hayley, pp. 324 and 344; Romney, p. 79.
64. Hayley, p. 315.
65. Hayley, p. 324.
66. Jackson-Stops, p. 530.
67. Colnaghi (1986) exhibition catalogue, *British Art*, London, p. 83.
68. Waterhouse, p. 22; Shawe-Taylor, p. 153.
69. Hayley, p. 92; Shawe-Taylor, p. 44.
70. Robinson, cited in Hayley, p. 323; Thomas Phillips, cited in Chamberlain, p. 375. Thanks to Lowell Libson for the Wilson parallel.
71. Shawe-Taylor, pp. 76–8.
72. Postle, in Strong (1991), p. 188; Pointon (1993) pp. 51–2.
73. Romney, p. 81.
74. Munro, J. (1994), *National Art Collections Fund Quarterly Magazine* (Summer), p. 59.
75. Graham-Dixon, A., *Independent Magazine* 2 November 1991, p. 65; Folger Library Art vol. c61, cited in Dixon, p. 72.
76. Hayley, p. 301.

77. Jaffé (1977), p. 30; Romney, p. 81. The stimulus of his native landscape is well established. George Barret RA, who had worked in Romney's studio, was one of the earliest artists to visit the Lake District. Through the Lockes at Norbury, Barret had links with the brothers Sawrey and the Reverend William Gilpin, who had Lakeland origins.

78. Shawe-Taylor, pp. 37–8 and 47.

79. Colnaghi (1986), p. 87.

80. Eitner (1955), p. 286.

81. Eitner (1955), p. 28.

82. Waterhouse, p. 308.

83. *DNB*, 'William Withering', vol. LXII, pp. 268–70; Withering was, with Priestley and Wright, associated with the Lunar Society in Birmingham.

84. Pieter van der Merwe suggested this in a letter to me of 20 October 1993; Nicholas Pocock is listed in the Yale sitters diary, but perhaps with regard to his son Isaac's apprenticeship to Romney.

85. Cross, D.A. (1998), 'Sawrey Gilpin RA', *Armitt Journal*, Lancaster University, **1**, pp. 64–85.

86. Jaffé (1977), p. 36; *Lonsdale Magazine*, 30 June 1822; Chamberlain, p. 117.

87. Royal Academy (1972), *The Age of Neo-Classicism*, exh. cat., London, p. 297.

88. Ward and Roberts, vol. 1, p. 100.

89. Hayley, p. 324; Romney, pp. 181 and 242–3.

90. Folger Art Volume c61, cited in Dixon, p. 72; Hayes (1991), p. 52; Romney, pp. 213 and 328; Hayley, p. 103; Waterhouse, p. 308; Bindman (1979), p. 86.

91. Gamlin, p. 206.

92. Romney, p. 85.

93. The ms. autobiography of composer John Marsh, extract contained in Romney File, National Portrait Gallery Archives.

94. Mannings (1991), p. 138.

95. Jaffé (1977), p. 11.

96. Waterhouse, p. 308.

97. Burke, p. 275; Sewter, A.C. (1941), 'Romney's Sketches for the Beaumont Family', *Burlington Magazine*, **79**, pp. 12–17.

98. This recalls one of Dr Johnson's justifications of portraiture. See the first sentence of this chapter. *The Idler*, **45**, cited in Friedman, pp. 9 and 45.

99. The present writer identified this for the Christie's sale.

100. Watson (1974), pp. 69–70.

101. Whitley, vol. 2, pp. 93–4, cited in Watson (1985), p. 40.

102. Chamberlain, p. 100.

103. *Odes to the Academicians* (1786 edition), London, p. 178; Sir Richard Pepper Arden, who also sat to Romney, was Master of the Rolls and an MP who had married the daughter of Richard Wilbraham Bootle. 'Pindar' himself (John Wolcot) sat to Romney in 1779.

104. Romney, p. 168.

105. Chamberlain, p. 149–51; Jaffé (1977), p. 44.

106. Dorment, p. 308.

107. Mannings (1991), p. 135; Waterhouse, p. 308.

108. Piper (1957), p. 176; Hayley, p. 302; letter, Cowper to Rose, 29 August 1792, in King and Ryskamp.

109. Hayley, p. 300.

110. Pressly, pp. x–xi. The father of Miss Joan Knatchbull (portrait in Parham Park, Sussex) corresponded with Romney about this. Draft letter, National Portrait Gallery sketchbook. Thanks to Alex Kidson for this reference.

111. Hayes, p. 104.

112. Thanks to Sarah Braddyll for this suggestion.
113. Ward and Roberts, vol. 2, p. 87.
114. Tomalin, Clair, and Dejardin, Jan (1995), *Mrs Jordan: The Duchess of Drury Lane*, Kenwood (1995).
115. Dorment, pp. 348–51.
116. Shawe-Taylor, p. 192; there are drawings in the Fitzwilliam Museum, Cambridge, for example BV 149, which are 'carved out of the flesh'.
117. Chamberlain, p. 306; Romney, p. 120; Rump, pls. 20–21.
118. Buttery, p. 109; Rump, pls. 25–6.
119. Romney, p. 164; Miller, Jonathan (1998), *On Reflection*, London, National Gallery Publications, p. 86.
120. Solkin, p. 187.
121. Allen (1984) p. 2.
122. Romney, pp. 127 and 162; Walker sonnet, V&A mss. 86cc32a 55; Chamberlain, pp. 187 and 377.
123. Chamberlain, pp. 187.
124. Shawe-Taylor, pp. 191 ff; Allen (1984), p. 1.
125. Shawe-Taylor, p. 205 and 214.
126. Pointon (1993), p. 192 and pl. 237.
127. Burke, p. 276.
128. Egerton (1990) p. 202, citing John Gage; Lister, pls. 10 and 12.
129. Waterhouse, p. 308; Piper, p. 212; Allen (1984), no. 12; Waterfield, G., and Quarrie, P. (eds.) (1991), *Leaving Portraits from Eton College*, exh. cat. London (Dulwich Picture Gallery), pp. 32 and 34.
130. Chamberlain, p. 324; sitters book, March 17 and 28, 1778, Ward and Roberts, vol. 1, pp. 85–6.
131. Pointon (1993), pp. 197–8.
132. All three are illustrated in Allen (1984), pls. 14, 19 and 15.
133. This notion is used of Miss Clavering by Pointon (1993), p. 192.
134. Gowing, L. (ed.) (1983), *Macmillan Biographical Dictionary of Art*, article on Romney, Jaffé (1977), p. 17.
135. Usherwood, p. 378.
136. Romney, pp. 83–4.
137. Burke, p. 275; Buttery, p. 105.
138. Numerous writers have repeated this association with Poussin, which appears to originate with Ellis Waterhouse. A more detailed examination of Poussin's theme of the dance in this context would be of interest.
139. Bindman (1979), p. 54.
140. Wash drawings at Manchester, Whitworth Art Gallery; Cambridge, Fitzwilliam Museum, LD 58; and on loan to Kendal, Abbot Hall Art Gallery. See also Usherwood, p. 378.
141. Jaffé (1972), p. 33; Fraser, p. 125. There are also Medea drawings at the Fitzwilliam Museum, Cambridge, and the Baltimore Art Gallery.
142. Chamberlain, pp. 102–3. Though more familiar as Lady Hamilton, in this volume Emma is almost entirely referred to as Emma Hart, the name she had during the active part of her relationship with Romney. Another indication of the friendship between Romney and Greville is that the latter stored wine in the artist's cellar.
143. Lord Bristol, cited in Fraser, p. 195.
144. Paston, pp. 84–5 and 127; Jaffé (1972), p. 71; Chamberlain, p. 167.
145. Fraser, p. 9.
146. ibid.
147. Chamberlain, p. 109.

148. Dorment, pp. 308–9; Hardwick, Mollie (1969), *Emma, Lady Hamilton,* London, Hamish Hamilton, p. 34.
149. Fraser, p. 172.
150. Chamberlain, p. 110; Jaffé (1977), pp. 35–6.
151. The sitters book for 1785 is lost; Watson (1974) estimates 180 sittings; on the surviving evidence she sat 118 times.
152. Dorment, p. 309.
153. Waterhouse, p. 317; Ward and Roberts list 45 but acknowledge problems of attribution; Romney lists 24; for a full treatment of these portraits see Watson (1974), which estimates 28 genuine portraits; Jaffé (1977), pp. 35–7.
154. Gamlin, p. 193.
155. Fraser, p. 39.
156. Shawe-Taylor, pp. 143–5 and 169–71.
157. Chamberlain, p. 168.
158. Watson (1974), pp. 60–61; Cross (1983) devotes a chapter to Diana.
159. Jenkins and Sloan, pp. 262–73.
160. Fraser, p. 88.
161. Romney, p. 183; Friedman, p. 134.
162. Jenkins and Sloan, pp. 252–61.
163. Goethe's *Voyage to Italy,* cited in Bowen, M. (1935), *Patriotic Lady: Emma Hamilton and the Neapolitan Revolution of 1799,* London, p. 58; Dorment, p. 324.
164. Jaffé (1972) pp. 37–9; Rutland mss. vol. 3, p. 311, Historic Manuscripts Commission, cited in Fraser, p. 91.
165. Rehberg's drawings were engraved and appear in Jaffé (1972), pp. 36–9; Jenkins and Sloan, pp. 260–61; Locke's are illustrated in Jenkins and Sloan, cat. 157.
166. Friedman, pp. 133 and 136; Wark, p. 2.
167. Folger sketchbook, cited in Jaffé (1977), p. 35.
168. Burke, p. 276.
169. Romney's words, cited in Chamberlain, p. 164.
170. Fraser, p. 172. This reference to Emma's poverty and wealth probably refers to her elevation from the austerity of Greville's regime to the relative extravagances of the Palazzo Sessa in Naples. It does not appear to be grounds for accepting the notion that Romney knew Emma before she came to the studio with Greville.

7. Patterns of friendship

1. Cumberland (1803), pp. 422–3.
2. Cross (1996), pp. 19–21.
3. Romney, p. 166.
4. There is a copy of the Macbeth canvas at the Garrick Club which is not by Romney.
5. 'Reed' is sometimes incorrectly spelled 'Read' in Blake's letters.
6. Reed, p. 5; *DNB*, 'Isaac Reed', vol. LXVII, pp. 391–2..
7. Sheldon, pp. 194 and 253.
8. Sheldon, p. 71; *DNB*, 'Thomas Sheridan', vol. LII, pp. 87–8; Kelly, Linda (1997), *Richard Brinsley Sheridan*, London, p. 7.
9. Bingham, M. (1972), *The Track of a Comet: Thomas Sheridan of Smock Alley,* London, p. 26; Kelly, p. 47, refers to the stammer of the Marquis of Buckingham.
10. Sheldon, pp. 5 and 41–6; Reed, 9 May 1780.

11. Reed, 30 April 1784; Evans is not to be confused with another bookseller of the same name (1739–1803); *DNB*, 'Thomas Evans', vol. XVIII, pp. 73–4; Romney, p. 166.
12. *DNB*, 'John Henderson', vol. XXV, pp. 398–401; Jaffé (1977), p. 28; Dixon, pp. 34 and 46. Henderson gave a reading from Hayley's *Two Connoisseurs* at Cavendish Square on 18 January 1783. Hayley (1823), p. 295; Richard Cumberland was also buried in Poets' Corner, Westminster Abbey, in 1811.
13. Hayley, pp. 301, 330 and 316.
14. Hayley, p. 316; Romney, pp. 165–6; Jaffé (1977), p. 26; Reed, Queen's Head, 16 October 1792; Shakespeare, 21 December 1793; Greene (1802), 21 December 1793. Thanks to Edwina Ehrman, Museum of London; see also n.6 above.
15. Romney, p. 232.
16. Hayley, p. 316.
17. *DNB*, 'Adam Walker', vol. LIX, p. 42; 'Richard Cumberland', vol. XIII, pp. 290–93; Ward and Roberts, vol. 2, p. 195.
18. Reed, Index, 16 October 1792.
19. They married the sisters Martha and Alice Dawson of Warton, Lancashire. Greene, p. 4.
20. Thompson, W. E. (1951), *Annals of the Royal College of Surgeons*, London, pp. 55–63. Thanks to Alison Fenwick for locating the tomb.
21. Taylor, John (1832), *Records of my Life*, London, cited in Venn, *Alumni Cantabridgiensis*.
22. Letter from Pamela Clarke, Royal Archives. Nicol's warrant dated 1 May 1780: Public Record Office, Kew, LC3/67 [116]; *Gentleman's Magazine*, 25 June 1828.
23. *DNB*, 'Francis Newbery', vol. XL, p. 312.
24. Mowl, p. 193.
25. Newbery must not be confused with his cousin, also Francis, of Paternoster Row.
26. Ward and Roberts, **2**, p. 111.
27. Reed, 25 December 1792.
28. *DNB*; letter to Romney, 7 November 1796, in Romney, pp. 239–40.
29. Jones, p. 8; letter to author from Laetitia Yeanolle, Folger Library, 29 June 1993.
30. Some claim that his country house was Heathfield Park, Sussex; Ward and Roberts, vol. 2, p. 111; Cumberland (1803), p. 422.
31. Romney's bank records with Child's Bank were pulped during World War II. Thanks to Elizabeth Allen for this information.
32. Reed, 27 February 1789 and 2 July 1789.
33. Reed, 23 March 1791.
34. Reed, 27 December 1792; Hayley, pp. 232 and 242.
35. Hayley, p. 233.
36. Carwardine letter, V&A ms. 86 cc 32a.
37. Ward and Roberts, vol. 2, p. 17; Braithwaite appears to have had a close relationship with Angelica Kauffmann, as he was a trustee of her marriage settlement.
38. Letter, Hayley to Romney, Barrow CRO, Z251/2.
39. Chamberlain, pp. 95 and 149; Ward and Roberts, **2**, p. 26.
40. Thanks to Stephen Freeth, Guildhall Library, London.
41. Chamberlain, p. 197.
42. V&A mss. 86 cc 32a/55.
43. Ward and Roberts, vol. 2, pp. 38 and 137.
44. On one occasion before seeing Cumberland's play *Wat Tyler*. V&A ms. 86 aa 25a.
45. Romney, p. 78.
46. Romney, p. 243.

47. Chamberlain, p. 246.
48. *DNB*, 'John Hoole', vol. XXVII, pp. 300–301; Williamson (1918), p. 248.
49. Ward and Roberts, vol. 1, pp. 109 and 124, 24 September 1786 and 6 August 1791.
50. Romney, p. 223.
51. NPG ledger, pp. 26–7; V&A 86 cc 32, cited in Pointon, p. 46; Watson (1985), pp. 95–7, cites the Yale Center for British Art collection of mss.
52. V&A 86 cc 32, cited in Pointon, p. 46.
53. Preston CRO DDGr, Hayley to Greene, 14 September 178(7)?
54. NPG ledger p. 16; Receipt Book, Fitzwilliam Museum, Cambridge, p. 13.
55. Cross (1997), vol. 2, p. 18; *Cumberland Pacquet*, 10 August 1784, cited in Curwen, J.F. (1928), *History of the Ancient House of Curwen*, Kendal, p. 186; *Gentleman's Magazine*, September 1810, p. 288.
56. *DNB*; Robinson's portrait of his son at Romney's tomb appears as an engraving in Hayley, Pl. 12.
57. Rawlinson's obituary in the *Derby Mercury*, 30 May 1849.
58. Thanks to Francis Greenacre, Bristol Art Gallery, citing the Sharples Collection Catalogue, p. 21; see also Knox, C. McC. (1930), *The Sharples*, New Haven.
59. Wilmerding, J. (1973), *The Genius of American Painting*, London, Mount, p. 329.
60. Nettleship, J.T. (1898), *Life of George Morland*, London, p. 11.
61. Thanks to the private owner for this information.
62. Information in the Barret box file, Witt Library, Courtauld Institute, London.
63. V&A ms. 86cc32 32a 53, Walker to Romney, 27 January 1802.
64. Letter from Isaac Swainson to his father of 26 September 1785 or 6, cited in a letter from T.W. Thompson of 5 October 1954 to the Librarian, St John's College, Cambridge.
65. Fitzwilliam ms. letter, John Romney to Hayley, 22 June 1806.
66. V&A ms. 86aa25, cited in Chan, p. 31.
67. Sir George Warren, account for *Miss Warren* portrait, ms. note, sold Sotheby's, 10 February 1970.
68. Hobson, V., *Index of the Honourable East India Company*, Cambridge, 1944, p. 478; thanks to Tim Cockerill.
69. Transcriptions made by Mr T. McCabe of the James Romney mss., lent anonymously for the purpose to Abbot Hall; *Quarto*, **18.2**, July 1980; There is, however, no memorial inscription at Bath Abbey.
70. Abbot Hall transcripts (see n 69 above) include some of his correspondence and the text of his play *The India Pavilion*.
71. V&A ms. 86cc32a, 18/1, dated 20 June 1774; Romney p. 308.
72. Romney, pp. 290, 306, 307 and 310.
73. V&A ms. 86aa25 a4; Romney, p. 311.
74. Parish Records, Dalton-in-Furness.
75. Esther Abbot was married to a Kendal hatter named Millers. Thanks to Tim Cockerill.
76. Hayley, p. 10. In 1764 in France he gave money to 'a poor Frenchman' (Greene Diary (1986), 'Expenses of Tour', 2 September 1764). In 1794 he gave £30 to his sister Jane, whose husband's debts were a constant problem.
77. Hayley, p. 182; Romney, p. 149.
78. Robinson, cited in Hayley, p. 322. Letter to Romney from William Cowper, in King and Ryskamp, 19 October 1792 and 5 November 1792.
79. B. Coll's map of Westminster (1754) indicates how near Romney lived to the countryside, though some building had continued north and west since 1754; Phillips, p. 10.
80. Chamberlain, pp. 348–9; Robinson in Hayley, pp. 322–3.
81. Romney, p. 86.
82. Romney, p. 274.

83. Hayley, pp. 287 and 326.

84. Cumberland (1803), pp. 421–2; Hayley, p. 326; Chamberlain, p. 255; Waterhouse, p. 306; Romney, p. 144.

85. He was rebuked on this count by the Reverend Samuel Greathead; Ward and Roberts, **2**, p. 64.

86. Quoted in Edwards, p. 278; V&A ms. 86cc32a/55 includes Walker's verse.

87. Hayley, pp. 224–5 and 251–2.

88. Hayley, p. 236.

89. Cumberland (1803), cited in Chamberlain, p. 53; Hayley, pp. 161 and 191.

90. Romney, pp. 56–7; Dixon, p. 20. Though John Romney says Thomas Dalton, it may have been his father, Captain John Dalton. Jaffé (1977), p. 16.

91. Fitzwilliam BV 64, 66 and LD 144; Jaffé (1977), p. 39.

92. Hayley, pp. 317–18.

93. Hayley, pp. 160; Cunningham, p. 120.

94. Preston CRO DDGr, undated letter, Hayley to Greene, 'Thurs a.m.' *c.*1788.

95. Cumberland (1803), p. 523.

96. Pressly, p. 121.

97. Illustrated Paston, p. 154; Hayley, pp. 253–4.

98. Dixon, pp. 120 and 132.

99. Hayley, p. 267.

100. Crookshank (1957), pp. 44 and 47; Chamberlain, p. 290.

101. Newton, E. (1962), *The Romantic Rebellion*, London, p. 13; Fuseli (1810), in Pilkington's Dictionary.

102. Pointon (1993), pp. 125–6; Romney, p. 298.

103. Thanks to Dr Esther Ross.

104. Flaxman, to Hayley, cited in Chamberlain, p. 236.

105. Chamberlain, pp. 54–5 and 91.

106. Chamberlain, p. 110; James Harrison (likely author of this anonymous volume) (1816), *Mémoires de Lady Hamilton, Ambassadrice d'Angleterre à la Cour de Naples: Choix D'Anecdotes Curieuses sur Cette Femme Célèbre*, Paris.

107. Letter, 29 November 1802, sold Sotheby's, 20 July 1971, transcript National Portrait Gallery archives; in 1910 Chamberlain valiantly upheld his respectability, p. 247.

108. 'A Memoir of Mr George Romney', *Lonsdale Magazine*, April 1822, p. 146; Jaffé (1977), p. 22.

109. Romney's *Italian Journal*, Fitzwilliam Museum; Farington (1975), *Diary*, 16 November 1798.

110. V&A ms. 86aa25a 5/2 & 5/3.

111. Wilton and Bignamini, p. 77.

8. John Boydell and the closet romantic

1. Friedman, p. 38.

2. Letter, Edmond Malone to Lord Charlemont, 6 June 1787, cited Ward and Roberts, **2**, p. 193. This source states that Dr Farmer, Master of Emmanuel College, Cambridge, was also involved in the gestation of the idea. Farmer also sat to Romney; Farington, *Diary*, December 1786; This year (1786) was also when Romney indulged himself by buying two farms at Ormsgill, adjacent to High Cocken, whose former occupants were lifetime neighbours of his father.

3. Romney, pp. 26 and 151–2; Friedman, pp. 66 and 132.

4. Newspaper cutting, in Edwards, p. 278.

5. Chamberlain, p. 149; Hayley, pp. 101 and 129.

6. Dixon, p. 48; Piper (1957), p. 194.

7. Friedman, p. 74, citing *The Times* of 4 May 1789.
8. Northcote Letters, cited in Chamberlain, p. 146.
9. Friedman, p. 75.
10. Munro, J. (1997), *Shakespeare and the Eighteenth Century*, exh. cat., Cambridge (Fitzwilliam Museum).
11. Hayley, p. 153; there are inconsistent details in Hayley and Romney. Some of the *Tempest* drawings may predate 1787. See Dorment, pp. 320–24.
12. See Romney's subscription ticket in V&A ms. 86cc32.2.
13. This sculpture survives in a public garden near the Memorial Theatre at Stratford-upon-Avon; illustrated in Friedman; a medal was struck bearing the Banks design (Cambridge, Fitzwilliam Museum).
14. *The Tempest*, Arden edition.
15. Hayley, pp. 127 and 175.
16. Hayley, p. 128.
17. Hayley, pp. 128 and 135, 140; 1790 was the year Boydell was elected Lord Mayor of London, and he invited Romney to the Lady Mayoress's Ball on 12 April 1791.
18. Hayley, pp. 126, 138–9 and 281; Foskett (1972), p. 132.
19. Chan, p. 79, suggests that Prospero relates to St Peter in Raphael's *Death of Ananias*; also see Greuze's *L'Orage*; Watson (1974), p. 71.
20. Romney, p. 151; the artist did besides earn £3,504 in 1786, more than three times his annual income before he went to Italy.
21. *Gentleman's Magazine*, **10**, December 1790, p. 1088–90; Friedman, p. 102; Romney, p. 153; Hayley, p. 141.
22. Wenham, pp. 57–8.
23. Pape, W., and Burwick, F., eds (1996), *Boydell Shakespeare Gallery*, London, p. 116.
24. ibid.
25. Farington, *Diary*, **1**, p. 198, cited Friedman, p. 130; Strong (1978), p. 13.
26. Hayley, pp. 208 and 260; Stuebe, I.C. (1979), *The Life and Works of William Hodges*, London, p. 70; Hodges, who sailed with Captain Cook in 1772, painted an excellent portrait of the great explorer and produced striking Pacific island landscapes with accurate ethnic details; for example, *The War Boats of the Island of Otaheite* (London, National Maritime Museum). After Cook's death he produced *The Death of Captain Cook* (London, National Maritime Museum).
27. Wind, E. (1930–31), *Vorträge der Bibliotek Warburg*, Leipzig, p. 130, abb 4, cited in Friedman, p. 136.
28. Morris and Stevens, pp. 51 and 54.
29. Dixon, pp. 64n–65 and 67; Boydell Gallery Catalogue, 1793, and Smith's engraving, London British Museum; a drawing of the Passions is at Yale Center for British Art, New Haven.
30. Even the version described as a 'sketch' (London, Royal Shakespeare Collection) is completed in some detail, especially the tiny flying spirits above the main group, where vivid colour contrasts with the virtually monochrome treatment of the Passions themselves. In Alex Kidson's opinion this version is not by Romney.
31. Friedman, p. 137; Morris and Stevens, pp. 51 end 54; there are drawings in the Fitzwilliam Museum, Folger Shakespeare Library, Walker Art Gallery and National Gallery of Scotland collections; Powell, N. (1952), 'Fuseli: The Infant Shakespeare between Comedy and Tragedy', *Burlington Magazine*, **94**, p. 172.
32. Wind, E. (1938), 'The Choice of Hercules', *Journal of the Courtauld and Warburg Institute*, **2**, p. 263, cited in Friedman, p. 136 n265.
33. Watson (1974), p. 73.
34. Romney, p. 147.
35. Friedman, pp. 70, 74 and 164 and pl. 70; Dixon, p. 251; Hayley, pp. 163–4; Romney, p. 152.
36. Northcote letters, cited in Chamberlain, p. 146.
37. V&A letter 86cc 32, 32a 37/1, Greene to John Romney, 27 January 1804.

38. Friedman, p. 34; Chamberlain, p. 147. After a chequered history the decision was made to have *The Tempest* cut down. Today only several heads survive (Bolton Art Gallery).
39. Illustrated in Milne Henderson, P. (1966), *I Maestri del Colore* Series, no. 250, Pl. 6, Fratelli Fabbri Editori, Milan (copy NPG archive library).
40. Pressly, vii; Boris Ford, p. 18.
41. Dixon, p. 154.
42. A notion expressed by Jean Wallis, 1998.
43. Hayley, p. 210; V&A ms. 86cc32 3/1.
44. Jaffé (1977), pp. 28 and 53.
45. For detailed expositions upon the drawings see the writings of Chan, Crookshank, Dixon, Jaffé, Wark and Watson.
46. Hayley, pp. 35–6.
47. Flaxman in Hayley, p. 310.
48. V&A ms. 86.32.cc.3/1.
49. Pilkington, *Dictionary*; Chamberlain, pp. 376–7.
50. Pointon (1970), p. 134.
51. Hayley, p. 367.
52. Romney, p. 102.
53. Hayley, pp. 72–3; Hagstrum (1978), in Essick, Robert N., and Pearce, Donald, *Blake and His Time*, Bloomington and London, Indiana University Press, p. 201; Hayley, p. 323 citing Robinson.
54. The best collections of these are at the Fitzwilliam Museum, Cambridge, the Dilworth Collection at the Yale Center for British Art, New Haven, and the Folger Shakespeare Library, Washington DC. There is also a significant collection at the Musée du Louvre and, to a lesser extent, in numerous galleries worldwide. The late Michael Jaffé, in the Preface to Patricia Jaffé's Fitzwilliam catalogue, states, 'Over 5,000 authentic drawings by Romney survive' (Jaffé 77, p. i). This is probably an under-estimate.
55. Hayley, p. 374.
56. Waterhouse, p. 39; Jaffé; Smith, p. 62; Romney, p. 54.
57. This would, however, have been an important commission from his old patron Sir George Warren, and it also involved more elements than usual in his portraits.
58. Boccaccio's *Decameron* gave rise to *Cimon and Iphegenia* (New Haven, Yale Center for British Art).
59. Hayley, p. 187.
60. Sketchbook of 1774, photographs in Witt Library.
61. Hayley, p. 131.
62. Folger ms. c61, cited in Dixon, pp. 126 and 137–9.
63. Watson (1974), pp. 54–5.
64. Hayley, p. 327.
65. Jaffé (1977), p. 44; this is reproduced as the frontispiece of the third edition and the textual reference is p. 115; Romney, p. 262; Chamberlain, p. 128.
66. Chamberlain, p. 248, cites Smith, J.T., 2nd edn 1829, *Nollekens and his Times*, London.
67. Allen (1984), p. 1.
68. Crookshank (1957), p. 48.
69. Dixon, pp. 39–40.
70. Gombrich, p. 298; Rump, G. C. (1984), *George Romney*, exhibition catalogue, Abbot Hall Gallery, Kendal, p. 2; Dixon, p. 30. Numerous sketchbooks survive intact; many have been broken up for sale. Intact examples include those at Princeton University Art Gallery, New Jersey; Yale Center for British Art, New Haven, Connecticut; Walter Art Gallery, Liverpool; Barrow-in-Furness Record Office, Cumbria.
71. Dixon, p. 40.

72. Gower, p. 48.

73. Sketches: Holborn sketchbook; drawing: New Haven, Yale Center for British Art.

74. Thanks to Alex Kidson for this observation.

75. Honour (1968), p. 101.

76. Dixon, p. 30; Wark, p. 2.

77. Wilton and Bignamini, p. 224.

78. Pointon (1970), p. 125.

79. Chan, p. 72; Hofmann, Werner, *The Death of the Gods*, pp. 19–21, in Bindman (1979), p. 12; Jaffé (1977), cat. 31 and 32.

80. Dixon, fig. 4, pp. 67 and 131; Hagstrum, p. 202; Pointon (1970), p. 125.

81. Walpole's annotation of the 1783 RA catalogue, cited Postle (1995), p. 265.

82. Hagstrum, p. 205.

83. Fraser, p. 177.

84. Sawday, pp. 44, 49; also see the true story of Anne Green, an infanticide who awoke in similar circumstances, p. 61; Romney, pp. 262–3; Jaffé (1977), p. 31.

85. Cover of Folger Shakespeare Library Art Volume c60, cited in Dixon, pp. 72 and 77–8.

86. Hayley, p. 374.

87. Flaxman's drawing is illustrated in Lister, R. (1989), *British Romantic Painting*, Cambridge, pl. 23.

88. Romney, p. 324.

89. Letter, Blake to Hayley, 2 April 1804, in Chamberlain, p. 238; Bindman (1977), pp. 21, 29, 117–18; letter, Blake to Hayley, 22 June 1804.

90. Dixon, pp. 69–70; illustrated in Jaffé, Smith; Ward and Roberts, 2, p. 199, refers to a study in oils of this subject.

91. It may not be a coincidence that he had dealings with both Horace Walpole, author of the macabre *The Castle of Otranto* (1764), and the eccentric William Beckford, whose gothic novel *Vathek* (1786) was likewise influential.

92. Thunberg, C.P. (1975), *An Account of the Cape of Good Hope and some parts of the interior of South Africa extracted from his travels* (4 vols.), in Pinkerton, J. (1814), *A General Collection of the Best and most interesting Voyages and Travels*, London, vol. XVI, p. 61; Chan, p. 100 n 4; Boase, T.S.R. (1947), 'Shipwrecks in English Romantic Painting', *Journal of the Warburg and Courtauld Institutes*, **10**, pp. 83–103; Cumberland's play *The Brothers* (1769) includes a shipwreck and his other works include protoromantic elements such as incest and suicide.

93. Blake's engraving appears in Hayley, p. 84; Chan, p. 73.

94. Chan, p. 78.

95. Chan, pp. 79–80; Chan, p. 100n. describes the Blake drawing as a watercolour. The present writer has only seen the pencil drawing (London, British Museum).

96. *DNB*.

97. Eitner (1955), p. 288; Bindman (1979), p. 155.

98. Symmonds, in Bindman (1979), p. 155.

99. Hayley, p. 217.

100. Chan, pp. 136–7; Dixon, pp. 25 and 29; Hayley, p. 212; Jaffé (1977), pp. 66–7.

101. Chamberlain, p. 186.

102. Hayley, p. 212.

103. Hayley, p. 77.

104. Dixon, pp. 106 and 151.

105. Dixon, pp. 112–13.

106. Dixon, p. 33.

107. Dixon, p. 32.

108. Dixon, pp. 69–70 and 172; Romney, p. 328.

109. Jaffé, Smith, p. 3; Shirley Gonzales, *New Haven Register*, 28 January 1979; Scrase, D. (1993), 'The Drawings of George Romney', *Arts Review*, p. 64; Marks, C. (1972), *Sketchbooks of the Greatest Artists*, London, pp. 203 and 207.

110. Dixon, p. 155.

9. Prisons and philanthropy

1. Watson (1985), pp. 22–3.
2. Walton, p. 17. Thanks to Richard Hall, Cumbria County Archives.
3. Greene Diary; Hayley, pp. 117 and 205.
4. Hayley, p. 204.
5. Watson (1985), p. 26.
6. Reed, *Diary*, 4 November 1785; Chan, p. 188 n27; Fitzwilliam Museum, Cambridge. The play *The Grecian Daughter* also inspired West's *Grecian Daughter Defending her Father* (New Jersey, Newark Museum), a rather more dramatic moment where the tyrant Dionysius threatens to slay the deposed king.
7. Denvir, p. 284; Sandby, P. (1862), *History of the Royal Academy*, p. 97.
8. Camus, A. (1957), *The Fall*, trans. J. O'Brien, Harmondsworth, p. 91; Morris and Stevens, pp. 44 and 48.
9. Chan, pp. 201–2.
10. The Howard League for Penal Reform is still very active today.
11. Chan, pp. 183–4.
12. Howard, p. 43; Pointon (1970), pp. xxiv; Chan, pp. 43–5; Wilton and Bignamini, p. 35.
13. Hayley, pp. 87–9; Bishop, p. 104.
14. Bishop, p. 104; Howard, p. 140; Deuchar, S. (1989), *Painting, Politics and Porter: Samuel Whitbread and British Art*, exh. cat. (London, British Museum), p. 41.
15. Goya drew prisoners and lunatics from his own experience.
16. Dixon, p. 245; Crookshank, p. 47. Romney's Howard drawings are located in several collections including the Fitzwilliam Museum, Cambridge, The Folger Shakespeare Library, Stanford University, The Tate Gallery, The Whitworth Art Gallery, Toronto Art Gallery and Abbot Hall Art Gallery.
17. Folger Library, Art volume c61 p. 72, verso 74.
18. Dixon, p. 245.
19. Chan, pp. 10, 14 and 60.
20. Bindman (1989), p. 73.
21. Hayley, p. 123.
22. Greene, 'Diary', 22 September; *The Bastille*, a fragment of a Blake poem, *The French Revolution*, 1791. In the *Italian Journal* of 1774 Romney rejoices at the Genoan achievement of liberty.
23. Thanks to the staff of Chichester Record Office.
24. Letter, Romney to James Romney, V&A 86aa25a; Romney, p. 92; Jaffé (1977), p. 52 citing *DNB*; Preston CRO DDGr, Hayley to Greene, 20 March 1790.
25. Bindman (1989), pp. 30 and 66; Jaffé (1977), p. 52.
26. Romney, p. 147; Gillam, J.G. (1954), *The Crucible: The Story of Joseph Priestley*, London, pp. 180 and 188–90.
27. Bishop, pp. 138–9; Hayley, pp. 144 and 153.
28. Hayley, p. 143.
29. Hayley, p. 148.
30. Hayley, p. 149; Jaffé (1977), p. 57.

31. Romney, p. 217.

32. Romney, p. 218; NPG ledger, p. 19. Carwardine was commissioned in 1792 as 'Colonel Propriétaire du Régiment des Volontaires Britanniques', a regiment unknown to the military historians in France approached by the present writer; Chelmsford CRO D/DPr 547. Was he involved, like Greene, in assisting refugees from the Terror? Cumberland's play *First Love* (1795) centred upon a girl whose parents died during the revolution.

33. Draft letter to Humphry about his illness in the NPG ledger; some of his patrons and critics have viewed many such pictures as 'unfinished'; others have been entirely satisfied with such versions of completeness. After Romney's death, Carwardine requested that he might purchase *'Twas when the Seas were Roaring* (untraced), an unfinished work, for his great staircase at Colne Priory.

34. Romney, p. 218.

35. Letter, 30 May 1791, V&A ms. 86aa25a 5/1, and two others in this sequence.

36. Letter from Hayley in the V&A ms., Thélassie sequence as above.

37. The 'Thélassie' drawings at Stanford are no longer thought to be correctly entitled. Eitner, L., (1993), *Stanford University Catalogue of Drawings*, Stanford p. 331. Caten Ten Cate of Holland was another of Hayley's mistresses. Referred to in the Fitzwilliam mss., Farington's Diary refers to the French couple domesticated with Romney. He appears to have considered leaving them a house in his will, possibly Prospect House, an indication of their importance to him. There may be a link between Thélassie and this couple.

38. Bishop, p. 100; V&A ms. 86aa25a 5/2 states that the 'Great Picture' was being painted during the Thélassie period, 1791–2; Romney himself sometimes modelled in clay but all his productions have perished.

39. Leech and Craik, **6**, pp. 180–81; Preston CRO DDGr box C2, letter, Hayley to Greene, 17 June 1798.

40. Preston CRO DDGr, 31 December 1790, letter, Hayley to Greene; this reference to secretaries is a literal one, as Romney often asked friends and even sitters to write letters for him. The word 'sultanas', with its resonance of oriental sensual indulgence, is almost certainly Hayley's hyperbole and a hint of his jealousy of his friend's success in this respect.

41. Fitzwilliam Museum, Cambridge, ms., letter, John Romney to Hayley, 22 June 1806.

42. Tillyard, p. 339.

43. Pakenham, T. (1969), *The Year of Liberty: the Great Irish Rebellion 1798*, London, pp. 45–6 and 269–74.

44. *DNB*; Chamberlain, p. 179; Bishop, pp. 84–5; Paston, pp. 133–4n; Drabble, M., (1985), ed. *Oxford Companion to Literature*, p. 913 n46.

45. *Cambridge History of English Literature*, **11**, p. 299n.

46. Ousby, I., ed. (1993), *Cambridge Guide to English Literature*, p. 927.

47. Barrow CRO ms. Z251/1, letter, Hayley to Romney.

48. *Elegiac Sonnets*, 1789 edition, facing p. 12. The print is identified thus: 'del. Stothard, sculp. Neagle'.

49. Tillyard, p. 339.

50. Ward and Roberts, **2**, p. 115; Romney dined with a Mr Pain on 4 July 1791, the anniversary of American Independence Day. This may not be Thomas Paine. Ward and Roberts, **1**, p. 124.

51. Foner, E. (1976), *Tom Paine and Revolutionary America*, ch. 6, cited in *Oxford Dictionary of Quotations*, third edition (1979), London, p. 368.

52. Ellis, H.M. (1920), 'Thomas Cooper, A Survey of his Life,' *The South Atlantic Quarterly* **19**, pp. 24–42.

53. Ward and Roberts, **2**, p. 164.

54. Alexander, D., in Turner, J. (ed.), op.cit., **28**, pp. 557–8.

55. Wardle, R.M., ed. (1979), *Letters of Mary Wollstonecraft*, Ithaca NY and London, p. 210; T.C. Rickman (1819), *Life of Thomas Paine*, London, pp. 100–101, cited Jaffé (1977), p. 57.

56. Jaffé (1977), p. 1.

57. Alberts, p. 214.

58. *DNB*.

59. In the sketchbook formerly owned by Kenneth Garlick, cited Jaffé (1977), p. 66.
60. ibid.
61. ibid. Hayley, p. 184.
62. Thanks to Christine Tranchant.
63. King and Ryskamp; letter, Cowper to Lady Hesketh, 29 January 93.
64. Bindman (1989), p. 73.
65. Jaffé (1977), p. 66; Greene, 'Diary' (unpaginated) illustrates this.
66. Bindman (1989), p. 67; Farington, *Diary*, 29 October 1797.
67. In Milton, H.S., ed. (1921, repr.1953), *William Cowper, Poetry and Verse*, Oxford, p. 104.
68. King and Ryskamp, letter, Hayley to Cowper, 26 August 92.
69. King and Ryskamp, letter, Cowper to Hayley, 21 August 1792; ibid., p. xxix; apart from cheering Romney and Cowper, Hayley wrote an *Ode on Dejection* for Wright; Blake engraved Romney's head of Cowper for Hayley's *Life of Cowper*, 1803.
70. Two ms. versions of this verse survive. They differ in line 9: 'But (Yet) this I mark' (Princeton University, Panshanger Collection). In Romney's brief correspondence with Cowper, the artist recommended his Turkish barber as a source of good-quality razor strops.
71. Hayley, p. 181.
72. Hayley, pp. 223–4; also see Hayley, p. 156.
73. Hayley, p. 174.

10. The fall of a rebel angel: years of decline

1. Farington, *Diary*, 29 October 1797.
2. Hayley, p. 239; Chamberlain, pp. 159, 163, 168 and 205.
3. Chamberlain, pp. 184 and 192.
4. This visit is implied by a passage in a letter Lawrence wrote to a Miss Hartley on 6 April 1787, cited in Goldring, D. (1951), *Regency Painter: The Life of Sir Thomas Lawrence*, Macdonald, London, p. 64. Thanks to Alex Kidson.
5. Hayley, p. 197.
6. Hayley, p. 313; Romney, p. 203; letter, 25 May 1788, in Maxwell, p. 121.
7. Romney, p. 230; letter Helen Valentine, RA Library 16 October 1997, re: RA Council Minutes, 22 May 1801; Haskell and Penny, pp. 135, 240 and 314.
8. Chan, citing British Museum Milton sketchbook, dated July 1792.
9. Hayley, p. 225.
10. Miss Romney's sale, 1894, lot 149, catalogue at Abbot Hall donated by Brenda Hart Jackson.
11. Hayley, pp. 221 and 226.
12. Bindman (1979), pp. 6, 21 and 164–5.
13. Maxwell, p. 137.
14. Hayley, pp. 196–7.
15. Hayley, p. 232; Romney, pp. 144 and 233. When Prospect House was sold, there remained several 'Grecian Lamps' and a 'six light chandelier with a brass arm and chain suspended from the orchestra', which were probably the vestiges of Romney's systems of illumination (Hampstead Assembly Rooms mss., Holborn Library).
16. Hayley, pp. 195–6.
17. V & A ms. 86aa25a, Romney to James Romney, 8 April 1794; Hayley, pp. 204–5.
18. Letter, Stanier Clarke to Hayley, 28 June 1793, ms. VI Fitzwilliam, cited Jaffé (1977), p. 62.
19. Hayley, pp. 199–201 and 401; Chan, p. 187.

20. Hayley, p. 203; Jaffé (1977), p. 63; Neve, C. (1978), 'Breakfast at Pine Apple Place', *Country Life*, 3, vol. CLXIV, August, pp. 310–11.

21. Hayley, p. 218.

22. Hayley, pp. 201, 210, 223 and 265.

23. Hayley, p. 280.

24. Thanks to Alex Kidson.

25. Strong (1969), p. 46; Mitchell, Charles (1944), 'Benjamin West's Death of General Wolfe and the Popular History Piece', *Journal of the Warburg and Courtauld Institute*, vol. 7, pp. 20–33; Honour (1968), p. 83; Kelly, p. 10.

26. Piper (1957), pp. 128–9.

27. Romney, p. 239; Jaffé (1977), p. 60.

28. Bedford CRO Wl/863; thanks to the owner for this information.

29. Pointon (1970), pp. 252–3.

30. ibid.

31. Jackson-Stops, p. 54; Allen, Brian (1984), no. 12.

32. Hayley, p. 212; Ward and Roberts, **2**, p. 115.

33. Pointon (1970), p. 125, fig. 118.

34. Ackroyd, p. 159.

35. *Paradise Lost*, Book 1, 1.45; Rump (1984), p. 3; Jaffé (1977), p. 69.

36. Bindman (1977), p. 22.

37. Chamberlain, p. 198.

38. Keynes, letter, Blake to Hayley, 22 June 1804; Viscomi, p. 48; thanks to James King for drawing my attention to this article. Dr Aileen Ward of New York University is not convinced that they met. Letter 9, September 1993; letter, Blake to Hayley, 22 February 1804.

39. Butlin, p. 304; Gilchrist, A. (1942), *Life of Blake*, 2 vols., Macmillan, London, p. 380, states that Blake's drawing of Romney was in the Rosenwald Collection, but it was not there by 1977; Bentley, p. 577; Essick, R.N. (1980), *William Blake, Printmaker*, Princeton University Press, Princeton, p. 182; Essick, R.N. (1980), *Separate Plates of William Blake*, exh. cat., p. 261; letter, Peter van Wingen, Library of Congress, 29 November 1993.

40. Letter, Blake to Hayley, 28 December 1804.

41. Dixon, p. 146; Shawe-Taylor, p. 7.

42. Wilson, p. 18; Bentley, p. 27.

43. Letter, Blake to Hayley, 22 June 1804; Wilson, p. 221; Dr Ward (see 5 refs above, n38) is doubtful whether Blake had access to Romney's drawings.

44. Dixon, pp. 146–7; Hagstrum, pp. 204–10 and 212 n14; Jaffé (1962), p. 1; Blunt, p. 41.

45. King (1991), p. 103; Pressly, pp. xi and 134–9; Blunt, p. 42; Hagstrum p. 211; Viscomi, p. 67 n1; Blake records his familiarity with Romney's tendency to leave his canvases unstrained; Romney, Long, Humphry and Reed all owned copies of Blake's illuminated books, Romney's purchases being made in 1794–6 (Viscomi has several references).

46. Bindman (1977), p. 133.

47. Letter, Blake to Hayley, 22 June 1804.

48. Letter, Blake to Hayley, 4 December 1804; Bentley, pp. 153 and 161; Butlin, p. 304.

49. Letter, Blake to Hayley, 23 October 1804.

50. Chamberlain, p. 198; Hayley, p. 241.

51. Hayley, p. 208; Romney to James Romney, V&A ms. 86aa25 1/1.

52. Hardwick, p. 19.

53. Hayley, p. 204.

54. Alex Kidson in conversation, 1998.

55. Bishop, pp. 214–15; Hayley, pp. 208–9, 220 and 258.
56. *Paradise Lost*, Book 12 ll 8–10; 610–13.
57. Hayley, pp. 75 and 214.
58. Hayley, p. 220.
59. Romney, p. 240.
60. Tscherny, N. (1986), *George Romney: Flaxman Modelling the Bust of Hayley*, Yale Center for British Art, Painting in Focus Series, p. 1.
61. ibid.
62. Hayley (1923), pp. 229 and 233–4; Cross (1995), pp. 15–19.
63. Hayley, p. 214.
64. Ainslie was the son of Dr Ainslie of Kendal; letter Barrow CRO Z250; Hayley, p. 221; Romney, p. 100; Reed Diary, 25 September 1794, refers to a visit he paid to John Romney in Cambridge, which may also relate to their anxieties.
65. Hayley, p. 83; Romney, p. 48; Hayley, pp. 220 and 236.
66. Chamberlain, p. 198.
67. Romney, p. 91; Hayley, p. 327.
68. Hayley, p. 327.
69. Ward and Roberts, **2**, p. 168; NPG ledger, p. 6.
70. Ward and Roberts, **2**, pp. 104–5.
71. Chamberlain, p. 143.
72. Chamberlain, p. 268.
73. Letter to author, Francis Russell, re: Shee's completion of *Edward Loveden Loveden* and *Miss Le Clerk*, 10 October 1991, refers to Shee's lists; Barrow, CRO Z244/1 and 2.
74. Hayley, p. 307.
75. Jaffé (1977), p. 30.
76. Gibbs, pp. 70 and 139.
77. Egerton (1990), pp. 54–5.
78. *DNB*; thanks to the staff at Montecello for information from Boyd, A., ed. (1983), *The Papers of Thomas Jefferson*, New York, **9**, pp. 482–3.
79. Gibbs, p. 53; Chamberlain, pp. 25–6; Paston, pp. 18–19; *DNB*.
80. *DNB*.
81. Cumberland (1805), **1**, p. 14.
82. Verse by George Romney Robinson, cited in Hayley, p. 337.
83. Pointon (1993), p. 26.
84. Haskell, F. (1970), 'The Apotheosis of Newton in Art', in *The Annus Mirabilis of Sir Isaac Newton (1666–1966)*, ed. R. Palmer, Cambridge, Mass., p. 318; Hayley, p. 314; Romney, pp. 263–7.
85. Keane, p. 45.
86. Foster, W. (1902), *Descriptive Catalogue of Paintings in the India Office*, London, pp. 1–2; Waterhouse, p. 309, unreasonably describes this work as 'a final flicker'; illustrated *Apollo* **84**, November 1966.
87. Hayley, p. 241.
88. Hayley, p. 242; see Storr, A. (1989), *Churchill's Black Dog and other Phenomena of the Human Mind*, London.
89. Hayley, pp. 155 and 232–4; 'gusto' in the eighteenth century meant taste.
90. Hayley, p. 213.
91. Hayley, William (1809), p. 256, quoting Tom Hayley.
92. The medallion was engraved for Hayley's *Life of Romney* of 1809; a verse in appreciation appears in Hayley, p. 236; Tom's disease is described in Hayley, p. 277.

93. Hayley, p. 293.
94. Farington, *Diary*, 30 December 1796.
95. Letter, Walker to Romney, 27 January 1802, V&A ms. 86cc 32. 32a 53/1; Chamberlain, pp. 218 and 239.
96. John Milton, *Paradise Regained*, ed. Bush, D. (1966), London, Book 4, lines 422 ff.
97. Chan, pp. 87–8; Romney, pp. 244–6.
98. Chamberlain, p. 236.
99. Hayley, p. 301.
100. Romney, p. 25.
101. Crookshank, p. 44; Chamberlain, p. 70.
102. *Providence Brooding over Chaos* was temporarily removed and hidden by the artist during the Gordon riots of 1780, to avoid him being thought a Catholic sympathizer.
103. Hayley, p. 242.
104. Romney, p. 10.
105. Chan, pp. 119, 125 and 181.
106. Hayley, p. 212.
107. Smith, *Elegiac Sonnets*, no. 18.
108. Chamberlain, p. 204.
109. She did not become his Countess until after the birth of their sixth child.
110. Bishop, p. 95; Farington, *Diary*, 20 December 1798.
111. Benjamin Haydon, quoted in Jackson-Stops, p. 30; Miss Iliffe and the children also came to Eartham and sat to Romney in the converted riding house. Hayley, *Memoirs*, **2**, 145.
112. Numerous letters in Preston CRO DDGr refer to Greene and his toxophilite skills.
113. Hayley, pp. 201 and 237; Chamberlain, p. 203.

11. 'An owl in the desert'

1. Hayley, p. 232.
2. Hayley, p. 233.
3. V&A ms. 86cc32a 1; Fitzwilliam Museum, Cambridge, Hayley mss. XIX, cited in Jaffé (1977), pp. 61–2.
4. V&A 86AA25a; Hayley, pp. 204–5.
5. V&A ms. 86AA25a 5/2.
6. Cumberland (1803), p. 418; Burton, p. 6; Ellis, p. 2.
7. Hayley, p. 199.
8. Ward and Roberts, **1**, p. 72.
9. Jacobs and Warner, eds (1980), *Phaidon Companion to Art and Artists of the British Isles*, London; Potter, G. (1904), *Hampstead Wells*, reprinted 1978, Camden History Society, pp. 85–90; Romney, p. 176; letter to author from Malcolm Holmes, Hampstead Library, 10 July 1993.
10. Ellis ms. Marylebone Library; Whitley, p. 17, cited in Pointon (1993), p. 44; Chamberlain, p. 213.
11. Hayley, p. 278.
12. Hayley, pp. 384–5.
13. Calloway, Stephen (March 1997), 'Behind a Blue Plaque', *House and Garden*, **52.3**, pp. 112–21.
14. Ellis, C.W. (1971), *Architect Errant*, London illustration facing p. 164; Williams Ellis lived for some years at Romney's house in the mid twentieth century; Farington, *Diary*, 30 December 1796.
15. Edwards, p. 279; Romney, pp. 251–2.
16. Information from Teddington Library, local history files.

17. Wilton and Bignamini, p. 197.
18. Lewis, W.S. (1961), *Horace Walpole*, London, p. xxii.
19. Bishop, p. 200; Paston, pp. 62 and 141; Hayley, p. 245.
20. Hayley, p. 283; Colvin, H.M. (1995), *A Biographical Dictionary of British Architects (1600–1840)*, Yale, 3rd edn, p. 157.
21. Hayley, p. 307.
22. Dixon, p. 116.
23. Chamberlain, p. 215.
24. Hayley, p. 251; letter from R. W. Steadman at Wilton, 12 August 1998.
25. Hayley, p. 245.
26. Hayley, p. 266. After the 1797 visit Hayley and Tom escorted the artist on the London route as far as Petworth. Hayley, *Memoirs*, **2**, 363.
27. ibid.
28. Hayley, pp. 208, 257 and 260.
29. 'Cross-Fleury' (1891), *Time-Honoured Lancaster*, Lancaster, p. 275. Thanks to Peter Williamson of the City Museum, Lancaster; Chamberlain, p. 211.
30. *Art Union*, March 1832, p. 22.
31. Thanks to John Martin Robinson; the portrait of Congreve has been cut down, as is clear from the photograph of an engraving after Lonsdale (Witt Library, Courtauld Institute); Lonsdale is also said to have been Portrait Painter to the Duke of Sussex and to Queen Caroline. Lonsdale may have been confused with Stewardson here (see note 75 below). More research is needed.
32. Greenacre, F. (1982), *Marine Artists of Bristol*, Bristol, City Museum and Art Gallery, pp. 95–9.
33. Romney, p. 26; the Pocock watercolour copies are referred to by Hayley in his *Memoirs*, **2**, 421.
34. Friedman, p. 162.
35. Cordingley, D. (1986), *Nicholas Pocock, Conway's Marine Artists*, London; thanks also to Pieter van der Merwe of the National Maritime Museum; *Gentleman's Magazine*, December 1835; *DNB*.
36. Chamberlain, p. 220; Romney, pp. 276 and 286. Cockin's paper was read on 20 February 1780 and is published in *The Royal Society Philosophical Transactions*, **70**, 1780, repr. Johnson and Kraus (1965), New York, pp. 157–63. Thanks to the Librarian of the Royal Society.
37. Hayley, p. 278.
38. Hayley, p. 264.
39. Hayley, pp. 284–6.
40. Barrow CRO Z254.
41. Hayley, p. 289.
42. Thanks to Dr Esther Ross.
43. Pierpont Morgan Library, New York ms. letter, 18 May 1800.
44. Arthur Evans, *North West Evening Mail*, 18 November 1989, p. 16.
45. John Romney says 1799, but 1798 is more likely; Romney, p. 253; Barrow CRO, lease, dated 1801, BD/HJ/38 no. 53 and estate map.
46. Farington, *Diary*, 1795; Barrow CRO BD/HJ/37–9.
47. Romney, p. 147; letter, Blake to Hayley, 21 March 1804.
48. Farington, *Diary*, December 1798, records Sharpe's report; 1798 was also the year Romney lent money to William Combe, the indigent Old Etonian satirist (letter in Barrow CRO Z mss.).
49. Shee, pp. 212–13.
50. Hutchison, p. 99.
51. Paston, p. 159.
52. 'And thus retire me to my Milan where / Every third thought shall be my grave.' Prospero's lines from *The Tempest*, V.i.310–11, could equally apply to Romney at this point.

53. Preston CRO, DDGr box C2, Hayley to Greene. Even Hayley was willing to be his amanuensis.

54. Hayley, pp. 293–4.

55. Quoted in Chamberlain, p. 223.

56. Farington, *Diary*, 30 March 1799.

57. Barrow CRO Z262.

58. Jaffé (1962), p. 2, refers to Hampstead Vestry Minutes and Hampstead Manor Minutes Book, Camden Library.

59. RA Council Minutes, 22 May 1801; thanks to Helen Valentine.

60. Thornton, P., and Dorey, H. (1992), *A Miscellany of Objects from the Sir John Soane Museum*, London, p. 62; letter, Helen Dorey, 28 August 1991.

61. Farington, *Diary*, 15 March 1809; sale catalogues for 1805 and 1807 are at the Yale Center for British Art, New Haven.

62. Farington, *Diary*, 26 January 1808.

63. Watson (1985), p. 20; Burton, p. 6; sale particulars pasted inside cover of Hampstead Assembly Rooms Minute Book, Holborn Library; Farington, *Diary* 15 May 1801.

64. 'Indication of Houses of Historical Interest', London County Council, 1901, part XXI; *DNB*. Mrs Rundle appears to have owned the house for a short period, perhaps storing some remaining property of Romney's. Later sales and thefts postdate her ownership; Hayley, p. 307; *DNB*.

65. Plan of Assembly Rooms, Holborn Library, 138 (iv).

66. Paston, p. 145; Gamlin, p. 230.

67. Postlethwaite, T.N. (1926), 'George Romney: Some Notes on his Ancestry', *Transactions Cumberland and Westmorland Antiquarian and Archaeological Society* **26** (new series), p. 349.

68. Chamberlain, p. 258.

69. Kendal CRO WDX 937, nos. 1 and 2: lease renewal, 31 January 1794, Leach mss., privately owned; thanks to Mr Leach and his tenant for giving access to the property.

70. Chamberlain, p. 223; John Todd, Map of Kendal 1787.

71. V&A ms. 86cc32 32a 53; Walker slightly misquotes Psalm 102.

72. Barrow CRO, Greene to Romney, Z246.

73. Hayley, p. 298.

74. Barrow Z240, CRO.

75. V&A ms. 86cc32a, 19 June 1802. He may be a brother of Jane Kennel, later John Romney's wife. She herself may be identical with the 'Miss Kenna' who also wrote letters signed by the artist during this period. Another artist claimed as a late pupil is Thomas Stewardson (1781–1859), but there is no evidence of this. His memorial claims royal appointments which are not substantiated by the archives at Windsor.

76. Letter, Pitcairn to Long, Barrow CRO Z248.

77. V&A ms. 86AA25, letter, Mrs Cockerell to Romney.

78. V&A 86cc32a, James Romney to Romney; Hayley, p. 298; Adam Walker wrote one of his last letters on 27 January 1802, V&A ms. 86cc32 32a 53.

79. Preston CRO DDGr, John Romney to Greene, 20 February 1802.

80. Thanks to Tim Cockerill.

81. V&A 86cc32a, 28 November 1802. A letter from Carwardine is quoted in a letter from Greene to John Romney, 25 November 1802; also see Greene to John Romney, 12 December 1802.

82. This portrait is engraved in Hayley.

83. Romney's family was not armigerous in his lifetime and no grant of arms is recorded at the College of Arms. Thanks to Timothy Duke, Rouge Dragon, 1994. 'Pictor celeberrimus' translates as 'most celebrated artist'. Thanks to Alan Farrar.

84. Watson (1985), p. 20; two wills survive: one at Preston CRO DDGr Box F4 and a later one at the V&A, 86cc32; Bishop, p. 311.

85. Preston CRO DDGr, will dated 15 November 1800. He also left £200 and a ring to Cockin, which would revert via a codicil to his nephew John Noble Pearson; the witnesses were all from Burton in Kendal, Cockin's home village.

86. Farington, *Diary*, 3 June 1803.

87. Chamberlain, p. 228.

88. Parish Records, Rusland.

89. Jaffé (1977), p. 1.

90. John Ruskin was the former owner of a Romney wash drawing of a woman standing in a landscape (Oxford, Ashmolean Museum). Thanks to Edwin Bowes, North West Museums Service.

91. Romney, p. 167. The American Romneys, including Bishop George Romney of Utah, are descended from Thomas Romney, the brother of the artist's father. Thanks to Dr Ralph Romney.

92. Chamberlain, p. 233.

93. Hayley, pp. 86 and 254.

94. Hayley, p. 62; Romney, p. 192.

95. Ackroyd, p. 48.

96. Pointon (1993), p. 122; *Arts Review* **38**, 14 February 1986, p. 63; Chittock, D. (1979), *Portrait Painting*, London, p. 86; Chamberlain, p. 264.

Bibliography

Ackroyd, Peter (1996), *William Blake*, London: Minerva.
Alberts, P.C. (1978), *Benjamin West: A Biography*, Boston: Houghton Mifflin.
Allen, Brian (1984), *George Romney as Painter of Children*, exhibition catalogue, London: Leger Galleries.
—— (1987), *Francis Hayman*, New Haven and London: Yale University Press in association with English Heritage.
Allen, Elizabeth (1996), 'George Romney', in *The Grove Dictionary of Art*, London: Macmillan, 27, pp. 117–20.
Behrman, S.N. (1953), *Duveen*, London: Hamish Hamilton.
Bell, C.F. (1938), *The Annals of Thomas Banks*, Cambridge: Cambridge University Press.
Bemrose, W. (1885), *The Life and Works of Joseph Wright of Derby*, London: Bemrose and Sons.
Bentley, G.E. (1969), *Blake Records*, Oxford: Clarendon Press.
Bicknell, Richard (1990), *The Picturesque Scenery of the Lake District (1752–1855), A Bibliographic Study*, London: St Paul's Bibliographies.
Bignamini, I. (1988), 'Art Institutions in London 1689–1768: A Study of Clubs and Academies', *Transactions of the Walpole Society*, pp.19–148.
Bignamini, I., and Postle, M. (1991), *The Artist's Model*, exhibition catalogue, London: Kenwood House.
Bindman, David (1977), *Blake as an Artist*, Oxford: Phaidon.
—— (1979), *John Flaxman R.A.*, exhibition catalogue, London: Royal Academy.
—— (1989), *The Shadow of the Guillotine*, London: British Museum.
Bishop, Morchard (1951), *Blake's Hayley*, London: Gollancz.
Blunt, Anthony (1960), *The Art of William Blake*, Columbia: Columbia University Press.
Brewer, John (1997), *The Pleasures of the Imagination*, London: HarperCollins.
Burke, Joseph (1976), 'English Art (1714–1800)', in Boase, T.S.B. (ed.), *The Oxford History of English Art*, Oxford.
Burkett, Mary E. (1987), 'Christopher Steele (1733–1767)', *Transactions of the Walpole Society*, vol. LIII, pp. 193–225.
Burton, N. (1986), 'Romney's House in Hampstead', *Camden History Review*, pp. 5–6.
Butlin, Martin (1981), *The Paintings and Drawings of William Blake*, New Haven and London: Yale University Press.
Buttery, David J. (1986), 'George Romney and the Second Earl of Warwick', *Apollo*, pp. 104–9, August.
Chamberlain, Arthur Bensley (1910), *George Romney*, London: Methuen.

Chan, Victor (1982), *'Leader of My Angels': William Hayley and His Circle*, exhibition catalogue, Edmonton Art Gallery.
—— (1983), 'Pictorial Image and Social Reality: George Romney's late Drawings of John Howard Visiting Prisoners', unpublished PhD thesis, Stanford University.
In the Notes all undated references to Chan are to Chan (1983).
Crookshank, Anne Olivia (1952), 'The Subject Pictures and Drawings of George Romney (1734–1802)', unpublished MA thesis, University of London (copy Courtauld Institute Library).
—— (1957), 'The Drawings of George Romney', *Burlington Magazine*, **XCIX**, No. 647, pp. 42–8, February.
Cross, David A. (1983), 'An Iconographical Study of the Principal Elements in the Masque in Shakespeare's *The Tempest*', unpublished MA thesis, Lancaster University.
— (1995), 'Romney's *Four Friends* and a Drawing at Yale', *Quarto*, Abbot Hall Art Gallery, **XXXIII**, no. 2 pp. 15–19, October.
—— (1996) (1), 'George Romney: Patterns of Friendship', *Transactions of the Romney Society*, **I**, pp. 19–21.
—— (1996) (2), 'The Reverend William Gilpin', in *The Grove Dictionary of Art*, London: Macmillan, 12, p. 645.
—— (1997), 'Romney's Pupils', *Transactions of the Romney Society*, **II**, pp. 17–20.
—— (1998), 'Sawrey Gilpin R.A.: Rival of Stubbs', *Armitt Journal*, Lancaster University, **I**, pp. 64–85.
Cumberland, Richard (1803), 'Memoirs of Mr George Romney', *The European Magazine*, **XLIII**, pp. 417–23, June.
—— (1805), *Memoirs of Richard Cumberland, written by himself*, 2 vols, London: Lackington, Allen and Co.
Cunningham, Allan (1829–33), 'George Romney', in *The Lives of the Most Eminent British Painters*, London: John Murray; Mrs Charles Heaton (revised edn), vol. II of III, pp. 137–209.
Curwen, J.F. (1900), *Kirkbie Kendal*, Kendal: Titus Wilson.
Denvir, Bernard (1983), *The 18th Century: Art, Design and Society (1689–1789)*, London and New York: Longman.
Deuchar, Stephen (1984), *Painting, Politics and Porter: Samuel Whitbread and British Art*, exhibition catalogue, Museum of London.
Dixon, Yvonne Romney (1977), 'The Drawings of George Romney in the Folger Shakespeare Library', unpublished PhD thesis, University of Maryland.
—— (1998), *'Designs From Fancy': George Romney's Shakespeare Drawings*, exhibition catalogue, Washington, D.C.: Folger Shakespeare Library.
In the Notes all undated references to Dixon are to Dixon (1977).
Dorment, Richard (1986), *British Painting in the Philadelphia Museum of Art*, London: Philadelphia Museum of Art in association with Weidenfeld and Nicolson.
DNB see Stephens
Edwards, Edward (1808), *Anecdotes of Painting*, London (Anderdon interleaved copy, British Museum c74).
Egerton, Judy (1984), *George Stubbs*, exhibition catalogue, London: Tate Gallery.
—— (1990), *Wright of Derby*, exhibition catalogue, London: Tate Gallery.
Eitner, L. (1955), 'The Open Window and the Storm Tossed Boat: An Essay in the Iconography of Romanticism', *Art Bulletin*, **XXXVII**, pp. 281–90, December.
—— (1970), *Neo-classicism and Romanticism*, 2 vols, vol. l: 'Enlightenment and Revolution', London: Prentice Hall.
Ellis, R. (1977), 'Romney's Two Hampstead Houses', *Camden History Review*, pp. 2–3.
Farington, Joseph (1975), *The Diary of Joseph Farington*, Kenneth Garlick, Angus Macintyre and Kathryn Cave (eds.), New Haven and London: Yale University Press.

Ford, Boris (ed.) (1990), 'Romantics to Victorians', *Cambridge Guide to the Arts*, vol. 6, Cambridge: Cambridge University Press.
Ford, Brinsley, 'British Artists in Rome' mss, The Mellon Centre for British Art, London (see Ingamells, 1997).
Foskett, Daphne (1972), *A Dictionary of British Miniature Painters*, 2 vols, London: Faber and Faber.
—— (1987), 'Ozias Humphry', *Transactions of the Walpole Society*, vol. XIX.
Fraser, Flora (1986), *Beloved Emma: The Life of Emma, Lady Hamilton*, London: Weidenfeld and Nicolson.
Friedman, Winifred E. (1976), *Boydell's Shakespeare Gallery*, New York: Garland.
Fuseli, Henry (1810), 'George Romney', in the Reverend Matthew Pilkington (ed.), *Dictionary of Painters from the Revival of Art to the Present Period*, London.
Gamlin, Hilda (1894), *Romney and his Art*, London: Swan and Sonnenschein.
Gatty, Hugh (1938–9), 'Notes by Horace Walpole on the Exhibitions of the Society of Artists and the Free Society of Artists 1760–1791', *Transactions of the Walpole Society*, **XXVII**, p. 55 ff.
Gaythorpe, Harper (1906), 'The Crankes of Urswick', *Transactions of the Cumberland and Westmorland Antiquarian and Archaeological Society*, New Series, VI, pp. 128–42.
Gibbs, F.W. (1965), *Joseph Priestley: An Adventurer in Science*, London: Nelson.
Gombrich, Ernst (1960), *Art and Illusion, A Study in the Psychology of Pictorial Representation*, New York: Pantheon Books.
Gower, Lord Ronald Sutherland (1904), *George Romney*, London: Duckworth.
Greene, Thomas (1986), 'Diary of his French Tour 1764', in Owen, Felicity (ed.),*Thomas Greene, Romney's Friend and Patron*, exhibition catalogue, Abbot Hall Art Gallery, Kendal; original ms. in Preston CRO DDGr.
—— (*c*.1802), a manuscript 'Life of George Romney', in a letter to William Long, Preston CRO DDGr, Box 55.
Hägstrum, Jean H. (1978), 'Romney and Blake: Gifts of Grace and Terror', in Essick, Robert N., and Pearce, Donald (eds.), *Blake and his Time*, Bloomington and London: Indiana University Press, pp. 201–12.
Haskell, Francis, and Penny, Nicholas (1981), *Taste and the Antique: The Lure of Classical Sculpture 1500–1900*, New Haven and London: Yale University Press.
Hayes, John (1991), *The Portrait in British Art: Masterpieces Bought with the Help of the National Art Collections Fund*, London: National Portrait Gallery.
Hayley, William: in the notes of this biography all undated references to Hayley are to Hayley (1809).
—— (1809), *The Life of George Romney Esquire*, London: T. Payne.
—— (1823), *Memoirs of the Life and Writings of*, together with *Memoirs of Thomas Hayley*, London: Colburn.
Holmstrom, Kirsten (1967), *Monodrama, Attitudes, Tableaux Vivants: Studies in Trends of Theatrical Fashion (1770–1815)*, Stockholm: Almquist and Wicksell.
Honour, Hugh (1968), *Neo-classicism*, Harmondsworth: Penguin.
—— (1979), *Romanticism*, London: Allen Lane.
Hudleston, Roy C. (1991), 'George Romney's Ancestry', *Transactions of the Cumberland and Westmorland Antiquarian and Archaeological Society*, **XCI**, pp. 145–59.
Hudleston, R. C., and Cockerill, T. (1992), 'Millom Families Part I': *Transactions of the Cumberland and Westmoreland Antiquarian and Archaeological Society*, **XCII**, pp. 91–8.
Hutchison, Sidney (1968), *The History of the Royal Academy 1768–1968*, London: Chapman and Hall.
Ingamells, John (1997), *A Dictionary of British and Irish Travellers in Italy (1701–1800)*, compiled from the Brinsley Ford Archive, New Haven and London: Yale University Press for the Paul Mellon Centre for Studies in British Art.

Irwin, David (1979), *John Flaxman (1755–1826)*, London: Thames and Hudson.
Jackson-Stops, Gervase (ed.) (1985), *The Treasure Houses of Britain*, exhibition catalogue, Washington DC: National Gallery of Art.
Jaffé, Patricia (Milne-Henderson) (1962), *The Drawings of George Romney*, exhibition catalogue, Northampton, Mass.: Smith College Museum of Art.
—— (1966), *George Romney, 'I Maestri del Colore* Series', no. 250, Milan: Fratelli Fabbri Editori.
Jaffé, Patricia (1972), *Lady Hamilton in relation to the Art of her Time*, exhibition catalogue, London: Kenwood House (Iveagh Bequest).
—— (1977), *Drawings by George Romney from the Fitzwilliam Museum, Cambridge*, exhibition catalogue, Cambridge: Fitzwilliam Museum.
Jamison, Kay Redfield (1993), *Touched with Fire: Manic Depressive Illness and the Artistic Temperament*, New York: Free Press.
Jenkins, Ian, and Sloan, Kim (1996), *Vases and Volcanoes: Sir William Hamilton and his Collection*, exhibition catalogue, London: British Museum.
Keane, J. (1995), *Thomas Paine: A Political Life*, London: Bloomsbury.
Kelly, Linda (1997), *Richard Brinsley Sheridan*, London: Sinclair-Stevenson.
Kenwood House (1961), *George Romney 1734–1802: Paintings and Drawings*, exhibition catalogue, Kenwood, London County Council.
Keynes, Geoffrey (ed.) (3rd edn, 1980), *The Letters of William Blake with Related Documents*, Oxford: Clarendon Press.
Kidson, Alex (1990), 'George Romney', in *The International Dictionary of Art and Artists*, Chicago and London: St James's Press, p. 720.
King, James (1991), *William Blake: A Biography*, London: Weidenfeld and Nicolson.
—— and Ryskamp, Charles (1984), *The Letters and Prose of William Cowper*, 4 vols., Oxford: Clarendon Press.
Leech, C., and Craik, T.W. (eds.) (1975), *Revels History of Drama in English*, London: Methuen, vol. 6.
Lister, Raymond (1989), *British Romantic Painting*, Cambridge: Cambridge University Press.
Maclean-Eltham, Barry (1996), *George Romney: Paintings in Public Collections*, Kendal: The Romney Society.
Mannings, David (1977), 'At the Portrait Painter's: how the Painters of the 18th Century Conducted their Studios and Sittings', *History Today*, **XXVII**, pp. 279–87.
—— (1991), 'The Visual Arts: The Augustan Age', in Boris Ford (ed.), *The Cambridge Guide to the Arts in Britain*, vol. 5, Cambridge: Cambridge University Press.
Maxwell, Sir Herbert (1902), *George Romney*, London and New York: Walter Scott and Charles Scribner.
Morris, Edward, and Stevens, Timothy (1968), *Early English Drawings and Watercolours in The Walker Art Gallery, Liverpool*: Walker Art Gallery, pp. 43–54.
Mount, C.M. (1964), *Gilbert Stuart*, New York: W. Norton and Co.
Mowl, Timothy (1996), *The Great Outsider: A Life of Horace Walpole*, London: John Murray.
Paston, George (pseud. of Emily Symonds) (1903), *George Romney*, London: Methuen.
Paulson, Ronald (1975), *Emblem and Expression: Meaning in English Art of the 18th Century*, London: Thames and Hudson.
Phillips, Hugh (1964), *Mid-Georgian London: A Topographical and Social Survey*, London: Collins.
Pilkington's *Dictionary*, see Fuseli.
Piper, David (1957), *The English Face*, London: Thames and Hudson.
—— (2nd edition, 1992), *The English Face*, London: National Portrait Gallery.
Pointon, Marcia (2nd edn, 1970), *Milton and English Art*, Manchester: Manchester University Press.

—— (1993), *Hanging the Head*, New Haven: Yale University Press.
Postle, Martin (1995), *Sir Joshua Reynolds: The Subject Paintings*, Cambridge and New York.
—— (1995), *The Subject Pictures of Sir Joshua Reynolds*, Cambridge: Cambridge University Press.
Pressly, Nancy L. (1979), *The Fuseli Circle in Rome: Early Romantic Art of the 1770s*, exhibition catalogue New Haven: Yale Center for British Art.
Reed, Isaac (1946), *The Diary of Isaac Reed*, ed. C. E. Jones, University of California.
Romney, John (1830), *Memoirs of the Life and Works of George Romney. . . Also some Particulars of the Life of Peter Romney his Brother*, London: Baldwin and Cradock.
Rump, Gerhard Charles (1974), *George Romney (1734–1802): Zur Bildform der Burgerlichen Mitte in der Englischen Neoklassik*, 2 vols, Hildesheim and New York: G. Olms.
—— *George Romney: Drawings and Paintings*, exhibition catalogue, Abbot Hall Art Gallery, Kendal.
Sawday, Jonathan (1995), *The Body Emblazoned: Dissection and the Human Body in Renaissance Culture*, London: Routledge.
Seidmann, Gertrude (1987), 'Nathaniel Marchant', *Transactions of the Walpole Society*, **LIII**, pp. 1–105.
Shawe-Taylor, Desmond (1990), *The Georgians: 18th Century Portraiture and Society*, London: Barrie and Jenkins.
Shee, M.A. (1860), *The Life of Sir Martin Archer Shee*, London.
Sheldon, Esther (1967), *Thomas Sheridan of Smock Alley Recording his Life as Actor and Theatre Manager in both Dublin and London*, Princeton, New Jersey: Princeton University Press.
Simon, Robin (1987), *The Portrait in Britain and America*, Boston and Oxford: G.K. Hall and Phaidon.
Solkin, David H. (1993), *Painting for Money: The Visual Arts and the Public Sphere in 18th Century England*, New Haven and London: Yale University Press.
Stephen, Leslie (ed.) (1885), *The Dictionary of National Biography*, London: Smith Eldes.
Strong, Roy (1969), *The English Icon*, London: Paul Mellon Foundation for British Art.
—— (1978), *And When Did You Last See Your Father? The Victorian Painter and British History*, London: Thames and Hudson.
—— (ed.) (1991), *The British Portrait 1660–1960*, London: Antique Collectors' Club.
Summerson, John (6th edn 1977), *Architecture in Britain (1530–1830)*, Harmondsworth: Penguin Books.
Sutton, Denys (1961), 'Romney, Precursor of the Romantics', *Country Life*, 22 June.
Symmons, S. (1975), 'The Spirit of Despair: Patronage, Primitivism and the Art of John Flaxman', *Burlington Magazine*, **CXVII**, pp. 644–50.
Tillyard, Stella (1993), *Aristocrats*, London: Chatto and Windus.
Tomalin, Claire (1994), *Mrs Jordan's Profession*, London: Viking.
Turner, Jane (ed.) (1996), *The Grove Dictionary of Art*, London: Macmillan
Usherwood, Nicholas (1984), 'Hints at the Irrational: Romney at Abbot Hall', *Country Life*, 9 August, pp. 378–9.
Vaughan, William (1978), *Romantic Art*, London: Thames and Hudson.
Viscomi, Joseph (1989), 'The Myth of Commissioned Illuminated Books: George Romney, Isaac D'Israeli and 160 Designs . . . of Blake's', *Blake: An Illustrated Quarterly*, **XXIII**, no. 2, Fall, pp. 48–64.
Walton, James (1984), *A History of Dalton*, Chichester: Phillimore.
Ward, Humphrey, and Roberts, W. (1904), *Romney: A Biographical and Critical Essay with a Catalogue Raisonné of his Works*, 2 vols, London: Thomas Agnew.
Wark, Robert R. (1970), *The Drawings of Romney*, California: Alhambra.
Warner, Oliver (1972), *With Wolfe to Quebec*, London: Collins.

Waterhouse, Ellis (rev. edn, 1994), *Painting in Britain 1530–1790*, Harmondsworth; Penguin Books.
Watson, Jennifer C. (1974), 'The Paintings of Emma Hart (Lady Hamilton) by George Romney: A Study of their Significance in relation to his Historical Works', unpublished MA thesis, Oberlin College (copy Kenwood House).
—— (1985), *Romney in Canada*, exhibition catalogue, Waterloo, Ontario: Kitchener-Waterloo Art Gallery.
Wenham, L.P. (1991), *James Tate*, North Yorkshire CRO Publications, no. 46.
Whitley, W.T. (1928), *Artists and their Friends in England*, 2 vols, Cambridge: Cambridge University Press.
Williamson, G.C. (1918), *The Life and Works of Ozias Humphry R.A.*, London and New York: John Lane.
—— (1921), *Daniel Gardner, Painter in Pastel and Gouache*, London and New York: John Lane.
Wilson, Mona (1948), *The Life of William Blake*, London: Rupert Hart-Davis.
Wilton, Andrew, and Bignamini, Ilaria (eds.) (1996), *The Grand Tour: The Lure of Italy in the Eighteenth Century*, exhibition catalogue, London: Tate Gallery.

Index

Page references in *italic* type indicate illustrations.

For works by Romney see subsidiary lists.

Index of works

PAINTINGS